professiona...
timely retu...
be

PA...

310

The Heart Is an Instrument

THE HEART

Is an

INSTRUMENT

Portraits in Journalism

MADELEINE BLAIS

Foreword by Geneva Overholser

The University of Massachusetts Press
Amherst

Copyright © 1992 by
Madeleine Blais
All rights reserved
Printed in the United States of America
LC 91–48358
ISBN 0–87023–772–1
Designed by Kristina E. Kachele
Set in Bembo and Bodoni Poster by Keystone Typesetting, Inc.
Printed and bound by Thomson Shore

Library of Congress Cataloging-in-Publication Data
Blais, Madeleine
The heart is an instrument : portraits in journalism /
Madeleine Blais : foreword by Geneva Overholser.
p. cm.
ISBN 0–87023–772–1 (alk. paper)
I. Title.
PN4874.B55A25 1992
814'.54—dc20
91–48358
CIP

British Library Cataloguing in Publication data are available.

Chapters in this book were previously published.
Their earlier appearances are listed on the last page of this book.

To Nick and Justine,
who think writing is easy.
"Just draw an A,
draw a B. . . ."

CONTENTS

V

ACKNOWLEDGMENTS

Most works of journalism are a collaborative effort and in addition to my subjects I would like to thank the following people for their guidance and encouragement:

Doug Balz, Lary Bloom, Philip Brooker, Ray Bubel, John Dorscher, Maggie Felser, Frank Girolamo, Kevin Hall, Nancy Hare, Athelia Knight, Meg Laughlin, Doris Mansour, David Maraniss, Michael Norman, Alison Owen, B. J. Roche, Leon Rosenblatt, Megan Rosenfeld, Julia Serebrinsky, Tom Shroder, Norman Sims, Bob Thompson, Gene Weingarten, Kathy Willens, as well as the late Howard Simons.

I would also like to especially thank my husband, John Katzenbach, for his immeasurable contributions.

FOREWORD

Geneva Overholser

What is it about really fine writers, how they delight, intrigue, *compel* us?

Style, you say. But style is not something you begin with. Rather, it's what you end up with, a result of far more fundamental traits. Traits such as an ear and an eye and a heart, traits that Madeleine Blais has honed superbly well.

This is a book well named: *The Heart Is an Instrument: Portraits in Journalism*. The heart is surely first among Blais's gifts. Whether she is writing about the famous—playwright Tennessee Williams, novelist Mary Gordon—or about the least elevated among us—a teenage prostitute infected with the AIDS virus, a homeless schizophrenic—she brings to her subjects an incomparable empathy.

It's not that she sides with them. She's uncompromising in her portraits. Rather, she seems to come to know them so completely that she can bring them to life: their strengths and weaknesses, their humanness. She makes the mighty into normal mortals. She makes the strange comprehensible.

One of the gifts she brings us is her ear, an ear that hears and records and remembers with remarkable clarity. This is a writer who recalls from childhood the curiosity-engaging quality of a headline like "Canadian Jury Acquits Man in

Death of Sleepwalking Wife" and can now listen when a twelve-year-old killer talks.

Then there's Blais's eye. What she sees is etched on her mind. With a masterly selectivity, she transposes it onto paper. The way a place looked, the feelings an experience evoked become real for us. This is true whether the subject is a fourth-grade teacher coaxing the best from her class or an old man taking a train ride that he hopes will lead to a long-sought honorable discharge.

Happily for the student, who will find this book both a delight and an aid, Blais also has a fine idea of just what it is that makes these wonders happen. Her work may be lyrical; her guidelines are down to earth:

> You are there to serve the subject, not the other way around.
> Do your homework; don't make people repeat information that is easily known. . . .

Ask concrete questions. Find an encouraging editor. Write things down exactly as you hear them. Use all your senses in an interview.

Such is the practical stuff of Blais's book. But the real power is in the work she gives us, in her ability to move people with a story.

Read twelve news stories on the problems of the mentally ill homeless. You will feel a detached dutifulness. Then read about Trish Livergood, in "The Disturbance." You will find a personal association with the issue.

"The Disturbance" is among the many stories that come to mind when one reads this sentiment from Blais in her epilogue: "It seems to me that one of the more crucial roles of the reporter is to give speech to the speechless."

She's right, and that's one virtue of journalism that ought to inspire a student. Yet another occurs to me, as a newspaper editor in an era when newspapers' health and purpose are under constant examination. That virtue is this: there is no medium that can compare with newspapering in telling a remarkable story about an issue that matters, in a timely way that reaches a lot of people.

If you aspire to the pleasure of living out your life as a newspaperperson, read this book. Not because writing can be taught. A heart, an ear, and an eye are gifts; if you are lucky enough to have them and smart enough to use them, they are gifts that can be honed.

Here, in the work of this wonderful writer, is a marvelous place to start.

THE
DISTURBANCE

The light was about to change, and Meg wondered what to do. As she peered through her windshield she saw one of those bag ladies who meander through the streets, a twentieth-century leper, a dirty disheveled insult to the image of the place where she roamed, Coral Gables, the perfect city, planned and placid.

Meg Livergood was out on company errands. A production coordinator at Porter Creative Services, she was driving her boss's Firebird. It was a hot August day two summers ago. As she cruised the Gables, heading back to her office, her mind was focused less on the steamy streets than on the trip she would be taking later that day to New York City with three friends, her first time ever in Manhattan. She was rushing back to the office so she could rush to the airport. She was feeling cheerful, she was feeling free. Meg is one of those women who had children at a young age—she was nineteen when she got pregnant with the first of two sons—and so, at thirty-four, she brings to the world of work the jazzed-up, uncaged enthusiasm of a Former Housewife. She smokes, a habit that she knows she has to give up. She drinks beer, but she stays thin. She works early hours; she works late ones.

It was just ill fortune that she happened down this side

street, got waylaid by that red light and sat in traffic, long fingers impatiently tapping the steering wheel, eyes sweeping a basically benevolent world until they stopped short at the repulsive vision of a tall hunched-over woman with a snarled nest of hair, dressed in ragtag aching disarray down to the brown men's shoes, eyes veiled, head down, proceeding at a slow pace as if in great pain, legs blotched and swollen, carrying a bundle wrapped in a piece of cloth, hobo style.

A sorry city sight to be ignored and forgotten: humanity bowed, humanity punished. And yet the sight drew Meg's gaze, sucked it in, with a disturbing, insistent, unarguable familiarity.

Meg stared, then stiffened.

Trish: her sister.

Meg Livergood debated whether to stop: this isn't my car, it belongs to my boss, what if I let her in it? What if she has lice? She looks shocking. She has never looked that bad. I can't put her in someone else's car. If it were my car . . . no, even if it were my car, I have a life too. I'm supposed to be at the airport thirty minutes from now. This isn't the first time Trish has been on the street. She's survived it before, she'll survive it again. But her legs. They look so bad. They look poisoned. But I've got to lead my own life, I have a right to my own life. . . .

The light changed.

Meg kept driving.

She didn't even look back.

In the Gables, where it is against the law to park a boat in front of one's house, Trish Livergood found sleep that night on the floor of a public ladies' room at the bus station. The floor was hard and damp and smelly, but sleep came quickly because earlier Trish had covered anywhere from ten to twenty miles in a frantic effort to outrun the race in her brain. In the morning, she washed her feet in the sink, and she dampened

Miami Herald photo by Carol Guzy

her long dark hair and soaped it up, but it didn't end up looking that great because she didn't have a comb.

She thought about breakfast. Usually, she got her food by going through the garbage bins. She preferred indoor garbage bins to outdoor ones. You get better food that way, it's slightly warmer. To her way of thinking the best places were Burger King and Kentucky Fried Chicken.

"You know how at the Burger King and the KFC they have that little door that says 'Thank You,' where you put your tray? One time there was this big piece of chicken and a biscuit and a whole bag of french fries. Back then, I was a vegetarian so I didn't eat the chicken, but I took the biscuit and the potatoes."

Usually, Trish stood and gobbled the food, worried only that someone might say: "Hey, that girl is going through the garbage." Once, in Coconut Grove, she found a really tasty piece of fish in a garbage can along the side of the road, and it was late at night, and no one got mad at her for taking it. Sometimes people would walk up to her and hand her food free. That happened at the bus station:

"The girl who works at the lunch counter saw me and she said, 'Hi, are you hungry?' So I said, 'Sure.' And she gave me this really nice brand-new salad. Once, at Lums, the manager said I could order anything I wanted so I ordered soup and crackers. I don't know what was wrong with me. I could have ordered something real nice. Another time a man put fifteen dollars in my pocket. Really. He didn't say a word, he just gave it to me. Lots of times I go into restaurants, and I can't order anything except a glass of water because I don't have any money, so, if I have enough money for a cup of coffee, I love it. It's so . . . I don't know . . . high class."

But, on that weekend two summers ago, there were no "God blesses" as Trish calls such sudden bounty, and she was so tired and so . . . hungry. See, she'd broken up with her boyfriend months ago, and she lost her job as a line person at Western Sizzlin for failure to concentrate, and she had been on the streets and off them for months, and she had only one real goal, which was to stay out of the hospital.

When was it that Meg took her to Crisis, the emergency room for mental patients at Jackson? Time had no meaning, all urgency with no purpose. When had the family given her money to rent a room on Miami Beach? When had she called them up for more money and why did they send Meg with the police to take her to Crisis? She could recall staying at Crisis for only a couple of hours, and, when she was released, they gave her four quarters to take the bus to St. Theresa's, and they gave her a piece of paper with the address. But she could never find her way around Jackson, even normal people have trouble with that neighborhood, and so she spent her money on a cup of Cuban coffee and she started wandering. In her pocket she had an old paycheck from Western Sizzlin for sixty dollars that she kept asking people to cash, and no one would, so she did something unusual for her, she ripped the check up into little pieces, and she walked and walked and walked until she found a nice bus bench in downtown Miami near where some men were doing construction work and where the sound of their machines made her feel safe. And then she thinks that on the next night she was in the Grove park when a man started beating her up for no good reason and knocked out some of her teeth and another man took her to a dark empty house and had sex with her, and he told a guy who was sleeping on the floor of the house he could "have some," too, so he did, but only once, which was halfway decent of him if you think about it because she really didn't want to have sex with anyone. And then the next day she went back to the Gables, and she kept going in and out of the post office because she had put two dollars in a mailbox along with a note addressed to no one asking someone to send her birth certificate to Trish at General Delivery in Miami because she desperately wanted some identification, and she was certain they had it at the post office, but they just wouldn't hand it over for some reason, and then she'd go to the bus station, and that's where she came up with her plan: wouldn't it be great to have enough money to take a bus to Colorado, a nice Greyhound bus that stopped all along the way at little towns, and so she decided to write a note to her grandmother, who lives about two miles from the bus station, and ask her for four thousand dollars because she also wanted money for a car and an apartment once she got to Colorado. She found a piece of paper, a McDonald's hamburger bag drifting down the street, and somehow she got a pencil . . . she has no idea from whom, and she wrote her message on the bag.

She took the note and walked to her grandmother's house and shoved it through a broken window pane in the door to the kitchen. The note to Granga, as Elinor Hanley is called by

Trish and by Trish's two brothers and five sisters, was intercepted by the attendant who provides constant care for the frail old woman.

"Meet me at the Miracle Theater on Miracle Mile at three P.M. with four thousand dollars."

If the note had ended there, the course of the next couple of years in Tricia's life might have been quite different. She might still be on the streets, empty-eyed and emaciated, and that would be only if she were lucky. But it didn't end there. Trish also wrote the following words:

"No shows are dead meat."

The note had an unusual effect. Instead of causing panic or consternation among the family members who saw the note, it engendered a giddy runaway feeling, close to joy.

At last: a mortal threat!

Finally: a criminal act!

Patricia Livergood is thirty-seven. She has been diagnosed as suffering from paranoid schizophrenia since 1972. She has been hospitalized twenty times, usually for a brief stay during which she is doped up, calmed down, and released. That's the system; most mental patients are indigent, like Trish, and the government has not chosen to subsidize long-term hospitalization. When Trish is not in the hospital, she tries to find work; she has had about thirty jobs, jobs she has held from a few months to a few weeks to a few minutes. Her disease causes her to concoct odd delusions about her life and her surroundings, to retreat into a catatonic stupor, and to neglect personal hygiene to a grotesque degree. The Livergood children—the other seven—recite horror stories about how their sister's disease stole her mind and their childhood. There is, at times, a sense of witness and intensity to their accounts that bears a resemblance to stories told by survivors of a cataclysm.

Schizophrenia is an ancient disease, an affliction shared by the victim and the victim's family. Families of schizophrenics often blame themselves, believing that some malaise in the household must be responsible. Their shame was once dealt with by the most extreme forms of denial: locking the "touched" family member in the attic or, later, spiriting that person away to institutions that earned the name "snake pits."

In recent times, people like Trish have been less hidden than they were in generations past. The idea that insanity is shameful, the reflection of weakness of character or morals, is slowly and grudgingly giving way to the modern medical understanding that it is a disease like any other, caused by a little-understood chemical imbalance in the body.

Still, the disease creates behavior that embarrasses normal people, that is almost impossible to live with, that sabotages most efforts at aid or treatment. It is especially difficult because it sabotages even sympathy. Unlike cancer or a palsy or a degenerative disorder, schizophrenia is not something you can see: a tumor, a tremor, or an obvious erosion. It is invisible, and in its thrall the victim often appears guilty of a diabolically willful malevolence. It can sometimes be controlled by drug therapy, but it can't be cured, not yet.

Schizophrenics in America today are left to wander the cities, to sleep on grates, and to stand in line for soup, the result of a well-meant policy of deinstitutionalization begun by President Kennedy more than twenty years ago, intended to free these people from institutional hellholes. The problem is that the hellholes of the hospitals have been exchanged for the hellholes of the street, thanks to an incoherent social policy on how schizophrenics should be housed and treated. They are often referred to as "the homeless," as if the absence of shelter, the inevitable result of their problem, were the problem itself.

The homelessness is a by-product of the schizophrenics' families' inability to tolerate the schizophrenic's disruptive presence beneath the original roof and of the recommendation by mental health professionals that patients live elsewhere for everybody's sake. Institutions are inhumane; halfway houses

are just that: halfway. These patients have a long-term disease
that requires long-term management. And the rage and guilt
most families feel toward their schizophrenic relatives make
them incapable of helping.

Some months ago, Meg Livergood wrote a letter to me at
the *Herald*. It was meticulously typed and presented, as if to
indicate that a troubled mind is not contagious. The Livergood family, she explained, had decided to tell their story
publicly—all of it, including details of a most intimate and
painful nature. It was a brave consensus, one that signaled a
dramatic change in the family dynamic: a new generation had
come to power, a generation of victims unburdened by the
guilt of having birthed and raised Trish.

Their hope, Meg wrote, was that a story about Tricia might
help make schizophrenia, the disease without walkathons and
poster children and charity balls, into a cause.

It was Trish's sister Amy who called the police and invited
them to meet Trish at the Miracle Theater two summers ago
and arrest her. Amy has always been a person of action. As a
child, she was the one who joined all the troops and all the
teams. In a family where drifting and dreaming hold a kind of
lyrical appeal (her father, a well-known Grove character, pur-
veyor of Martinburgers, is sixty-four years old and plans to
spend this summer strolling the boulevards of Paris), she is
sometimes teased for betraying the family honor by having
goals and meeting them. "I tell them all the time: I don't want
to be like you, a thinker and not a doer." She follows the
comment with her characteristic laugh.

Second from the youngest, Amy was the first to finish
college; she recently bought a townhouse. She works selling
advertising for Community Newspapers, Inc. A stunning,
strapping woman, she was the one her sister Lizzie and her
brother Jimmy contacted about the note, pressing her to do
something. Lizzie and Jimmy are the two Livergood children
who still live at the family home, nicknamed the Camp-

ground because it is something of an indoor/outdoor house. The missing windows are great for cross-ventilation.

"Lizzie and Jimmy were about having a cow; they kept saying this is the moment we've been waiting for, this is extortion. What are you going to do, you have to go to the police. I drove over to Miracle Mile with a detective in an unmarked car and I saw her right away, sitting on the bus bench. She was dressed the way she usually is dressed when she gets real sick. I give her my old clothes all the time, nice clothes, Calvin Kleins, but she loses them, so she ends up at the Salvation Army and she always picks out a bag lady outfit. That time she had on polyester pants that were too short with an elastic waistband. They were checks, black and white. I remember she was sitting there all hunched over, and she was real tan and real skinny. And the detective looked at me and looked at her and said, 'God she's thin. Is she normally built like you?' and I said, 'no.' At the police station I asked if I could get her anything, and she said a McDonald's would be nice, and so I got her a hamburger and a pack of cigarettes, which she always wants.

"You know, if Mom were still alive, we wouldn't have done this. See, Mom would have comforted Granga, and Granga would have felt protected by Mom. Mom would have brought Trish to Crisis. You have to be one sick dog to get into that place, but I really think at that time she would have been admitted for a few days. But you never know. They might have let her out in two hours. I can't count how many times people in our family brought her there, different members: I've been, Meg's been, everybody's been, and after a while you begin to think, what's the use? Fool me once, shame on you; fool me twice, shame on me."

If you ask family members to pinpoint when they first thought of Trish as insane, there is a puzzling discrepancy. Some say from her early childhood, some say at adolescence, some say in her early twenties, when she began using drugs heavily. Her sister Sue remembers that after Trish returned from college, she started to pace one day and kept pacing and pacing, and finally ran into the restaurant where Sue worked, careened around it wildly, and left. It was a coworker who said, "Something is wrong with your sister," and then Sue knew.

Everyone agrees: Trish was a major source of chaos in a house full of chaos.

Amy recalls:

"Trish had been a problem all our lives and all her life. Her actions sometimes seem so deliberate, and so mean, it's hard to believe she's not doing it all on purpose. She used to call us names and put us down all the time. When we were growing up, she paced the house all night long. One time she stood still and stared at one orange for two days. She would sit in your car and pee in her pants and laugh and laugh. And if you asked her why she did it she would say didn't you always wonder what it would be like to pee in your pants. When she's sick, she has this laughter called inappropriate laughter. She has bouts of violence. She hit Granga, she hit my mom. When she's crazy, she can be very, very strong. She jumped over a six-foot-tall wall with a fence on top of it at one hospital. She brought a parade of street people into our house, Jesus freaks, druggies, cons for sure. She went swimming-pool-hopping with Meg's kids; they were three and five. She told them she was their mother and taught them how to play with matches. She let a nine-year-old drive her car. She burned her arms with cigarettes. She wandered the streets in the middle of the night, a serious threat to her own physical well-being. She exposed herself to the neighbors. She took the family dogs, Scruffy and Annie, out in a torrential rain, and brought them somewhere so they would be lost forever, and she succeeded. The family never saw the dogs again. She threw away my mother's beloved plants, including a six-foot-in-diameter staghorn fern that was her great pride. You want to know her rationale for doing that? Well, that's why you have a house to keep that stuff outside, animals and plants. She said only assholes keep that stuff in their house. One time Mom asked her to clean the shelves in the kitchen, just to give her an activity, so she emptied out the cupboards and threw everything away.

"This merely scratches the surface. Try this. Our house had no air conditioning, but sometimes Trish would turn off all the fans and close the windows and close the shutters so you'd come home to a hotbox, and Tricia would be sitting there saying, 'I don't know what the big deal is.' You could never bring a friend home because of what Trish might be up to. When she wasn't hitting people, she would poke, poke, poke, especially your face when you were sleeping because she had trouble sleeping at night, and she would get really mad at us for keeping these weird schedules of waking up in the morning and going to bed at night.

"Plus, the nightly tirade of making her take her medicine. She didn't want to take her medicine because then she'd be like us. Who'd want to be weird like you, she would always say.

"So you quit fighting. She would stop taking it and pretty soon she'd get really sick and you're back at square one. You take her to Crisis, and they say they can only admit the craziest. So you take her home and sit around waiting for her to be the craziest.

"These are not isolated instances, a once-in-a-while thing. This was routine in our family.

"We tried private institutions. State hospitals. We tried not putting her in the hospital and keeping her at home, we tried halfway houses, we tried different kinds of drugs, we tried no drugs and outpatient psychotherapy. We tried going in weekly for shots."

The family's level of desperation rose to such heights that they urged Trish to get a one-way ticket to join the Rajneesh commune in Oregon when the cult was combing Miami flophouses for converts.

"To us," says Amy, "calling the police and sending her to jail was just another avenue. Hey, let's try this."

Imprisonment promised safe haven compared with the street. There would be more supervision, better medical care, actual group therapy, all kinds of things that she had never had in the mental health system. "In America," says Meg, "its better to be criminal and crazy than just plain crazy."

And so Trish was taken by the Coral Gables police to the Dade County Women's Detention Center. Most of the women she met there were in on prostitution charges, which they called "pros." She resisted any temptation to say she was in for "extor," and instead told them she had been arrested for sending a note to her grandmother. Most of them told her that if that was all she had done, she could expect to be back on the streets real soon honey.

The family was contacted by the state attorney's office and asked whether they were firm in their resolve to prosecute. It was up to Granga, because she was the one who had been threatened. Encouraged by the others, Granga, who is now ninety-one and all bird, all bones and flutter, was unwavering:

"Absolutely."

Trish was found incompetent to stand trial, so she was sent to the Florida State Hospital in Chattahoochee until her mental health improved to the point where she could understand the charges against her and be sentenced. There she took lessons in courtroom terms and she started work on an autobiography that included a list of all the men she had ever had sex with, even the ones who had raped her, and thoughts about her family and her childhood. The words fill every inch of page after page of legal paper, and reflect an overcrowded mind. Chattahoochee was her all-time favorite mental institution. They had barbecues and dances, and at Christmas everyone got a present: "It has a real nice Southern flavor."

Her family did not attempt to contact her, although she did on occasion contact them. At Chattahoochee, two years after

her mother's death, Tricia wrote her a letter, asking for cigarettes.

Happy hour at the Taurus bar in Coconut Grove on Friday
nights is a boozy open-air salute to tropical leisure, and a
newcomer hyper from a hard week downtown might not
detect the group within the group, but veterans always keep
an eye out for the Livergood family, for that slew of brothers
and sisters, handsome, outgoing kids now in their twenties
and thirties and for their father, Martin, the man in the signa-
ture white cap, playfully tilted, who sells Martinburgers at the
Taurus on Saturdays and Sundays.

The Livergoods have a wonderful aura of moveable feast.
Like any big family with grown children who manage to get
along, there is something enviable about their intimacy, a
clubby sort of magnetism. They are like a resort town, permanent throughout the seasons, and the people who hang
around the family are like tourists, eager for contact but af-
flicted with a wistful feeling of having trespassed.

During the time that Trish was at Chattahoochee, the
other family members continued their Sunday morning tradition of meeting for breakfast at 9 A.M. at Monty Trainer's
restaurant. The tradition started four years ago, right after
their mother died. To the Livergood children the miracle of
Sunday breakfast is not that they get together week in and
week out and that everybody tends to be in a good mood,
but that Martin buys. Martin is one of those colorful fathers
who they wouldn't want to have missed, but sometimes the
children wish that a touch of practicality had tempered his
pipe dreams.

All cancer is cruel, and Norma Livergood was cruelly sick
with hers for about two years before she died. The Livergood
daughters are very nurturing to each other, but the one arena
in which it's every woman for herself is the contest over who
looks and acts most like their mother. They all want that
championship.

While Martin Livergood dreamed big, Norma Livergood sold tires and bras at Sears to support the family.

Martin Livergood's children sometimes call their father Mr. Bigwig, Mr. Dreams. He became a hippie in the sixties, and while there was a certain drama in having a father who didn't go to work, his rebellions carried a hefty tariff, like the time in 1967 when the family had no phone, no car, and lived in a one-room cottage in the Gables for a year.

Norma Livergood quietly provided throughout. She washed the clothes, she cleaned the house, she bore the burden of Trish. Her only failing was as a cook; her kitchen repertoire seems to have consisted of one dish: grease-spitting hamburgers the shape and size of golf balls cooked at a too-high heat. But her husband compensated there. There was nothing he liked more than concocting a big aromatic pot of something. Something about feeding hordes has always appealed to him. Among his failed businesses was one called International Harvest Corp., in which he proposed that shrimp boats be equipped with plants that turn the trash fish inevitably scooped into their nets into protein powder to feed the masses. He still has faith in the idea, and a certain misty-eyed sentimentality overtakes his voice when he recounts its failure, like a belle bemoaning a lost beau: "It was going to go some place. . . . It had dynamite potential . . . and to think I was only one boat short."

Norma Livergood met Martin, both only children, in Chicago. She was nineteen and he was twenty-three when they married, and he had already started a career in sales. Up until 1961, when Martin Livergood started a magazine called *Beachcomber,* which lasted one issue and plunged him into a debt of about a quarter of a million dollars, the family lived well. The magazine was supposed to appeal to people who hung out on the beaches. Given the fact that the target audience consisted mostly of ne'er-do-wells, or, if that is too harsh, of people who tend not to hold in high regard the

notion of a fixed address, a liability to any circulation department, it is probably not surprising that the enterprise died.
Not a single issue survives.

Since 1961 Martin Livergood's two longest-running gigs
have been at the Village Cobbler in Coconut Grove in the seventies, when home-made leather sandals were the countercul-
ture rage and, later, when the requests for sandals dipped from
about eight pairs a day to one or two, at the hamburger stand he
started called Martinburgers. "Yum-Yum time," he shouts to
healthy-looking people in their 100 percent cotton clothes,
strolling down Main Highway in the Grove in search of
personal happiness and something to buy. He makes enough
money to pay the rent on a modest apartment behind the Taurus. Meg says, "He is trying real hard lately and he's fixed up
that apartment real cute; it's such a riot." At this apartment is a
huge framed version of Norma's favorite poem, "If," which
was read at her funeral. For two years after his wife's death, he
stayed on at the Campground, and it was a huge relief to his
children when he decided to strike out on his own, but less of a
relief when he showed up with a very young girlfriend at one
gathering, causing Lizzie, the youngest, to want to call her bad
names. He can be seen, tall, striking, with a beard and a pot-
belly, walking the streets of the Grove every morning on his
way to coffee and the crossword puzzle at any of several sidewalk cafés that he frequents, the white cap as his herald, revealing, as hats often do, a secret wish to be something of a legend.

It built slowly, the decision of the Livergood family to tell
Trish's story and their own, and it might not have happened at
all if Patricia, after her release from Chattahoochee, had been
able to make it without their intervention, even allowing for
an extremely liberal definition of what making it might mean
for someone with Trish's disability.

This is Trish's view of the family, from her autobiography,
written in that frantic cramped script while she was feeling
what she calls "paranoid," her all-purpose word for when she
is unmedicated, out-of-sorts, and hallucinating:

"I don't feel my family is qualified to control my life. I don't want anything to do with them. I just don't like them. They suck. They are like monkeys in a cage."

Trish sits on her narrow cot at the boardinghouse in Cutler Ridge, hunched over a precious pad of paper upon which she writes all her goals:

"—get my picture in Easy Rider magazine
—join health spa
—buy a bike
—get some underwear"

Trish Livergood lives here now. After her release on probation from Chattahoochee last summer, she was placed in this home along with several other deinstitutionalized patients and enrolled in a rehabilitation program in which she has taken a video workshop and courses in kitchen skills, where she learns such things as how to place those movable letters on a menu chart: fried or baked fish, macaroni and cheese, black-eyed peas and okra, tossed salad, chicken, apple pie. This task consumes an hour.

She goes to group therapy and takes Trilafon, a pill that she says has miraculously calmed her.

There is no more scavenging for food from dumpsters; meals are provided by the boardinghouse.

The days go slowly. Her training classes end at one, and after that there is the TV in the living room of the boarding-house or the 7-Eleven about a mile down the street where she can hang out. Then she thinks about these guys that keep coming around that are a little like, well, strays, and they won't leave her alone. They all want sex. Part of a long line of reject boyfriends; who was the first one? The one who got his money by pretending to lose coins in cigarette machines. Sometimes he got up to six, seven dollars a day. Maybe the problem is where she meets these guys, sitting out in back of the 7-Eleven drinking beer. Some of those people are nice, like the guy who lives in the meter room, he's nice, and so is the guy who lives with the guy who lives in the meter room at the back of the store. But then again the only thing they ever want to do is drink beer, and she's not against beer or coffee and cigarettes, she likes them, but not every minute. Then there's this latest guy, he comes and gets her, and hardly says a thing, and then he drives her to a construction site and tells her to look at the lake, which is no lake, it's nothing but a rock pit, and then he wants sex, and when it's over he says hey, want to drive with me to the gas station to get some gas, so she says OK but he changes his mind and just drops her back off at the boardinghouse and says maybe he'll come by next weekend, too, so be ready.

She has tried to buy guns twice. The problem is you can't get much of a gun, really, for under two hundred dollars. She looks at guns when she gets all hung up on the possibility of suicide. She would pick a private place, like at the beach.

She goes back to writing her lists. She is trying to remember all the things she shoplifted recently and hopes to repay, like a lunch at a restaurant from which she simply walked out, and also two bottles of Lancer rosé wine, which she saves on a small nightstand to use as vases, in case someday someone gives her flowers.

The price of a clean narrow bed in a room with three other beds and three meals a day and a television that is on continuously from one in the afternoon until eleven at night is three hundred dollars a month. Her landlord, Betty Wade, accepted Trish with the understanding that when her Social Security check came through she would be reimbursed for any back charges.

But it wasn't that simple.

Getting public assistance became an ordeal. After Trish was released, she was denied disability because she had worked in the past, and so—by bureaucratic reasoning—was capable of working in the future.

When she couldn't get money to pay Mrs. Wade, she turned to her family, first to Meg, the sister who had driven by her in the street a year before. Meg cringed: "She takes up a ton of your life if she has half a chance." Yet she listened.

Trish asked: "How sick do you have to be to get benefits?"

And Meg thought: That's a good question. Let's ask the whole world.

It was Meg who first proposed contacting the *Herald,* but she wanted the entire family to support the project. In unanimity, she felt, there was impact. Any big family is more than the sum of its individual members; it is also the family as a unit, a massive singular entity that is unique in nature, capable of acting with peculiar force, a sort of combination tornado, chorus, and posse.

Meg never forgave herself for driving by her sister that summer day. ("What would my mother say if she knew?")

Meg's most riveting feature are her eyes, large, woeful, beckoning, luminescent blue. She says all her life she has had trouble looking directly at people. It was from years and years of avoiding looking at Trish.

The first person Meg called was Amy, because she expected her to be the most supportive.

Amy was. She had long felt that the problem with the Livergoods is that they are all reaction, no action. Her response to being victimized by Trish as a child is to refuse to be victimized as an adult. To be silent would be to give the disease the last laugh.

Amy promised herself she would tell all, even the gross part that there was no way to make sound not gross: all those times when Trish wouldn't do anything about her period. It would just be coming out of her, dripping all over the house, dripping all over you, and to this day when people compliment Amy on how well she gets along with everybody, she always says to herself, "I think it's great there's that whole huge public out there and not one of them is dripping menstrual blood on me."

Meg expected some resistance to the idea of contacting the newspaper from the oldest Livergood sibling, Kathy. The Livergood children divide themselves in half: the first four had one kind of childhood, the kind with a big house and lessons and studio pictures with the Easter Bunny, and the others—born after financial reverses—had a different kind, a scrappier sort of hippie existence, one in which curfews and limits were mostly self-imposed. Trish and her problems colored the childhood of the first group; they tyrannized the upbringing of the second.

Now thirty-eight and a display artist at a department store, Kathy has a role in the family as elegant oldest sister. She has long fingers, a face that is beautifully composed, and a natural style that causes her to look put together in anything, even a frayed sweat shirt. She is divorced, with teenaged children. Everyone teases her about her soft-spoken air of career-girl perfection; they call her Mary Tyler Moore. When people outside the family used to ask Norma Livergood why Kathy turned out differently, she would say Kathy had a different mother. Kathy's mother volunteered to work on charities, she belonged to a country club, and her husband was a prosperous seller of ads for magazines like *Newsweek*.

Kathy had for a long time made it clear that if she had her choice she would not have anything to do with Trish ever again. In Kathy's earliest memories Trish had behaved in an irritating way. When they bathed together, she would kick and kick until Kathy was forced into a corner of the tub. She ruined dinners with her creepy nonstop stare. "Mom," Kathy would say, "make Tricia stop staring."

"Tricia, stop staring."

But of course she never did.

But there was an even fresher wound that led Meg to think Kathy would object.

"I think Trish killed Mom. I really do," Kathy says. "The stress she caused that woman. . . ."

But Kathy said all right. She wasn't wild about the idea, but she would not stand in its way. It was the call of blood. Although she had no wish to be burdened by Trish and her problems, she would not burden the family with her misgivings as they traveled yet another avenue for help.

Trish is the next oldest, thirty-seven, and then comes Sue, a year younger. Martin calls Sue the Aunt Mary in the family and says everyone should have an Aunt Mary. Sue organizes, Sue plans, Sue remembers everyone's birthday.

Sue is known within the family for having suffered one particular disappointment:

When Trish graduated from Gables High she was sent away to college by her parents. The following year, when it was Sue's turn, she was told that there was no money for it. As it turned out, Trish would be the only Livergood child the parents sent to college. Trish chose Vernon Count in Rhode Island from an ad in the back of *Seventeen* magazine. To this day, the Livergood children believe she was not sent off so she could have a broadening intellectual experience, but so the parents could ship the turmoil out of state. Six months later, Trish was asked to leave the school. She had not gone to classes, she had run up huge bills.

Sue is cheerful, pretty, outgoing. She is married to a handsome, husky guy, the brother of Meg's husband, and together they own and operate a bike shop in Key Largo. They are planning to sell the business and they recently moved to Miami, in the Hammocks, in West Kendall, a citadel of easy houses, easy living and outward suburban propriety. Sue has been asked if the Livergood family, with its maverick streak, is disappointed because she has chosen such a conventional place, and she usually responds, "Don't worry. We're just renting."

Once for an entire year Sue's family watched "Ozzie and Harriet" reruns. People come to her for advice so much that when the *Chicago Sun Times* had the Ann Landers contest, she applied.

Sue is the grown-up.

Sue not only agreed to publicity, she also volunteered to go to Social Security with Trish and to serve as go-between with Trish and the rest of the family.

For months Trish had been getting letters of rejection from Social Security and all her phone calls met with rebuff. But when she materialized in the drab, crowded waiting room with her sister, and with a reporter brandishing a reporter's notebook, she was not turned away with the usual dispatch but instead ushered to a desk with a man behind it who had a phone upon which it was possible to place a long-distance call to a person in Baltimore and inquire about a case review. Throughout, Sue tried to act like Ann Landers. Here's a problem and it's our job to solve it, so let's get it done as pleasantly as possible. The initial joy in learning in early March that Social Security was conducting a review that could result in retroactive benefits was dissipated in May when Sue learned that Trish's file is still sitting in Miami. "Boy, if I knew they weren't going to send it out right away, I would have called every day."

John is the child who has moved away, and Meg expected major objections from him. He is a big guy, rugged looking, into computer sales; he was always strong and sturdy and used that to create an aura of invincibility around the others. The myth of his strength goes back to the playpen: as a baby he dismantled and wrecked two, three, or four of them, depending on who remembers. "Top quality, from Marshall Field" recalls his father, his voice filled with admiration even now.

John was the leader of the younger pack, and sometimes their tormentor. Both Jimmy and Lizzie remember John dangling them by their legs over the second-floor balcony of the Campground, and when the younger children watched TV he sometimes made them stay put by brandishing a belt. He liked to pin Lizzie to the ground and start to spit, only to suck it back at the very last minute. "Normal things, sort of," says Lizzie. He owns a nice house in Atlanta, earns ninety-six-thousand dollars a year in the computer business, and has interviewed for only three jobs in his life, all of which he got. "Distant and disconnected" is how he sometimes describes himself, especially when it comes to family matters. He has sayings for when a subject makes him uncomfortable:

"That's all the emotional attention I can devote to that subject right now."

"Sorry, the memory disc is full."

"The board of directors is falling asleep."

He said yes.

"Are you sure," asked Meg, astonished. "I mean, you know what you're getting into. . . ."

"Yes."

"The family name. . . ."

"Really. Yes."

Amazingly, they all said later: The board of directors didn't fall asleep. No one knew exactly what was going on in his mind when he said yes, and no one questioned him, because they did not want him to reconsider.

Meg assumed Jimmy would be a piece of cake.

Jimmy, who wants to be known as James, is said to be by all the others the best looking in the family. He was certainly the most photographed as a baby, a statistic that sets off a secret fury in his siblings. He is a waiter at a place where he has to tell the customers "Hi, my name is James," and he is always talking about moving away. He is the artist in the family, though he does not pursue that gift very actively, unless you count the time recently when he spray-painted black the flowered couch in Granga's living room. He jokingly calls himself a life-long bachelor.

Jimmy's the most sensitive, and he feels the most guilt about everything, not just Trish. "Oh God, I remember how Amy and I used to send Trish to the 7-Eleven in the rain to get candy, just to get rid of her . . . sure, sure, if you think it will do any good."

Jimmy was indeed cake.

Lizzie is the baby. She says there is one quick way to sum up her position in the family: "There are no baby pictures of me." The other children used to tease her and tell her she was adopted, and when they ran off and abandoned her, she had a song, "Everybody hates me," which as the years went by turned into a more upbeat version: "Everybody doesn't like me."

Lizzie said it was fine with her, but as far as she was concerned the logical solution for Trish and people like her was to build a big underground city somewhere and when they do something beyond the pale they should—and she makes a swooshing sound—be sent down a one-way chute for all of time.

Granga will talk to anybody about anything as long as the Livergood children are present. She assumes most strangers work for the city.

Granga had purchased the house in the Gables for the family in 1968 after the horrible year in one room, the one that Meg tries never to think about: "Oh God, we had to sleep in shifts. I slept outdoors on a porch. It was no fun." Granga's generosity in buying a house for her daughter and that husband of Norma's and their great teeming brood of kids, for the whole noisy crew, was undercut slightly by her intention to live there as well. "Martin and I never got along," she says. "Sons-in-law are like that sometimes. Oh, we say hello. The other day at that thing [her ninety-first birthday party] he waved, I waved. That's about as far as it goes."

Granga's voice often changes its register; it has the weak, scratchy quality of a record that's been played too often. "If Trish moves back here, I'm leaving. I'll go to Epworth Village in Hialeah. Have you ever been there?"

"But," said Meg, "no problem, Granga, Trish isn't coming back."

"Epworth would be a nice place. . . . Sue?"

"It's Meg."

"Oh, I thought you were Lizzie. Don't forget about my funeral."

"I won't, Granga."

"Promise now. . . ."

"I promise."

The young woman mouths the instructions of the old one: "Mass at the Church of the Little Flower . . . make a nice donation . . . not cremated, buried . . . about one hundred dollars."

Her memory is a river that is sometimes deep and sometimes shallow, and you never know which it will be when.

Monday through Friday Martin Livergood does not work. He is a boulevardier in a culture that he says has no respect for men of his leisurely leanings. "In this country," he says, "it's a bummy thing to do, to go from coffee shop to coffee shop." He wakes up early and has coffee and breakfast at any of two or three spots in the Grove. He might do an errand in the late morning, talk to his meat man in South Miami, or go to Norman's and get something fresh for dinner that night if he is cooking for company, something he tries to do once a week or so.

On the weekends when he's doing the burger gig, he tries not to drink until five or six. Then he has a beer or two and goes out to a nice restaurant, where he enjoys a couple of strong vodka drinks and a bottle of wine, and then maybe an after-dinner drink or two. When he recites his week's schedule, he laughs and says, "God, I sound like an alcoholic."

He gave his blessing to Meg for publicity, but he didn't think it would do any good. He says that he despises all that crap from the *mea culpa* crowd, that a child like Trish is a cross to bear. He remembers Trish when she was very young, and ornery, and all the old excuses: "The child's left-handed." . . . "She's stuck in the middle between two sisters." . . . "She has that weak eye that turns inward."

Then, when she got really sick, she beat up Granga, she beat up Norma. "She wouldn't sleep. We worried she would set the house on fire. She used to put rope around our doorknob and try to keep us locked in our room. I used to say, 'Don't worry, Norma. I have a knife.'

"Norma's father was the same way, you know. He died in an asylum. Norma was afraid of him. He was an insanely meticulous dresser of the straw-hat days. He spent most of his time doing his fingernails, but once in a while he'd lose it in the middle of the night and start crowing like a rooster."

As far as Martin is concerned, even if Trish always was imbalanced, it was drugs that tipped her over for good. "Trish went on a bad drug trip when she was twenty years old or so and she never returned.

"I've erased Tricia out of my life," he says softly.

He is not sure he ever wants to see her again.

"You know," says Sue, "For a parent it is as if the child has died."

Almost, but not quite.

The baby in the studio picture of Trish, cooing, pampered, in a hopeful, gorgeous dress, has not died so much as disappeared, and a mocking impostor has taken her place.

At first Tricia herself did not want a story done. "I have to live and work in this town," she told Amy. "What will all my friends in Miami think?"

Amy considered the question. "But Trish, you *don't have* any friends in Miami."

Trish said, "I guess you're right."

Later she would joke about how a story about her should begin:

"Attractive, popular, should be with normal people. . . ."

For the first time in her life, encouraged by social workers, Trish is reading about her disease. "Schizophrenia means split mind, and it might make you think you are someone else better than who you really are, like Jesus, though I personally have never thought I was some great person. When I'm sick, I just zoom and I don't have any feelings at all."

She has started reading a book called *Is There No Place on Earth for Me?* by Susan Sheehan, about a mental patient. "The girl in the book is named Sylvia Frumpkin, and she's all right but really I don't like her very much. In a hospital ward, you can just tell, she's a real management problem, kicking and spitting at the nurses and not taking her medicine, and I don't like to be prejudiced, but people like that are really crazy."

There is one part of the book that intrigues Trish, the afterword in which the author states that Sylvia Frumpkin has improved dramatically and has not been hospitalized in recent times.

Trish is incredulous. "How did she do that?"

"I would love," says Trish's sister Sue, "To go before a Senate subcommittee on schizophrenia. Can you imagine explaining to them that your sister's friend lives in the meter room at the 7-Eleven and that he has a roommate? It's a whole silent world."

She keeps a notebook recording all the appointments she has made for Trish, the trips to Social Security, the sessions with Trish's counselor, the appointments that she had urged Trish to make with the dentist at the clinic. Sue decided that this is the year to do what she wants with her time; both children are in school. She has made Trish her project. With each triumph she says to her, "Let's not get a lot excited."

Then Trish starts talking what Sue calls Bigwig Talk—job, apartment, car, marriage—Sue says, "Time and place. A day at a time. Don't pressure yourself, Trish, if you know what I mean.

"Maybe you could get one of those squeegees and a bucket and a rag and go around cleaning windows at a shopping center."

"Maybe," says Trish, "but really, I want a real job. And another thing, Sue. I want to get my own place. The boardinghouse is kind of baby care."

"Time and place, Trish, you know what I mean?"

Then Trish asks for a match for a cigarette stub she has retrieved from a public ashtray. Sue looks askance at the stub, and Trish says, "I knew you wouldn't like it."

Trish looks forward to Sue's visits more than anything. "All my sisters and brothers are nice, but Sue's visits are real special." Sue brings her clothes from the other sisters, and one miraculous time Meg sent down a brand-new box of makeup, which instantly replaced the Lancer wine vases as Trish's most prized possession. "This," says Trish, "is a true God bless."

"Trish, this all stops if you stop taking your medication," says Sue.

"I know."

"Absolutely, Trish."

"You don't have to worry about it. I already decided I'm not going to ruin my life just because of one little pill."

It was the end of a visit in late March, and Sue had dropped Trish back at the boardinghouse. While Trish was in the bathroom, Sue counted her pills. She wanted to count them again at the next visit to make certain the correct amount had disappeared.

"Sue," said Trish, returning to the room. She addressed the floor rather than her sister directly. "I've been thinking."

"Oh oh. What's up?"

Trish looked up. Her brown eyes were lighted by blue makeup applied with some care. Her hair was down and she twisted a strand as she spoke. "Well, you know Easter is coming up."

"What about it, Trish,?"

"Well, I was thinking, if the family is going to get together, I'd like to come."

Sue braced. She kept her voice very calm and gave her sister a level look.

"Trish, I have to be honest. Not everyone in the family is sold on seeing you again. You've put a lot of them through a lot."

"Well, I've been taking my medicine."

"They've heard that before."

Trish didn't respond.

"I'll ask them. I'll do what I can. I think you've changed. I really do. You know this is the first time you've admitted you have a disease. But. . . ."

"I was kind of lonesome at Christmas, that's where I got the idea to come down there for Easter, and I thought the whole thing through."

"Trish, you know what your social workers say. It's very important for you not to hang around with the family. It doesn't mix. It's very stressful for everybody."

"Well, I don't think I should be excluded from the family because it's stressful." Her voice was flat and low, and she looked down and away as she spoke. She folded her arms and moved her tongue around inside her closed mouth while she nodded her head back and forth. This was as close as she had gotten with Sue in these visits to rebellion and passion. And then she spoke.

"I am part of the family even if I have schizophrenia."

That night Trish and her friend Anita went to the 7-Eleven and sat in the back amid debris, hoping to collect the usual crowd of men, who provide beer and companionship and compliments, especially to Trish. Her teeth are a liability: brown raggedy stubs. They appear to ache even if they do not. When she walks, she lopes, with her head leading the way, as if striving to arrive everywhere a millisecond before the rest of her. But she has an appealing slim figure, and her cheekbones are enviably high. In certain lights the pinched, preoccupied brow softens, and there is a trusting freckled innocence to the way she looks that takes her back in time, ten, twenty years.

"I feel depressed tonight."

"I don't know why."

"Granga's scared of me. I guess I went too far.

"That note I sent her. I didn't mean for it to be threatening. I said dead meat just to be, you know, social, the way people call each other dead meat. What I should have done was put the word 'borrowed' in it. Sue says Granga's scared of me now. I guess I went a little too far. I was hallucinating she had lots of money lying around the house.

"I had the best childhood. We were all just one big happy family. It was fairyland. We lived in this one 150-year-old Victorian house in Chicago, and I had a beautiful room and lots of Ginny dolls. I miss my mom. Mom's Irish. You have to know something about Irish people. They love to talk, and Mom's big characteristic is talking. At her funeral they read a poem she really loves by Kipling about how if all around you everyone is losing their head and if you can keep yours, well son, then you are a man."

The idea that Trish would join the family at Easter aroused different emotions in different people. Sue, they said, we've heard it before. You're the only one who believes she has a future. What if she decides to tear the restaurant apart?

"She won't," said Sue, "she's fine. She's different this time, I'm telling you."

"Well, then, why so soon? Why now? Why Easter?" They worried that the reunion was simply showmanship, all song and cabaret designed to satisfy the great maw of a newspaper article, and not because of some genuine family longing.

"Trish asked me herself. She wants to come." Jimmy and

Lizzie said they might have to work; after all, Easter's a pretty big day at restaurants. Martin kept wondering why celebrate Easter anyway; to him, religion is ridiculous, it's the wearing of costumes and the worship of ghosts. "Dad," said Sue, in her steady voice, looking to soothe, not outrage. "No one's asking you to go to church."

Then Martin decided he had to work.

"For thirty years," Sue said, "Dad has made a big point of never having to go to work, but suddenly on Easter he has to sell Martinburgers."

Some family members told Sue: "You know, Granga's pretty old. If Trish comes, she might have a stroke or a heart attack."

"Keep them apart," said Sue. "Don't tell her Trish is there. Half the time Granga doesn't even know who I am."

John said he could live with it, but he was from out of town now and so the problem doesn't belong to him in the same way it belongs to the others. In his typical language, flavored by years around computers and corporations, he described his sister as "a supreme resource drain."

Worrying about Trish and how she would behave was easier than worrying about themselves and how they would behave. But it was a test for everyone.

Trish's goals now, from her notes:
"To acquire a lot of clothes, jewelery, makeup, shoes etc.
To live in the country (mountains) of North Carolina.
To have a good relationship with someone I like and get married.
To be about fifteen pounds thinner.
To have a car and a good job for a while.
To be involved in life and be happy.
To be on the bright side instead of the dull side."

Behaving in the manner of a benign despot, Sue went ahead and made reservations, picking a place she likes, the elegant

Biltmore. ("I'm the classicist in the family.") The time was set for noon; at eleven the immediate family would gather at the Campground for a photo session that would re-create a similar picture taken almost twenty years ago with two major differences: No Mom, no Trish. It was decided by the majority that Trish should not be in the photo because her presence would symbolize a return to the fold that had not actually occurred and that may not even happen.

On the night before Easter, Kathy called Sue to say she wasn't sure about the next day, wasn't sure if she could take it. Sue said, give me a break.

Of all the children, Sue and Amy were the least apprehensive. Amy was furious at the others:

"Sometimes Meg and Jimmy and Lizzie act now as if they are so hurt by Trish, so scared. I don't buy it. They're not children anymore. They can handle Trish.

"From what Sue says, maybe she can have a little life now. Sue says she's going to get Social Security, but even if she didn't, why couldn't we all chip in a few dollars a month, we're all working, we could help. Theoretically, if she were retarded, we would have no hesitation about helping her.

"I think the people in my family would rather be mad at Trish than sad about her. When you're mad you can hate someone. When you hate someone, you don't have to care about them. When you're sad you feel more helpless. You're more aware . . . *this is Trish.*

"I'm not a martyr. I don't go around helping every different kind of weirdo. But I do feel unconditional love for my family. I would not turn my back on any of them, not one."

On Easter Sunday, Trish put on an outfit that Amy had sent down: a silk T-shirt and white pants. Amy told her to be sure not to wear striped or colored underpants and she heeded this advice. Trish told everyone in the boardinghouse that she was going to order a steak, which stands in her mind as the ultimate food luxury. Trish knew that her brother-in-law was coming to get her at eleven. She tried not to get ready too early, but by ten she was waiting. There was a great debate over who would actually have to go and get Trish. She didn't know that one of the reasons that Meg's husband was serving as chauffeur was that he had accidentally shot his youngest boy with a BB gun and the boy's foot had become infected.

For Meg's husband, picking up Trish was an act of penance.

Everyone agreed the reunion went much better than expected, except Trish, for whom the day worked out just as happily as she had hoped for, with the single quibble that the restaurant had a buffet breakfast and she could not get a steak.

She spoke to everyone, including Granga.

The consensus of the party postmortem was that Trish did seem to be doing better than she had in years. Lizzie allowed as how that one-way chute to the shadow city for shadow people might not be necessary after all. John and his bride listened politely while Trish told the same story about babysitting John over and over, about taking him to the park, and how he had gone to the bathroom there, at times punctuating her accounts with THE laugh. Not a laugh, THE laugh. Kathy had feared Trish would be appalling: "And except for her teeth, she looked good. The thing I noticed is that in the past when she had problems it always seemed as if maybe she could slip back into a normal life, but now I don't think that's possible."

Martin came, and ate, quickly. He did not speak to much of anybody, but when he left he put his arms around Trish, hesitantly at first, and then a little less awkwardly, and seized her, surrounding her slender bony body with a quick fierce wordless hug.

❦　❦　❦

The single most glamorous development in the life of Trish Livergood since being rescued by her family was her appearance on "Donahue," when she and her sister Meg promoted what has become a family cause: eliminating prejudice against mental illness.

"Let me tell you," says sister Meg, "what schizophrenia isn't. It isn't something maliciously concocted by Trish to ruin our lives. It's an actual illness, oftentimes seen on a CAT scan image as a physical effect on the brain. I know that I can't treat a schizophrenic any more than I can treat a diabetic because I am not a trained professional. With that knowledge, the guilt, fear, frustration, and anger have disappeared. And once I could relate to schizophrenia as being real—just as diabetes is real and as something that must be vigorously and continuously managed—I was able to love my sister as I love all of my brothers and sisters."

Despite Trish's strides, Meg warns, "My sister has always danced on a very high, very weak thread. Until there's a cure, that's an on-going truth. The difference is that now she has a net beneath her."

For the "Donahue" show Trish and her sister Meg got to fly to New York, to take three limousine drives, and to stay at a swank hotel where they could order whatever they wanted from room service.

"The food came up on a table, and all the dishes had those silver things on top of them," recalls Trish, puffing on one of her ever-present cigarettes. Whenever the subject of "Donahue" comes up, Trish's face, which seems prettier now, less harsh and with fewer lines, breaks into a huge grin. The rest of her—a pleasingly lanky collection of tall person bones—is animated as well.

"During the commercials, do you have any idea what he does? I mean can you just guess?" Although these are questions, the sense is that she wants to provide the answer on her own. "He," she says pursing her lips a bit, mimicking the style of an inveterate gossip with a true tidbit, "flirts."

She pauses to let the information float gently forth, like a leaf in autumn.

"He flirts with all the women in the audience and I'm not kidding. It was quite an experience going on that show."

But that was not her biggest break in the past few years, not by a long shot. Her biggest break is that she has a real job now—twenty-six hours a week, earning about ninety-eight dollars after taxes. The siblings gratefully give most of the credit to Sue, who over the years has shouldered their mother's former responsibility as Trish's protector.

With the assistance of a social action program called Fellowship House, Trish started out on jobs with minimal responsibility; her first was to pick up trash in the parking lot of the Wometco movie theater complex a couple of hours a week in the early morning. From there she graduated to a job in maintenance at Herman's World of Sporting Goods, cleaning bathrooms and sweeping floors. This occupied her two hours a day, five days a week, and even when Trish got so depressed that all she could do was stay in bed and drink coffee and smoke cigarettes, she made herself go to Herman's for those two hours. "That job," she says, "was the one thing I couldn't afford to lose."

Because of the episodic nature of her disease, she had to be hospitalized twice and missed work. Both times it was caused by the same thing—the doctors thought she was doing so well they reduced her dosage. Other than those two episodes, she always showed up.

Her sister Meg had this to say about a recent incident: "The family gathered for Thanksgiving dinner last year and Tricia came over. She had just changed jobs and just turned forty and it was a little too much. We noticed that she would laugh a little too hard, she would snap at people where she normally wouldn't and if you knew what to look for you could see she was slipping." Later, back at her own apartment, "she threw out all the food she had bought and she was screaming at people." Meg and other relatives went to get her under the pretext of going for a cup of coffee and took her to the hospital, where she remained for several weeks as doctors got the episode under control and stabilized her medication. Then she did beautifully.

In time, Trish's diligence paid off.

She spoke to her counselors at Fellowship House about taking on a harder job for longer hours. Trish said, "I want to be more in the flow of the mainstream." She was told she could apply to be a cashier at Toys R Us near Dadeland.

"You have to take a four-page test:

"Did you ever have a problem with alcohol on the job?

"Do you have friends who steal?

"Do you think you should get the same punishment for stealing food as other things?

"Would you give a person who didn't have enough change a break on the price?"

"The basic trick," says Trish, "is to answer no to every-thing."

Trish dresses nicely for work, in stylish short skirts and pretty blouses. People tell her she looks like Cher and like Olive Oyl, and she takes both comparisons as compliments. She walks to work from where she lives, and always gets there a half-hour before her shift so she can cool off in the break room and relax with a couple of cigarettes. At her register she is the very picture of intense concentration and polite pa-tience. She is on her feet all day, and at the end of eight hours she says, "It's just the weirdest feeling. I'm tired but I'm not sleepy."

Back when she was living on the streets and owned nothing she used to save everything, including rubber bands, paper clips, old straws.

"I'm more selective now," she says, and the Fellowship House apartment is proof of how much better off she is these days. She is proud of all her possessions, including prescrip-tion glasses, two charge cards (Lerner and J.C. Penney's, each with a limit of $450), a TV with remote control, a Sony radio, a statue of the number forty for holding candles left over from her recent birthday, several pairs of shoes, a pretty tin box that used to contain candy, a bag of blow pop lollipops for her girlfriend Angel, who likes them for some reason, a hanging Santa bear, several packages of pretty soaps not yet opened, a dress for her twentieth high-school reunion, which unfortunately she missed because she was in the hospital, a photo album with pictures from when she was young and had all her real teeth and pictures from now with the new fake teeth, two purses, lots of makeup in a shoe box, four or five pairs of earrings, an icebox stocked with juice, bread, ice cream, and frozen chicken thighs, a cupboard with whole-wheat pancake mix and noodle soup. She also has a roommate who shares her food and has "a real nice personality."

Because of the large volume of business, Toys R Us allows for a variance of five dollars between the amount of business done that day according to the tape and the amount of cash in the register. Trish's variance is one of the lowest. It has always been under one dollar, and most days it is under fifty cents. In the words of her boss, "She's an excellent worker, just super. She's accurate, dependable and good with the customers. You couldn't ask for more unless it was more people like Trish."

Trish even has a plan for the future. She wants to study word processing and find work in that field. Her goal is a full-time job, with vacation pay and retirement benefits and a little office. She wants to make enough money to buy her own condo.

"Right now," she says, "I'm strictly dreaming, but if I could live anywhere in Miami it would be at a place like King's Creek, which are real affordable spacious condominiums near Dadeland." She has ideas about how to furnish a condo: "I want a black leather couch. I insist on a black leather couch. They cost about one thousand dollars. And I would like a full-size or a queen-size brass bed and a stereo and a TV stand and a tall cabinet you can put all your stuff in. Maybe even a dog, like a basset hound because they're docile, or if I'm really living all by myself maybe it better be a German shepherd."

She would like to swim in the pool in the common area

every day and eat only healthy food. She would have as her vehicle not a car but a red F-10 Chevy pick-up truck. She imagines herself sitting outdoors at night on one of those little balconies, maybe having a cigarette or two if she hasn't given them up by then, listening to her favorite Elvis tape (*Fools Rush In* and *I Can't Help Falling in Love with You*) and just thinking, relaxing, and watching while the smoke drifts off and disappears, joining the clouds in a sky she can almost touch.

"When I told my sister Sue about my fantasy, Sue said 'That's not a fantasy. That's reality. That's your goal.' Imagine that!"

MOTHER
KNOWS BEST

One day last summer on her way to stardom in New York City, ten-year-old Tamara Jones consumed the following items: orange juice, a Danish, Perrier water, a doughnut, root beer soda, part of a tuna fish sandwich, a brownie.

Then she puked.

Afterward she had a late afternoon snack of some blueberry frozen yogurt, and at dinner she picked at a piece of chicken and fell asleep at the restaurant.

It had been a long day: a modeling session for McCall's patterns, an audition for a detergent commercial, then some hanging around at a dessert parlor that specializes in entertainment by children. This was followed by the upset stomach and a trying interview with an agent. Dinner was at the Lion's Rock Restaurant on the East Side with her mother and her manager, Barbara Jarrett, and Mrs. Jarrett's husband. After falling asleep at dinner, Tamara woke up long enough to fall asleep in a cab on the way home to a sublet in SoHo. It was a tough day, but as Tamara, an Aries, is fond of saying, "There are regular people and then there are Aries."

For the past three summers, mother and daughter have left Miami for Manhattan, leaving Tamara's father and sister at

Photo by Keefrey

home. Rev. T. Luther Jones is the coordinator of chaplain services at Jackson Memorial Hospital. Allison is a darling teenager who nurses her own dreams of becoming a model, while listening to the Beatles records.

Tamara is fifty-eight inches tall. She weighs seventy-four pounds. Her long straight hair is dirty blonde. At the moment she is "in size," which means she is a perfect children's size 10, and that is one reason she is finding work as a model. Janice Jones first noticed the girl's talent when she was a baby of five weeks. The mother had gone to a movie with Allison, then three years old, Tamara was there because she was being breast fed. But this is what startled the mother: Tamara, in swaddling, could not keep her eyes off the screen. She was so absorbed that she could not even eat. By the age of one and three quarters, the child was dressing in outlandish outfits and there is one family photo with this prophetic legend, "The entertainer pauses in the midst of routine in front of the stereo."

At four she was taken to professional photographers for her first portfolio shots. Janice Jones remembers being asked for the child's résumé and almost panicking: "What résumé? She sleeps and goes to the bathroom." The photographer told the mother that Tamara has a "Tatum O'Neal Paper Moon quality." In New York now, her manager, Mrs. Jarrett, says she is reminiscent of the "young Brookie Shields."

This is how Tamara describes her start in show business:

"Well, my mother decided for me. She thought I might like it and then I decided I like it." Sometimes Tamara tells people she would like to be a dentist when she grows up. When she says that, adults always laugh. Her mother says there are many career opportunities open to the child, and not just in theater and modeling. "For instance, she could be a Jane Pauley or Barbara Walters."

Monday, May 12, evening. Mother and daughter are at the Miami Beach Center for the Performing Arts, seeing the musical *Annie* for the third or fourth or possibly fifth time. Tamara is wearing a long romantic dress and her mother a short romantic one. The girl's face is all bones and lines and angles; she favors her father who has an aging handsomeness that is nevertheless stern. He looks like a minister in a Hawthorne story. Janice Jones's face is composed of many circles;

the cheeks, the eyes, and the nose are round. Allison's features resemble the mother, though she, like her sister, has a willowy quality. Allison was not at the play; she was sent to school last year in Mississippi. The Reverend Mr. Jones was also missing; his absence is calculated. Tamara and her mother plan to reconnoiter with the casting agent from the movie *Annie* during the intermission, and Tamara says, "Mommy didn't want Daddy to come tonight because she doesn't want the man to see how tall he is." Rev. Luther Jones is six feet, three inches tall. Children who want to be stars should try to be short and look younger than they are.

The curtain rises. Tamara and her mother are attending this production with an air of critical authority. After all, they have seen the original on Broadway. Annie is on stage, singing "*Maybe*."

In the darkness of the theater, the mother speaks above the song: "Tamara sings better. Tamara sings better than that."

"Mother, I can't hear."

"This Annie just isn't impetuous enough," Janice Jones continues. "The production is coming off as nothing but a series of tricks."

Rapt silence from Tamara.

The mother: "What happened to the dance? They didn't do it like they did it before when we saw it in New York. What happened?"

Tamara, with slight exasperation: "Mother, it comes later."

Intermission.

Mother and daughter head for the lobby. There are several men there. One is in deep conversation with two women. Like radar, pretending to be looking at some posters, Tamara scoots near them and eavesdrops. She returns to her mother with this intelligence. "It's him, Mom, it's him."

Janice Jones politely interrupts and the old man signals that he will be with her momentarily. When he does join them, she suggests Tamara for a part as one of the orphans, if not for Annie herself. The man recites a weary spiel: the director has a certain image of what he wants the children to look like and you wouldn't believe how many kids in L.A. look like what the director is looking for and you also wouldn't believe how a lot of those kids are only nine and they've already had seven years of dance.

Not to be discouraged, Janice Jones tries one more ploy.

"Well, will you at least take one of these pictures of Tamara? I just picked them up today and they were made only last week. It would be wonderful if Tamara could be just an orphan because I could be a tutor on the set and I have my master's degree and I teach school right here in Dade County and I helped Tamara and she has never scored less than the ninty-ninth percentile in anything. . . ."

While she speaks she has produced the pictures. Barely glancing at them, the man says, "Very good. That's great."

Blinking lights signify the end of the intermission.

The man turns to Tamara:

"Nice meeting you, doll."

On the way back to their seats, Janice Jones says, "Tamara, how did you know that was the right person?"

"I knew he was somebody. You could just tell."

"Did you ever see those ladies before?

"Mother, I don't know every stage mother in Miami."

This summer Janice Jones and her daughter moved to New York. They subleased a one-bedroom, fifth-floor walk-up in SoHo, an artist's neighborhood with low buildings just south of Greenwich Village. For Janice Jones, just about everything is better in New York than in Miami; even her back problem disappears. Her dream is to convince her husband, Luther, to get a job as a minister in this city; he is reluctant because he will not qualify for retirement benefits from his current job unless he stays four more years. She has also told him he could get work as a model. He has posed locally in Miami for the Diplomat Hotel and Intercontinental Banks.

There was terrible news in the Jones family last spring,

news that threatened to spoil the entire summer, if not the next few years.

It came from the orthodontist: Tamara needed braces.

"I cried," says the mother.

"I did too," says Tamara.

It looked as if the child's career might be suspended, indefinitely.

But then in mid-July came this phone call from Janice Jones. As usual, she spoke in a circle, telling anecdote within anecdote before arriving at the point. Her habit is to speak a great deal, in a pleasant modulated voice, nonstop like Muzak, as if to compensate for some sense of emptiness in the air:

"Hi, we're in New York. It's a long story how we got here. Remember how I told you Tamara needs braces. Well, the orthodontist caught the problem just in time, thank God, and he was able to leave the top teeth alone except for the night brace. And the braces on the bottom barely show. We had almost given up hope and at the beginning of the summer I went home to visit my dad in Jackson, and then I also went to my high school reunion, and I wore pink and black because those were the colors in the fifties and, well I meant it as a little joke, and Allison was away at camp and Luther had to work and Tamara went to water skiing camp where she got a beautiful tan by the way, and she learned to ski quite well and they only take eighteen kids and you have to qualify to get in and the camp is international. . . ."

And, and, and, well, somehow mother and daughter made their way to New York. Soon their days were filled with shoots and auditions, dinner at Sardi's, discount tickets to all the big shows and, budget permitting, phone calls home to Miami.

Allison: "I love it when they call. We talk just like we're talking together. Like the ad says, it's the next best thing to being there. Mom fills me in on everything she and Tamara are doing, and Tamara asks me what I'm doing. I really miss that kid."

Allison hopes that when her own braces are removed, she can be a model. "It sounds so satisfying and it's glamorous. I never wanted to be something more in my life than a model. I used to want to be an ice skater but I grew out of it. I can't explain it, but I gotta be one. If Tamara keeps working very hard and she can taste it, can taste acting the way I can taste modeling, I have no doubt she'll make it."

Tamara worked very hard this summer. Sometimes she and her mother were out of the apartment sixteen hours a day. The mother slept in the bedroom, and the child stretched out on the roomy couch in the living room. They awakened, on good days, to the sun pouring through a skylight. Tamara's time was spent working, looking for work, or taking lessons to be better at work when it arrives. Tamara had taken lessons in tennis, swimming, roller skating, tap, ballet, jazz, voice, brogue, diving, piano, singing, and baton. Allison used to take lessons, but at about nine or ten, she felt she had to choose between school and lessons and school won. In her diction, Janice Jones sometimes chooses long-winded euphemisms favored by teachers, and thus lessons are often called "skill development."

On one July day, Tamara had a ten o'clock appointment at Theo's studios. Before venturing forth, Janice Jones packed the following items: about fifteen selections of sheet music, a tape recorder, a clean casette, two cameras, one Polaroid, one Instamatic, a subway map and a bus map, toothpaste and brushes, a bulging appointment book, subway tokens, a thick black portfolio containing extra pictures and résumés, a Magic Marker and stapler and a fine Flair pen and scissors, all for adding and clipping things to Tamara's résumé. "In case it's necessary to make up special materials on the run." She also made some tuna fish sandwiches for the road.

Tamara was dawdling, munching on a Danish, curled up on the sofa. She told a résumé joke she heard on TV: "OK, a lady went to a dating service and the man there was making a résumé. The man asked the lady to tell him every single thing she did before she went to the dating service. She said first she got up and made some oatmeal. The man wrote down 'gourmet cook.' Then she washed the dishes. The man wrote down, 'loves water sports.' Then she said she ran down to the store. The man wrote 'great jogger.' Then she went crosstown to get her hair done. The man wrote 'travels extensively.' Ha ha."

Janice Jones delights in Tamara's jokes, no matter how often she hears them. At Sardi's Tamara loves to order piña coladas, "without the rum." Each time, Janice Jones laughs.

Today, she didn't. "Tamara, excuse me," came the voice of authority from the kitchenette. "The time is late. Would you please brush your teeth and not say another word until you're out the door?"

Tamara did not say another word. Janice Jones decided they would take a cab to Theo's "to save Tamara's muscles." She slung the various baggage over her shoulders and arms: "So many people have told her she has the best portfolio in the business. We were here two days and she had Saks."

Theo's studio. 10 A.M. McCall's patterns. The young woman who has escorted them upstairs offers coffee and doughnuts. She is some sort of assistant, and like many others who populate the fringes of the narcissistic world of modeling, she will probably remain fawning until she has reached the point where she can afford to be temperamental. Tamara says she would like some water.

"Perrier?" asks the young woman who is doing the serving.

"Oh yes," says Tamara. "My favorite."

"Trendy kid."

A slim young man approaches the child.

"Tamara?"

"Yes."

"Tammy?"

She cringes slightly. Tamara is pronounced with the accent on the first syllable. She answers when the accent is placed elsewhere, just as she answers to the truncated Tammy, which she does not like. She will even respond to the utter trans-mogrification Tomorrow Smith. It's all part of the business.

"My name is Joseph," says the young man. "I'm going to do your hair."

Janice Jones stations herself nearby and watches while Joseph combs Tamara's hair and prepares the hot rollers.

Janice Jones: "They say show business is crazy. I was so worried when she got those braces, but the moment she got them, she's had more offers of work. I think it's because she has a vulnerability now."

Tamara studies her face in the mirror, the straight nose, big eyes, high cheekbones, a look that combines knowledge and innocence in a way that is unusual in a ten-year-old. Joseph tells Tamara he is going to give her an old-fashioned look that morning. Her face lights up and she says, "I love the twen-ties." Tamara says she has many looks. "I can be sad, I can be abused, I can be dead, I can be happy. What's bad about me, you can't make me look younger, I can't look seven. No way. Unless maybe I had a surgical thing done to me."

11:30. After the session, Tamara changes quickly, and the team takes a cab to the Chrysler Building for an audition for a television commercial. Tamara signs in at the reception desk on a sheet of paper, after Kim and Dawn and Wendy. Tamara says that you have to be "very nice to those people and pronounce their names right," because the woman behind the desk could be married to the man in charge or she could be somebody's cousin: "You never know." She sat down across from her mother, waiting to be called. "Here, wear this," said her mother proffering a piece of pink yarn for her hair. "No," said Tamara. "Yes," said the mother. "It will give you a pep-permint-stick look." Janice Jones wants her daughter to ap-pear as young as possible. Parents are not allowed to be pres-ent at auditions, so when Tamara is called, the voice of her mother trailed the child: "You're to tell them you just came from McCall's." When Tamara returned she recited the line from the audition: "Mom calls it an Oxydol white."

1 P.M. An appointment at Something Different Dessert Shop on First Avenue. Tamara drank a root beer in the cab on the way. There were several other children there, and Tamara was not given an opportunity to solo. Janice Jones told her to give the picture and résumé to Peter Sklar, artistic director of Beginnings, which bills itself as the first professional show-case for children in New York.

Tamara said, "No."

"Please," said the mother.

"I don't want to," said Tamara. What she did want was a brownie.

"This is one of the aspects of the growing child," Janice Jones explained pleasantly. "Sometimes they won't always do exactly what you tell them to do."

Although there was no real action for Tamara that day at Something Different, they hung around for two hours, with Janice Jones periodically slipping away to a pay phone to confirm other appointments and to see if Tamara's manager had scheduled anything at the last minute.

After the third series of phone calls, she returned to the restaurant. Her pace was adrenalized and there was a sweep-ing, swooping purpose to the way she collected her posses-sions in seconds. "Hurry up," she was saying. "You have an appointment at the Ann Wright Agency at three and it's three o'clock now." They were soon hailing a cab, while Janice Jones recited one of her many truisms about the world of theater: "In this business you sometimes have to turn on a dime."

While her mother chatted, Tamara read a magazine called the *City Kiddie Scoop*. It contained interviews with other child stars: Adam Rich, who plays Nicholas Bradford in "Eight Is Enough"; Gary Coleman of "Different Strokes"; and Quinn Cummings of "Family." The advertisements in this magazine are for cookies and ice cream.

In Manhattan, there is always a rush. Tamara's mother told the cab driver to go to 136 East 57th Street. Out of the cab, through the lobby, and into the elevator. On the way up the girl was told to comb her hair. The child explained, "They don't like it if your hair is messy." Tamara had the hiccups. "My stomach," she said in a small voice. "Tamara," said her mother, "I told you never read in the car. It makes you sick."

"My stomach," Tamara whispered after they were ushered to a bench to await the agent. "I think I'm going to puke."

She rushed off to the bathroom, and when she returned the agent called her in.

Agent: "Well, now, let me look at your card and see what the story is. I can write down how much you've grown and things like that." She rifled the card file. "How long are you in town for?"

"Indefinitely," answered the child responding to her mother's coaching. Janice Jones had told her to say that because agents don't like to promote somebody who lives in Florida for a job in New York. "Besides," says Janice Jones, "in a way it's true."

"What have you been doing?"

"Some commercials. Modeling. This morning I did something for McCall's pattern book. I'm going for a movie but I forget what it's called."

The agent eyed the child: "I see you've got braces. Hmmmmm."

"With modeling it doesn't matter."

"For commercials, it is a problem. They are very particular about that in New York."

The agent finally located the card and started updating it. "Height?"

"Let's see. I think I'm fifty-eight inches. Yeah, that's right. Do you want to look at my portfolio?"

"OK. Some of these pictures make you look old."

"See, we didn't meet the photographer before we got those pictures taken. My mom took all the makeup off when she saw what was happening." This is an anecdote her mother tells almost every time she opens Tamara's portfolio.

"Well, I think we should keep you a little girl for a while longer, don't you think? No sex stuff."

Tamara nods. "Would you like to see some new pictures. Here, you can keep them."

"Now I'd like you to read for a voice-over. This is not for on-camera work because of the braces."

"I'm getting so I can talk without them showing. I am practicing."

"But it's still the agent's obligation to let them know. And most don't want braces. Here read this. . . ."

Tamara had been handed a worn document from which she read: "Ladies, you know you have a delicious cream topping when you have Dream Whip on your shelf. . . ."

"Very good, honey."

Later, Tamara sat in a nearby health food restaurant. She ate a dish of blueberry frozen yogurt and she played with the Polaroid as if it were a toy. Her mother was off making more phone calls.

"I didn't like that lady," said Tamara. "That agent was a finicky little cat."

Reunited, mother and daughter relaxed for the next couple of hours before cocktails at 7:30 with her manager, Barbara Jarrett. Dinner at the Lion's Rock was without event. Mrs. Jarrett mentioned something about the movie *Annie,* but Tamara wasn't interested: "I'm bored of it now completely to death."

A long day: McCall's, Oxydol, and Dream Whip. The child fell asleep at the restaurant, again on the way back to SoHo, and finally, close to midnight, at home. Tamara says that on audition days she likes to sign off with a little prayer: "Thank you very much, God, for this day. As you always said, 'No good deed goes unrewarded' so please reward me. This is the time."

In late August, Luther and Allison received a phone call from Janice and Tamara. The news was good: they were coming back.

The news was bad; it would not be for long. They said they needed to "regroup," to get their winter clothes. Tamara and Janice would stay in New York truly indefinitely, or, at least for as long as Tamara is "in size."

"It looks as if Tamara has landed kind of a biggie," said Luther Jones. "*Seventeen* magazine."

Will he and Allison join them in New York? "I have no plans to go. Janice says I should come up and take a shot at modeling, but I hate to risk those retirement benefits."

His feelings about the absence of his wife and daughter are tempered and almost biblical. "There have been hardships and separations since the dawn of history."

Labor Day weekend. Mother and daughter arrived back in Miami. Luther Jones left for two weeks in the naval reserve. The *Seventeen* magazine biggie is on the back burner for a while. That's show business. But the child has landed a White Cloud bathroom-tissue commercial. That's also show business. Her mother says: "It's a fifty-second commerical, and she has a major part."

Janice Jones has applied for a hardship transfer from her job as a teacher at Pine Villa Elementary school. Her hardship: "After work I am too far away from home to do anything with my child's talent, and Tamara has to have her lessons right after school because she has to wear her night brace continuously for fourteen hours." At the moment, they would like to return to New York, but they are not sure when they will be able to.

Janice Jones was surprised and amused to find that Allison would like to be a model like her sister. She laughed indulgently. "At that age, their ideas change all the time. I said to Allison, 'Where's the ballet? Where's the charm school? Where are all the things you never wanted to do that lead to modeling and acting?' Allison is just like her father. Ten years after you make a suggestion, ten years later, something will suddenly dawn on her."

Before Tamara's birth at Jackson Memorial, Janice Jones had

prepared a tape recorder to record her first cries, but her husband neglected to bring it to her room on time. And, even though she had natural childbirth and Luther worked at the hospital, he neglected to arrange to witness the birth. "He is like that sometimes," she said.

"Allison was sweet and adorable," Janice Jones smiled. "But there was something different about Tamara as far as I was concerned."

Tamara's mother says she was not given the same opportunities she has given her children; her parents didn't believe in skill development. "My parents didn't really understand my urges. They never had a piano in the house. I begged for lessons to such an extent that they finally agreed to rent a piano. I had perfect pitch. I had a temper fit because the black notes wouldn't play.

"I had it in me."

Tamara's mother remembers that when she was very young and all dressed up, people in the street used to pause and smile. "I was Shirley Temple . . . but don't print that."

❦ ❦ ❦

Tamara Jones is an undergraduate student at Florida International University. Tamara looks back on those days in New York with great fondness. It was a life led in italics followed by exclamation points: *a breathless round of auditions! try-outs! appointments! and interviews!* that soon yielded to harsher realities. Her parents separated and then divorced. The chance to be in *Annie* which Janice Jones so coveted for her daughter never materialized. "To this day, I'm not sure why. I was certainly scrawny enough to play an orphan." After high school, she tried moving back to New York on her own, but she never felt comfortable. She went to Paris, but she was assaulted on the subway and headed back to Florida to the State University of Gainesville. The transition was painful.

The slightly derisive tone she uses when she says "from Paris to Gainesville" makes her feelings obvious even now. She returned home to Miami.

In her manner and appearance she combines elements of both parents. Physically she still resembles her father more than her mother. Perhaps in honor of his work as a minister she now volunteers at her church teaching Sunday school. She keeps passages from the Bible on her refrigerator door to memorize so she can recite them later in silence during moments when she feels hassled. She has inherited her mother's drive and enthusiasm and she even sounds like her when she excitedly conveys that in her life now "lots of things are happening kind of quickly on the edge." She is close to her sister, Allison, who works with her husband in a business selling automotive parts.

She still works as a model, often in Miami Beach which in the course of the eighties went from being a seaside ghetto for the elderly into a chic hot spot where Hemingway wannabes in wrinkled khakis drink foreign beers and fancy coffee on the porches of deco-style hotels painted the color of dinner mints and where Tamara is one of the bevy of utterly beautiful young women. She earns up to $750 for a day's shoot and that's how she pays tuition and rent on the one-bedroom apartment in a more sedate part of town. She has a stereo and VCR, a phone with an answering machine, a futon, and a desk with a white tile top that doubles as a dining room table.

She hopes to major in history, and she tries to keep her career as a model quiet at school because when other students find out they project all kinds of attributes on her. "They think you're dumb or you're stuck-up. Unless someone really presses me, I just say I'm a free lance or I work in photography."

Her portfolio reveals pictures of a young woman with a look that varies from sultry shots in lacy underthings, to poses of utmost propriety in elegant attire against a divan, to the clean-cut outdoorsy appearance of pure good health, which is in fact the unmade-up version of her. Her straight hair is cut at chin length which lends itself to variable styles; she is tall and thin and keeps in shape by swimming. She says that in front of the camera, her primary goal is to convey self-respect. In May 1991 she married and she goes by the name Tamara Jones McKee.

SANDY'S
BABY

"**B**ack two rows, keep quiet," bellows Mr. Lingles, the principal, his face entertaining its customary expression of exasperation.

It is awards day at Lingles School, and the object of the principal's wrath are the oldest boys, the ninth-graders, who occupy the two back rows. They are in a taunting mood, a not unusual state of affairs. There are ten boys in all and only one of their number sits apart, David Montalvo.

This is a school where many of the students have what are called behavior problems, which translates more than anything into an inability to sit still and concentrate.

David Montalvo is there for other reasons. "He couldn't go to a public school," says his mother. "They would eat him alive."

Not that the same sort of cannibalism doesn't exist at Lingles. The setting may be smaller, but there is plenty of room for the cruelty of boys. It is that special radar for defect.

The room, a windowless library, is charged with the roiling energy of kids on the last day of school. The boys who do not win awards try to disguise their disappointment with hooting contempt for those who do.

In the ninth grade at Lingles everyone has a nickname. The

Photo by C. W. Griffin

only point of commendation about the nasty names is the democratic urge that assures that everyone gets one. No one is exempt.

"Tits," they call the boy who is slightly overweight.

"Baldylocks," for the kid with a crew cut.

"Urine," pronounced loudly as Your In, is for the classmate who drank some (by mistake) at a party (a long story, typically adolescent in its plot twists and not worthy of a full recounting here).

It is time for the Most Prolific Reader award, an honor that might be coveted in some settings, but that here is so hopelessly out of reach for the majority, for whom reading is an

overwhelming obstacle, that the notion of reading for pleasure is as farfetched as electric shocks for the fun of it, and
besides, they figure that this year's award will go to the same
boy who won it last year.

They're right.

"David Montalvo," says Mr. Lingles.

David rises.

His appearance is startling. The eyes are a little too high in
the head and the eyelids are oddly skimpy, leaving a part of the
eye always exposed, even in sleep. Both eyebrows are inter-
rupted in the middle by a bald patch. His face, from the side,
appears flattened, and there is a scarred marbling above the lip
and on the chin. A vertical slash in the middle of his forehead
fosters an impression that his face is like a piece of fruit
chopped in half and then rejoined haphazardly. (Can't he have
plastic surgery, people sometimes ask his mother; can't the
doctors do something? She sometimes answers: Do something? Do something? He's had forty operations just to get to
this point.)

"E.T.," hisses one of the boys.

He is in many ways the boy who fell to earth, and his
extraterrestrial quality is not lost on his classmates with their
diabolical perspicacity when it comes to ridicule.

David appears not to hear.

They hiss another name.

He peers through thick glasses at the certificate. His thumbs
are fine, but the fingers in both hands are misshapen and
stunted.

They hiss yet another name.

He starts to lift his unfinished fingers as if to cover his ears.

"Stubs," they call him.

"Zipperface."

When David was born his eyes had no lids.

They were set disproportionately, weirdly apart, one higher
than the other.

The nose was a flattened protuberance that looked as if someone had smashed it with a hatchet.

The mouth was a gaping hole that overtook the lower half of his face.

All his fingers were deformed, and the big toe on the right foot was missing.

The skull was misshapen.

He was exactly as one doctor described him, in language remarkably direct, devoid of all fancy polysyllabic evasions, shocked and colloquial:

"He's a mess."

To his mother his face looked as if a volcano had erupted, or a bomb blast had gone off in it. It was red and angry looking.

In another era, the best and only hope for a child like David was the circus.

David Montalvo was born without a face.

Now he has one.

The operation that saved David from a life as a freak came into prominence in 1968, the year before he was born. It is called a cranio-facial.

It is a life-threatening procedure. Surgeons open the skull from ear to ear and peel the forehead down like an orange. It requires up to twelve hours of anesthesia.

David has had this operation. Twice.

For David, modern operating theaters are a miracle of ingenuity, of true creation: where there was nothing, there is now something.

"They took bone from the hip and put it here," he says, pointing to his upper jaw. "They took two ribs out and put them here and here," he says, pointing to the cheekbones.

He touches his nose: "The skin for my nose came from the back of the ears."

"Let's see. They took the skin from inside my right arm and built eyelids with that."

He places his hand on his chin: "My chin was fine, but it

was too big compared to everything else so they removed some bone and I can't remember where they put it. But I know they put it someplace else because they never waste anything."

Ultimately, David relied on his own resources to cure his condition. Parts of himself were used to make other parts.

"Most children with clefts have a cleft lip or a cleft palate or a cleft lip and a cleft palate. David," said Dr. William Silver, who to this day supervises his orthodontia, "had a cleft face." Silver has promised him a set of perfect teeth, as long as he puts in his rubber bands.

Dr. Gilbert Snyder, the surgeon who did the first procedure that in many ways saved David's life said, "I wish you could have seen his mother sixteen years ago. She had this quality like a character out of a Henry James novel. I remember that when I first saw David I gave her a booklet on clefts that I gave to all the parents of children with this problem, and there was one thing that made her stand out. She read it. And later she asked me question after question. She wasn't going to give up.

"You know, to this day, no one knows exactly why there are clefts. As far as we know, they are something that falls from the sky.

"There was a popular movie at the time of David's birth about a woman who had given birth to a monster that pretty much explains the position David's mother was in.

"She had Rosemary's Baby."

She was a very young woman of nineteen and he was her first baby. At seventeen, Sandy Montalvo had run away from home and moved to Florida. Why Florida? "Where else if it's January in Indiana?" Her father was an officer in the navy. The family was living in South Bend, where her father was in charge of the ROTC program at Notre Dame. Sandy used to believe her parents were perfect, but if they had been perfect, what would have prompted her to run away? She thinks now: her father had an officer's need to control everything, and her mother had the need of an officer's wife to redound to her husband's credit, to trade continually in veneer and create at any cost the impression of a happy household. "Beneath the picture of false perfection was a real inability to communicate with me, and with my brothers too."

She landed in Palm Beach. She found a job as a bookkeeper for a company that sold parts for cars. She lived in a one-bedroom furnished walk-up over a garage. She moved in with her sneakers and her jeans and some old towels and dishes, mismatched, from her mother. Her parents had finally given their blessing: "If they went ahead and agreed with what I wanted to do, at least they'd know where I was. They wanted me to go away to college, belong to a sorority, play lots of games, fulfill their dreams for my childhood. Looking back, I wish I would have."

She met Gary right away, through a friend.

If she thinks about it really hard, she can almost see what she liked about him: "He *appeared* to be gregarious and fun. And, one other thing: he was always in trouble like I was in trouble. We were both the type who did everything the hard way and had to always walk the extra mile."

They were eighteen when they decided to marry. Both sets of parents opposed the match but gave in. Gary got a job with the University of Miami as an air-conditioning mechanic. When she got pregnant with David, they moved into a trailer along South Dixie Highway by the Serpentarium. Her mother-in-law gave her a shower before the baby was born and she was given the usual paraphernalia.

Around the third month she had the Hong Kong flu.

She took no drugs.

She had no alcohol.

"I wasn't even old enough to drink. In those days you had to be twenty-one."

If the baby was a boy he was to be named Gary but when she saw her child for the first time she changed her mind and named him David William, after her two brothers: "I had a feeling Gary wouldn't be hanging around for long, but my family would."

To this day she keeps the obstetrical notes that describe her progress during labor and delivery, as if there must be some special way to read them to decode why what happened happened, to divine the course of events that resulted in David.

> Date and hour of onset of labor: June 7, 1969.
> Duration: First stage, nine hours and 40 minutes; second stage, 28 minutes; third stage, three minutes.
> Condition of infant prior to transfer to nursery: Infant has several anomalies. Resp. color and cry app. satis. on transfer to nursery.

After any birth, especially one in which the mother is anesthetized, the first time she awakens and the baby is not nearby, there is a moment of emptiness and panic.

The nurse's bedside notes:

1:30 p.m. Pt. asking abt. baby—becomes very upset. Physician called. Pt. medicated.

"I remember that," she says now, "I remember waking up in this skinny little room, or maybe it just seemed skinny because I was on a stretcher, and looking up at all the nurses, this sea of faces and nobody was saying a thing."

The next day she is described as eating fairly well, and sleeping much of the morning. By mid-afternoon she was staring at the walls again, this time "with intensity," and 3 P.M. marked the first visitation with the baby, right before he was to be taken to another hospital and given his first surgery so he could be fed. She insisted on dressing the child in a blue-and-green flowered sleeper with booties to match. She concentrated on the parts of him that were normal and was grateful to her tears for blurring the rest.

Later in the day, the baby gone, for all of time for all she

knew, she ate lightly, showered with assistance, and was visited by her parents who flew in from Indiana ("Please come,"
she had said to her father on the phone, when she found out
about her son's condition. "Daddy, I had an ugly baby.")
When she first saw them, she stared beyond them in a trance.
After they left, she watched TV for a while, complained of
pain, received some medication, drifted off to sleep and then
at ten minutes after two in the morning awakened, sobbing.
She would cry out again. The nurses tried to calm her but
whenever they left the room, they could hear her from the
corridor, talking to herself—babbling, until finally one of the
nurses asked her what was wrong.

"They took my baby and put it in a can and put the lid on,"
she kept saying. "They put it in a can."

Then the notes say, *"Reassured pt. baby was OK,"* and finally
it was reported that at six in the morning the patient "slept for
the remainder of the night."

Postpartum course: "Uncomplicated except for reactive depression."

Sandy remembers: "When my mother took me home from
the hospital I couldn't even dress myself."

The patient knew the truth:

The baby was not OK.

The phrase "Infant has several anomalies" reverberated in
her mind; she would come to loathe those words.

"It was as if his features had developed autonomously and
there was no central steering committee," says Dr. Snyder, the
plastic surgeon who performed the first operation on David,
when he was eight days old, at Children's Hospital. He at-
tempted to repair the cleft in both lips, and Dr. Silver fitted him
with a device so that he could eat. Without these two interven-
tions a baby like David would not be able to create enough
pressure to swallow and would often end up starving.

These two doctors were the only two at the very beginning
who suggested to David's mother that he might, if not pros-

per, at least survive. They were the only two who offered their support.

The others talked one game: permanent institutionalization in a home for profoundly retarded children. Sunland. Orlando.

They said he wouldn't walk, wouldn't talk, he was hydrocephalic, he would lie on a mat all day long, and no mother could love him. They were, in many ways, victims of a prejudice as primitive as it is ancient: If a person is deformed on the outside, that person must be deformed on the inside as well.

Sandy's baby has just turned sixteen. Turning sixteen is a symbolic event for any child, but for one like David the portents weigh even more heavily. It has been a summer of reckoning, an interlude filled with growth and the fear of it. If you're still a kid, summer is supposed to be, theoretically at least, heavy with aimlessness, but in Sandy Montalvo's small suburban house near Dadeland even the slow time of year isn't slow.

"My mother," says David, "is overprotective, loud and she has a temper. And if she decides to do something, it gets done."

"Listen, David," said his mother. "You're sixteen. I don't want you living at home forever. If you want to get your license, you're going to have to study the booklet and show us that you know all the answers before we take you for the test. We're going to have to find a new school for the fall, and I want you to get some vocational counseling. And now that you are getting older, it's up to you to decide whether or not you want any more operations. When you were a little kid, it was my choice. But now that you are older, and the doctors have done most of what they can do, you're going to have to help us decide. There's a lot of pain and a lot of risk."

"Mom, can I play my tapes?"

"Not until you've finished your chores."

"Don't forget," says David, "her father was a commander."

She has a long history of stubborn behavior.

When David was born, she allowed him to be placed in Sunland. But, against nearly all the advice, she made plans to visit him on Labor Day, the first three-day weekend. She and Gary drove to Orlando and they rented a hotel room. She took the baby out of the facility and held him all weekend long. There are pictures of a young woman, her hair pressed straight in defiance of the natural curl, clenched back with a wide headband, wearing loud shirts and bell-bottoms in the style of the day. Photographed from a distance there was nothing unusual about the bundle in her arms. That weekend she made a curious discovery: despite all the predictions to the contrary, her son was responding very much the way she supposed a normal baby would respond. He loved to be held, his deformed eyes fastened on her perfect ones and she was certain that from time to time his contorted mouth shaped itself into a smile.

She became pregnant again. When David was a year old, she gave birth to a second son, Todd Michael, who was fine.

Seven months later, her marriage ended.

More and more she would take David out of Sunland for longer and longer periods of time.

David's grandmother, Gary's mother, often vacationed in Georgia and she would sometimes bring the boy down to Miami. "Even when he was little he was sharp. He always wanted me to read to him. I told Sandy: There's nothing wrong with that boy's brain. He's too sharp for that place." Soon after, she took him out of Sunland for good.

After Gary left, David's mother got a job processing checks at Southeast Banking Center at their computer center from five in the evening until two in the morning. A high-school girl who went to school on the afternoon shift spent the night with the children.

That's when Sandy met Rafael Montalvo. He was in charge of teaching new employees how to use the computers.

"He had an instant dislike for me and tried to get me fired. He went to the supervisor, who told him there was no way I would be fired so he ought to settle down and teach me what I had to learn."

On Christmas Day, when David was two and a half and his brother one and a half an event occurred as inexplicable as David's defects. She put her younger son to bed and several hours later when she went to check on him, he was not breathing. The diagnosis was crib death.

It is a struggle for Sandy to speak of Todd Michael, and her words are choked:

"When Todd died, it was one of those experiences. It's very difficult for me to explain to other people, the pain, the complete desolation, it's something you never get over.

"There isn't anything else you can do because it's so final.

"Todd was perfect, and he died. David has all these problems, and he lived.

"This is not something I can talk about easily."

She would go on to have one more baby, this time a perfectly formed girl, Cecilia, who is now eleven. People often tell her mother that Cecilia looks like an actress, the one with all the eyebrows: What's her name? Hemingway? The beauty is similar to her mother's; she has a wide open face and shining complexion. What is most stunning about the faces of both mother and daughter is their incredible clarity.

When David gets on Cecilia's nerves, she waits for him to make a phone call and then she does everything she can to distract him, from making loud noises to claiming that the house is in great danger.

When Cecilia gets on David's nerves, he goes into his room and locks the door and lets her bang on it as much as she wants.

David's stepfather is strict with Cecilia and easy on David. David's mother is strict with David and easy on Cecilia.

David is considered by everyone in his family to be lazy, and the most commonly proffered argument to prove this point is made by his mother: "He would NEVER clean his room if I didn't make him."

Both parents worry about Cecilia's perfectionism and they offer a quick list of the more outrageous examples:

On vacation, she makes her bed in the hotel room before the maid comes.

Every night she lays out a fresh outfit, as well as two Q-tips and a piece of dental floss already cut to the right size.

If she makes a mistake on a paper for school she won't use white-out, preferring to start all over again.

Parents always remember certain incidents in the lives of their children with the force of a photograph, a split second lifted out of the continuum and preserved for all of time in the mind's eye:

David's mother always remembers the time when he was four or five and he appeared to be very sad one morning as she washed the dishes.

"What's the matter, David?"

"I don't want to go to school today."

"Why not? You always liked school."

"Well, I don't want to go today because no one likes my hands."

Cecilia's father always remembers the time when she was four or five and she was bringing a new friend home. She stood outside, the door was swung open but she waited to enter while she cautioned her friend: "When you see my brother, you will see he is different, but I don't want you to stare."

David and Cecilia's mother likes to think they have for each other a profound sense of loyalty.

David attended public schools through the sixth grade. His mother petitioned the south area office of the Dade County

School District to see that he was properly placed, and when it was first suggested that he be assigned to a classroom of children with physical disabilities, she refused to accept the placement. "But," she was told, "your son is different."

"That's right, he is different. But he's not in a wheelchair. You will make him feel even more different than he is. David can ride a bike, he can climb a tree. He can hold a pencil."

At a certain point when David was still in grade school Sandy Montalvo was taking her son to a different doctor every day.

"I realized I had to let up. With a child like David if you're not careful, he will take up your entire life and that's not good for anybody.

"As it is, we have this strange twinness. When David's doing fine, I'm doing fine. And when he's not doing well, I'm not doing well.

"Every time he goes into surgery, as they wheel him into the operating room, I literally feel as if something is being ripped out of me.

"I went to see the movie *Mask* with David, the one about the child with the deformed face. Cher played his mother. There are major differences between that movie and our life. In the movie nothing could be done to improve that child's condition. And in the end the child died, so everybody in the theater could leave the movie feeling great: The problem is over.

"With David the problem is never over. It just takes on new forms."

David's biological father does not see him often. For his sixteenth birthday he gave David fifty dollars in cash, delivered to him by his grandparents. He took David to a concert, once.

"Most kids, they call their stepfather by his first name and they call their father Dad. For me it's just the opposite."

Rafael Montalvo, David's stepfather: "Seeing David for the

first time really was a shock. He was a monster back then. I did not feel at first a tremendous amount of attraction for the kid.

"The first time I started feeling something for David was when he was going up to New York for surgery for the second time, and Sandy said, 'I think you should come with us.' They were preparing to give him a shot to sort of calm him down and as I understand it it is a very painful thing.

"I always had this thing in my head: boys don't cry, and David knew this, and I could see him fighting back the tears, and I saw these big things coming down his cheek, and he said, 'Dad, it hurts,' and for the first time I began to wonder what he was going through, and I took my hat off to him. I felt respect."

"Dennis," says David, turning to his best friend. "Do you remember Leah? Well, there's a girl in my school this summer who's so pretty she puts Leah to shame." They look like typical teenagers, sitting on a curbstone, watching girls go by. David's mother may have thought of it as a summer of reckoning, but to David, it was just plain summer. David never acts as if he has any special problems. It is at once admirable and frightening. By refusing to appear vulnerable, he might be making himself more so.

Most of David's conversations during his sixteenth summer, at least those conducted outside his parents' earshot, centered on one theme.

"What I look for in a girl," said David, "is blond hair and personality."

He is trying to work up the courage to ask the preacher's daughter, who happens to have been blessed with many charms including the evocative name Lana, for her picture. He might succeed. One reason he likes her: "Her father always says she's supposed to set an example."

When his mother took him to Atlantis Academy to look

over his new school and to sign him up for a couple of summer courses, he was given a copy of the most recent yearbook to keep. His mother was heartened by the enthusiasm he showed toward this document, although she was not sure why he found it so captivating.

"One, two, three, four, five, maybe six, definitely seven, absolutely eight. Wow, eight really good-looking girls. Wait until Dennis sees this."

He has only one faint complaint about girls in general:

"A lot of them don't say a word while they slowdance."

"My biggest fear about David is what is he going to do? Can he function without being taken advantage of by everybody?" says Rafael Montalvo.

"David likes to talk. If he could he would just sit around all day talking.

"I always tell him: David, you have to prepare yourself for something. Now is the time when you should be preparing."

David's stepfather also saw the movie *Mask*. It was a father and son outing, and afterward they went to Burger King and sat and talked:

"I told David that one of the things in the movie that impressed me and I thought we ought to talk about is that the boy is attracted to one of the girls in his high school not just as a friend, but as a man to a woman, and she likes him, but only as her friend. Does that happen to you? He said, 'Not really.' I asked him about does he ever feel he would like to go to bed with a girl, kiss a girl? Have you ever felt that way toward a girl? 'All the time.'

" 'But,' I said, 'you haven't really tried to kiss a girl.'

" 'Not yet.'

"And so I told him, it's going to take a special type of person to have a physical relationship with him. At your age, I said, it will be very difficult, but later in life it will not be so hard.

And then I made sort of a joke. In the movie the boy meets a blind girl and I said, 'Maybe you could meet a blind girl.'

"And he said, 'I wouldn't want someone like that.' "

On a recent visit to the office of Dr. S. Anthony Wolfe to discuss his future, the doctor reached over, cupped the boy's chin and tilted his head upward. Dr. Wolfe was examining the results of the most recent surgery in which two of David's ribs were used to make his upper jaw protrude more in an effort to diminish the crushed flat look to David's face, especially in profile.

"Good," said the doctor, "Good."

The doctor had just cut the wires, but David still had trouble moving his mouth so it still sounded as if he were speaking through clenched teeth.

"So, Doctor, can I have steak for dinner?"

"Steak? I don't want you eating anything that will stress your jaw. For right now I'm going to prescribe an edentuous diet; that means a diet for people with no teeth. What a baby or a seventy-five-year-old lady might eat."

David's mother stirred in her seat. "David," she said, "Do you want to show Dr. Wolfe the list you brought." Then she addressed the physician, "Now that David is turning sixteen, it is going to be more and more up to him whether he chooses to have any more operations. There is a lot of pain and a lot of risk. He wrote down some of the things he wants to ask you about."

David started to read from the list.

"Chin scar: remove.

"Eyebrows: more.

"Nose: some nostrils.

"Forehead scar: make smaller."

Dr. Wolfe listened intently. He has a handsome face, and because he is a plastic surgeon, the handsomeness creates an impression of someone endowed with a beauty he generously wishes to universalize. He nodded thoughtfully: "We're down to the final buffing. Everything sounds possible. The hardest will be the nostrils. But, let's see, if we take a little bit of skin from here," he said, leaning over and touching the back of David's left ear, "We might do all right."

It was time to leave and David turned to the doctor, and politely, hesitantly, said to the doctor:

"Doctor, may I ask one more question?"

It was a solemn moment. His mother looked at him with pride and relief: a mantle had been passed. David was taking charge of his medical destiny.

The doctor hunched forward, "You can ask as many questions as you want."

David cleared his throat and shifted in his seat.

Long pause.

"Can I," asked David, "eat French fries?"

The night shift. Children's Hospital. Miami.

"Sit still, Jeremy, sit still."

The nurse is gently holding the child, coaxing him to take medicine from a dropper she inserts in his mouth.

"That's a good boy."

Her voice is continuous exhortation with one goal in mind: the alleviation of his suffering. He has a condition known as failure to thrive. At the age of two he weighs less than twenty pounds. He is bones and eyes.

The nurse, glowing with purpose, in white slacks and loose white sweater, glides on soft shoes from one room to the next: for Jonathan there is insulin, for April an adjustment of the complex tubes providing her with nourishment, for another child, who is sleeping, a simple touch of the hair.

Four years ago, Sandy Monalvo entered nursing school. She received her accreditation this spring.

For a while she had thought about becoming a recreational therapist. "That's someone who plays with the kids at the hospital. When David was little I remembered those places as the one place where I felt peace. But at the time there were a lot of federal cutbacks for that type of program."

The decision to become a nurse was the decision "to do something for myself."

An accident forced upon her a professional's familiarity with medicine and hospitals and children who are ill. By going to school, she made it formal. Now her knowledge is recognized, in the uniform and the respect and the salary. She loves her work.

"I wanted to do for other people the same kinds of things I was getting from the nurses when I brought David to the hospital."

She starts work at midnight, and it is now almost eight in the morning, time to punch out.

But before leaving, she must brief the incoming nurses on the patient load. She has a folder, which she flips through. The technical language rolls off her tongue, it is a code she speaks with fluency: vital signs are stable, afebrile, DV.2; 50 cc's an hour; the tent is functioning well.

She comes to one more patient, a little girl.

She wants to explain that the child isn't docile.

She squirms during shots. Only someone who knows Sandy's history might wonder about a connection between the description of the patient and a description of herself, and detect the note of admiration in her voice:

"She's a real fighter."

"I wonder," said Cecilia, as she sat beside her brother at the Department of Motor Vehicles licensing station one July day, "if Mom and Dad will take us out to dinner if you get it."

"Will you," said David, "quit saying that."

"Saying what?"

"If you get it."

The process of obtaining his driver's permit took David five and a half hours, but to him every minute was weighted with tension and theater. Cecilia kept fidgeting and telling David,

"This is the most boringest thing in the world," to which her mother replied, "I'll remind you you said that when it's your turn to get your license."

At least part of the time was spent racing around town to obtain forgotten documents. They discovered upon arrival that the licensing people require two forms of identification so David's mother drove home and got three; school records, a birth certificate, and a copy of the 1974 court order making David the adopted son of Rafael Montalvo. She has fought insurance companies for sixteen years to have David's operations covered ("This isn't just plastic surgery. This is survival.") Getting three instead of two was instinctive: she is used to the vagaries of bureaucracies, the sudden introduction of new rules.

During the first two hours of waiting David kept checking his wallet to make sure he had enough money; his mother had made it clear that paying for the license was his responsibility. He kept showing Cecilia the spot in his wallet he had taken care to clear for the license if the day proved to be a success. "Wait: Not if, *when,* Cecilia, I really mean it. Don't say 'if you get it' anymore." It took David about twenty minutes to finish the test.

He stood while the examiner corrected it.

She looked up and said something, and the significance of his smile was unmistakable.

"So far so good," he said to Cecilia.

He asked the examiner if he could keep his copy of the test as a souvenir but she politely explained that it was against the law.

Next, the eyes.

He was asked to look, close up, and identify small letters in a machine. The examiner made a face, indicating displeasure. She turned to the tall, gangly boy, fragile and thin in a muscle shirt that revealed few muscles, his CAT cap with the Jack Daniels insignia, hiding his face. "That's the best you can do?"

An hour and a half later, after an emergency visit to an ophthalmologist, David presented a form saying his eyesight could not be improved beyond his current performance.

She stared and squinted and seemed to pore over every squiggle in the fine print.

David kept brushing the back of his hair with his hands in one of those useless adolescent campaigns to defeat nature, and in this case to tame what is clearly a beautiful and natural curl.

"This is restricted to daylight hours," said the examiner.

It was, for David, better than nothing.

He grinned in ecstasy and entertained the delicious fantasy of going home, the proud possessor of this magical plastic rectangle, and finding his friend Jimmy and "really smearing it in his face."

Time to wait in line for the chance to pose for the official photo.

"Mom, do I look all right?," he said, pressing his hair flat.

"David, you look fine."

And then she paused as if to curb her tongue, but in the end could not resist issuing one of those maternal edicts: "You know I don't know why you keep combing your hair down like that. It would look great all curly."

"I don't," said David, his patience obviously taxed, his voice lowered so as to reduce the public nature of the discussion, "like curls."

He was summoned for the official photo and instructed to remove his hat and his eyeglasses, both of which provide proportion and symmetry to his face, and without which the scars and misshapen parts take on a cruel prominence.

"Can't I at least wear my glasses?"

"Sorry," said the examiner, "Gotta see the eyes. That's the rule."

Then David had to wait to see whether the picture turned out all right.

He was summoned once again to the counter, and with a routine casualness that did a disservice to the meaning of the moment, the examiner handed David his license.

David turned toward his mother and Cecilia and made a thumbs-up gesture and engaged in a whirling motion clearly indicating victory.

"Oh, Mom. Look, they gave it to him," shouted Cecilia. "He passed. He passed." And then, with the peculiar tenacity of an eleven-year-old, she revived the subject of the evening's repast. "Please, Mom. Please."

"But I went to the grocery store last night and I'm going to make string beans and meat loaf."

"Oh Mom, I'm just not in a mood for that. Why can't we take David to his favorite restaurant? Why can't we go to the Red Lobster?"

Her mother looked doubtful. "We'll have to see what your father says."

On the way home David kept opening and closing his wallet and scrutinizing the license. He said he didn't like the picture very much. Nobody likes the picture on their license, his mother said.

"I hate mine."

"It's not the picture," she said, "It's the status."

"David," said Cecilia, "I have a question."

Her voice strained with overdone neutrality.

It was lofty with fake objectivity, as if the inquiry were utterly idle and not designed to recruit him in the insurrection she hoped to stir.

"What would you rather have for dinner tonight? Meat loaf," she said in a low drab meat loaf sort of voice, "or," and here the voice was coy and musical, light and lilting, "Would you like to go out and . . . celebrate?"

"If there has been any benefit to having a child like David . . ." his mother started to say, and then she paused.

"Benefit is an odd word. What I mean is. . . ."

She paused again, and then seemed to change the subject.

"Let me tell you something that happened while we were on vacation. We were at the beach and there was a man there who had cerebral palsy and he had it bad. He moved in this tangled way, and you could see how much effort it took. He was with his wife, and a toddler and a newborn baby. I could hear other people commenting on him. 'Don't you feel so sorry for someone like that?' and 'That looks awful!' I was thinking: people who have everything, people who are used to having everything work, have no idea of the adjustments a man like that has to make.

"He took his family to the beach!"

"The beach is not the most comfortable place in the world, all that sand and sun and heat and oil and still he was able to enjoy his life. It's incredible, that people have the gift for this, the energy. The will."

The family did celebrate David's triumph. Although technically he had obtained a driver's permit, which merely gave him permission to learn how to drive, the word "permit" was quickly dropped in favor of the more elevated expression, "license". Lost in the avalanche of good will that greeted this accomplishment was the suddenly insignificant fact that David had never really been behind the steering wheel of a car.

From the legal pad David used to communicate after his most recent surgery, a request to his father:

"I need to find a spot where I have not gotten a shot.

"I want you to squeeze my hand hard enough to where I will not feel the pain of the shot.

"Even if you think you will break my hand."

The dream that plagued David's mother in the days and nights following her son's birth, in as much detail as she can summon:

"I would dream they put the baby in a garbage can, one of those big ones you put on the sidewalk for the garbage men to take, and it had a black plastic bag inside and they put a top over it. I would be looking for the baby and couldn't find him. After I had looked everywhere I would lift the top off that can and there he was. I never saw the baby's face when I opened the can, I just saw a hole. I would wake up screaming. 'You have to take the baby out of the can.' "

Awards Day. Part Two. Lingles School. After an end-of-the-year banquet, consisting of hot dogs and chocolate cake and consumed with bolting haste, the students reconvened in the school library for the final formal ceremony of the year. The paper awards had all been bestowed; now it was the big time, now it was the trophies.

When Mr. Lingles stood before them and said that he was now going to make his final award, chastened silence reigned and even the bullying swagger of the older boys earlier in the day had given way to a different mood: paying attention was their way of showing sentiment.

"I have one more award but before I tell you who it is for and why this student is receiving it I want you to take a good look at the muscleman on top."

He held high the last trophy. He was careful to cup his hand over the part of the pedestal engraved with the name of the recipient.

"It goes to a student who has done a lot more growing in a short amount of time than a lot of us will ever do in a long amount, someone who was born with something they could not control but they had to live with and overcome.

"Some of you have given this student a pretty hard time.

"You've taken his book bag and hidden it.

"He has taken more mouth and guff and teasing and insults than anyone should ever have to take from anybody."

The principal paused, he looked directly at the ninth-grade

boys in the two back rows, and gave them each, one by one, a level gaze for what seemed like a very long moment.

"Some of you have helped him simply by being you."

Then one of the boys spoke back. His voice was clear and low and filled with something that sounded remarkably like deference. The others looked at him with approval, and he seemed to represent the whole group, when he said, so everyone in the room could hear, "All right, David Montalvo. Come up and get your award," and the headmaster nodded in the direction of David, who slowly stood and walked toward the podium.

In one hand he gripped the trophy, and with the other he shook the hand of the headmaster, finally turning so everyone could see his prize, and at that moment applause began to fill the room, following David as he moved down a corridor into the school parking lot, where he was surrounded by students who wanted to congratulate him, including girls, some of whom were blond, with personality, and as he left Lingles School for the last time, starting on the walk home, he thought to himself how his mom was really going to like this, and there was about him a jauntiness, a bounce to his step, that teenagers' conviction that life is as light as sneakers, and every now and then the sun would catch the shiny part, the part with the engraving, which David couldn't help reading over and over again, and he didn't even care if it was corny; it was better than being called E.T., or Stubs, or Zipperface:

David Montalvo.
Mr. Courage.

🐦 🐦 🐦

The last time I saw David was at a gourmet store called Norman Brothers where he was bagging groceries and weighing vegetables. He had on his trademark hat and although still gangly, he had begun to fill out a bit. He said he liked the job and it was obvious he worked at it with great enthusiasm. He kept up his usual banter with the customers, all of whom seemed to appreciate his diligence and good will. He said he was saving his earnings so that eventually he would be able to go away to college.

THE TIME
OF HER LIFE

———

There is no way to take a true picture of time, the blur of hours and motion of minutes. I used to think of myself as a champion keeper of the calendar, expert at knowing as far in advance as possible the precise destiny of every second. This was my kingdom, a place I could control. But then I made a new friend, another mother, with children the same ages as mine, a boy of eight and a girl of four, whose sense of schedule put me to shame. Here was a true maven, a marvel of efficiency in using up time before it even exists. I asked if she would take me on a time tour of her week. She said fine, but in order to do this, I had to make a phone appointment: Thursday morning at 11:05. "Which do you want?" she asked. "A week that's maxed out, or just a week week?"

Be wild, I thought, be a gypsy: Go for broke.

"Maxed out," I said, "Definitely."

So here goes, if not a full portrait of time itself, at least a kind of snapshot of the way some of us live.

On a typical maxed-out Monday, my friend wakes up at 6:30. She leaves at 7:45 to take the children to school. Her son is dropped off at 8 and her daughter at 8:15. She goes to her gym at 8:30, changes, swims until 9 and then aerobicizes until

10. Then she showers, does her hair and dresses for work, having picked out her outfit, stockings, and jewelry the night before. From 10:45 to 11 she drives to her therapist, stopping to pick up a muffin (usually something whole grain) and a bottle of water. The food she eats in the car, the liquid she

drinks during therapy. She leaves at 11:50 and arrives at her office at 12:10, making one stop at the florist to pick up her standing weekly order of a five dollar bouquet for the office. Because she's a regular customer, the bouquet she gets is usually worth much more. She counts on hitting enough red lights to be able to put on her makeup; she doesn't put it on earlier because she generally cries in therapy. In her job as a therapist, she sees individual patients from 12:30 to 7:30 and then leads a group from 7:30 until 8:45. Meanwhile, her son takes the bus home after school and is met by a sitter. Together they pick up his sister at her child care at 4. The sitter helps them pack clothes and their special blankets for the overnight at their father's house. My friend hires good dependable sitters with cars and pays them eight dollars an hour. (Her top-paying patients pay her eighty dollars.) When my friend leaves work on Monday night, she either goes to the grocery store to shop for the week's provisions or meets someone for dinner. Either way, she is home by 10:30 or 11. Tuesdays are her early day; she gets up at 6 in order to run four and a half miles in forty-five minutes, a double loop around a small lake, and still be out of the house by 8. At 8:30 she starts seeing patients, all day, until 5: nine in all, straight through, without a break. Lunch is always a sandwich packed the night before, not just a hunk of bread and slab of meat slapped together but, because she is a gifted cook, usually something inventive, tenderly compiled, say a half-piece of pita bread with munster cheese, sprouts, and a dab of gourmet salsa. On Tuesdays at 5:01 she leaves the office in an absolute dash to get to her daughter's day care before it closes. Wednesdays are structured so that she gets a break in the middle of the morning for her weekly manicure. A patient finishes at 9:50; she goes for the appointment from 10 to 10:30 and is back in the office for the next patient at 10:40. This is a recent indulgence. She never used to worry about her nails because she never really worried about her looks at all. She is a tall, slender, beautiful woman with thoughtful blue-gray eyes. When she tries on clothes, almost everything looks great. She is out of her office by 2:30. This is her son's early day for getting out of school, and often he beats her home. He lets himself in with his own key. Usually he is not alone for more than fifteen minutes. They then spend from 2:30 until 5 on a special outing, at the arcade, the comic book store, or the library. Together they pick up her daughter, and when they get back shortly after 5, she starts dinner, and during the warm months she often mows the lawn, though once in a while, lately, because there is no other time for exercise that day, she leaves the children in front of the TV and does an abbreviated twenty-two-minute jog. There are tenants on the bottom floor of their house, and she does not leave the children unless she is sure the tenants are at home. Because she is never confident that the children ate as well as she would like at their father's on Monday, she likes to insist on a good dinner on Tuesday and Wednesday nights: no pizza, no hot dogs, nothing gobbled on the run. Ideally this is a civilized interlude when they all sit down and eat together, though sometimes the meal degenerates into a pitched battle between the children as to who is going to tell her what first, with her daughter sabotaging her son's conversation by putting her feet on the table and with her son sabotaging her daughter's conversation by opening his mouth to reveal half-eaten food, saying, "train wreck." The temptation, she says, is "to drink twelve glasses of wine." A standard good dinner might include roast chicken, a fresh vegetable, rice or pasta. After dinner, she bathes the children, helps her son with his homework, and puts them to bed (she calms the children with a book, a board game, or some quiet conversation) and then her time to herself begins. From 10 to about 12:30 is for phone calls, correspondence, TV, or just sitting in an armchair, zoned out, home, happy enough, cosseted by fatigue.

Sometimes she has trouble sleeping; it was hardest when she and her husband first separated. One or the other of her children woke up every hour. Oddly, the less sleep she gets, the less she needs, and sometimes she is up until 1 in the morning fussing, cleaning. "You'd think my house would be immaculate."

On Thursdays, she sees five patients from 8:30 to 1:35. At 11:05, she has half an hour free, and unless her husband is out of town, that is their time to talk about the children and also their divorce settlement. They used to talk at night, but she found that when they talked late at night, she felt depleted, snappish, vulnerable. That is why she carved out of her schedule a time during the workday for them to talk, a few sunlit minutes, crisp and efficient. Thursday afternoons, she picks up her children and takes them back to the house, where they are met by a sitter at 3:30. She returns to work by 4:10 in order to meet with two more patients and lead a group that gets out at 7:30. At 5 or so, the children's father picks them up for an overnight. Friday morning, she gets up at 6 and goes for a long run. Fridays are devoted to professional consultations as well as sessions with patients. She finishes up at 6:30. A sitter has met her son when he gets home from school, and as on Mondays, the two of them pick up her daughter. Friday nights are for puttering. Sometimes she will get a home video for her children, and usually Fridays are when she gets to open her mail. Saturday mornings at 7:30, the cleaning woman comes. The minute she arrives, my friend dashes out of the house to go for a quick run in order to be back and showered in time to take her daughter to ballet from 9 to 10. The cleaning woman stays with her son while he plays Nintendo. Every other Saturday, her husband comes at 11 and the children spend the next twenty-four hours with him. If the children are with their father, she spends the day on errands: dry cleaner, hairdresser, florist again, picking up her own personal bouquet for the house, six dollars on a regular weekend, nine dollars if she's having a dinner party. Sometimes on Saturdays she goes to the Power Pack aerobics class at 4 at the health club, where she pays reduced membership fees because she has agreed to use it only on weekday mornings and weekend afternoons. During the summer months, she loves the beach:

all that warmth, just pouring down. She used to read all the time when she was married; she likes that aspect of herself, that part of her that delivered her psyche to a wash of words and imagined the lives of others. But now she is too distracted to read; her life is its own surfeit of plots and subplots. There is no use reading about invented lives when she is spending so much energy reinventing her own. She sometimes thinks that the orgy of reading was really just a way of being alone, and now she is alone enough. Besides, books are filled with unexpected twists and turns, and she feels she cannot take any more emotional surprises. Sometimes, despite her better intentions to have an active, productive Saturday on her own, she is overcome by the absence of her children. She often feels a horrible pang when she sees them disappearing out the front door with their father. It is, she says, as if all the meaning in her life has just walked off.

Sundays are a late day, a luxury of sleep. Sometimes she stays in bed until 8.

On Monday, the week begins anew. At least summer, with its odious, preening spontaneity, is finally over. What chaos it is to accommodate vacations, hers, her patients', her soon-to-be-former husband's, plus all those camp schedules, and the baseball games, especially the ones that are rained out and must be rescheduled, and then the usual epidemic of potluck picnics and last minute invitations to someone's cottage for an all-day barbecue. There comes a moment every summer when she finds herself filled with longing for the peace of the school year, when every week she launches the same vessel with its cargo of hours, borne ceaselessly into a maelstrom, consoling in its very predictability.

❧ ❧ ❧

"The Time of Her Life" generated several angry letters and one mildly supportive one:

"The busy woman in 'The Time of Her Life' enjoys two advantages most women don't have: money, so that she can afford luxuries like a cleaning woman and eight-dollar-an-hour baby sitters; and job flexibility, which most women don't have regardless of how much they make. This is not a snapshot of the way *I* live."

"The article about a certain woman's time management techniques really opened my eyes.

I too have two children. What I *don't* have is:

1. An hour and a half to work out every morning.
2. An eighty-dollar-an-hour job.
3. A pool of eight-dollar-an-hour sitters that I can call on (with their own cars!).
4. A flexible enough work schedule to take off half days at will.
5. The ability to make ends meet on only one job.

I resent the *Post*'s insinuation that this woman's life is anything but ideal. All she has is free time."

"Move over, Art Buchwald and Erma Bombeck—surely the writer wrote this piece with her tongue planted firmly in her cheek—but, alas, I think she is serious.

As a full-time caregiver, I can't imagine having enough time to indulge myself the way her eighty-dollar-an-hour therapist friend does.

If she really believes anyone with this abundance of time for herself is a 'snapshop of the way we live,' she has never encountered the real world of 'maxed out.'"

"Reading about the ultra-structured week of the upscale, newly single mother in 'The Time of Her Life,' I did not experience the rush of sympathy and identification I was expecting. Instead, I found myself thinking, 'This woman has a nice life.'

But though I shook my head in envy over her autonomy, her support system, and her budget, I found myself nodding in agreement over her determination to live a balanced life (and that seems to be the point of all the planning and scheduling). She is right.

Most women, rich or poor, are struggling to meet multiple role expectations. In the case of the single mother, anxiety and guilt can be strong enough to eliminate balance altogether, as the woman postpones the arrangement of her own life in order to be on call for her children."

As for the subject of the piece, she used to say that she was sometimes grateful there was no love interest in her life:

"Throw a man into this mix and well. . . ."

Well, one day not so long ago while rushing to the service station to get gasoline for her mower so she could mow the lawn before heading back to the office to lead a group in therapy, she met someone with a broken-down carburator who, upon seeing her forgot all about his engine trouble. Now, she finds she has less time in some ways, but more in others because of the way he pitches in. Still, the basic shape of her ways and days remains the same; they are thinking about getting married but first she has to find the. . . .

A ROOM
OF HER OWN

At first it was impossible to sleep; every time she closed her eyes she saw his face. So sometimes late at night Carol Fennelly would put on the nightgown her dead lover had given her as an engagement present. It is pastel and long and silky, not secondhand like most of her clothes, but purchased brand-new from a real store, Victoria's Secret. Then she would light one of the candles next to her bed, illuminating a room unlike any other at the shelter for the homeless where she lives. It is a small space (she estimates the dimensions as twelve by ten by eighteen), and although the walls are typical government issue, bland and civic and institutional, almost zealously nondescript, she has domesticated them with a vengeance, turning them into a beckoning tumble of color and icons and artifacts. In her pink slippers she would move about in a soft glide, almost ghostly, and she would light another candle and another and another. Their glow would join the flickers from a comic bulbish appliance called a plasma ball that she sometimes leaves on all night. It belonged to her companion of thirteen years, and it produces jets of color, reckless ricochets of pink and purple. She would put on music, especially a tape of love songs he had put together for her. The peace of this moment would be a consoling contrast to the tumult of his final days: the fights, the screams and the harangues, the slamming of doors, the threats to throw her furniture out the window, the calling of terrible names:

> Lady in red
> Is dancing with me
> Face to face
> Nobody here
> Just you and me
> It's where I want to be.

And so while the music played and the shadows throughout the room pulsated and contorted, she would try to get Mitch Snyder to pay a visit.

But of course he never did.

She hesitates to call this room at the Community for Creative Non-Violence a shrine and prefers to think of it instead as a refuge, a place for restoration after her long public days as a spokesperson-by-default at the shelter, where all the unpaid workers are equal but some are more prominent in their equalness. The days begin at five in the morning, grueling whirlwinds of glad-handing and politicking and working the phones for favors in a kind of upper-class panhandling (her goal is not spare change so much as free rides on jets for visiting celebrities who will create good will for the shelter at media events) and cajoling her contacts at assignment desks throughout the city ("How about a cold weather story? We have fifty volunteer nurses in our health clinic right now giving free flu shots to our residents!") and smiling a lot, smiling all the time, telling everyone yes, yes; she's fine, just fine.

He killed himself in the room next door. The last time anyone spoke to him was about five in the afternoon on Tuesday, July 3. After that he stopped answering his pages,

and he was discovered, with his cat, by a fellow worker at the community on Thursday, July 5. He left a note addressed to Carol: "I loved you an awful lot. All I ever wanted was for you to love me more than anyone else in the world. Sorry for all the pain I caused you in the last 13 years." He also mentioned where he had hidden eight thousand dollars in cash that belonged to the shelter. It fell to his unofficial widow to make the public announcement. Those who saw her that day say that she looked ravaged. Normally a pretty woman, with curly brown hair and two somewhat protuberant front teeth that make her look younger, more eager than her forty-one years, she stood puffy faced and dark eyed outside that now-famous building at Second and D NW and spoke very quietly. The words she used were simple, spare, plain, and true. In her distinctive speaking voice—it is both soft and forceful—she told the crowd of about fifty reporters and photographers that Mitch Snyder, famous activist, government gadfly, street angel, always said good things happened when it rained.

"Well, today," she said, "he was wrong."

Before he died she had sequestered herself with a friend "to get some space, I never wanted to leave the center; it was for personal survival what I did." A week later she moved back in.

The day was thick with heat, humid and motionless, but at the shelter the merciful air conditioning was on. She could not imagine sleeping ever again in the room they had shared, so she turned it into the archives, the official repository of the boxes and papers and important records of the community, including what Carol Fennelly likes to call "the guys." "The guys," she says, "are actually a coed crowd," consisting of the ashes of thirty men and women who froze to death in the District and who, Mitch vowed, would never again be homeless. Often it was she or Mitch who was called by the morgue to come and claim them.

Slowly, she lugged their bed and their dining room table and their dressers into an adjoining room, and, standing amid the cartons and the dust, she felt invigorated by the disarray. Grief transformed itself into activity. Her plan was simple. She would set about making sense of her life by making sense of her things. She put the big tapestry on the wall above her bed; it is filled with blues and magentas, and the pattern consists of two mandalas, the wheel of life. She bought it on layaway twenty-one years ago when she was unwed and pregnant, and living under her parents' roof in her home state of California; it was a symbol of her hope that someday she would have her own place. On the bed near the pillows she placed the collection of about a dozen teddy bears she had given to Mitch over the years.

In the days and weeks and months that followed she concentrated on making her room as cheerful and as aesthetically pleasing as possible.

In the room's single window she arranged her greenery, mostly tough, can't-lose plants such as ivy and philodendron, cousins to the weed in their tenacity. All her photos she put up on the wall opposite her bed above the old wobbly desk; pictures that provide an instant history of her life. There's a picture of her dressed as a clown back when she was into amateur clowning as one of the ways to attract crowds at CCNV events; she had made the headdress herself by gluing red fringe to some pantyhose. There are several pictures of Mitch, one with his friend Cher, who is part of a group of celebrities who have supported the shelter, most of them inspired by the made-for-TV movie called "Samaritan" in which Martin Sheen played Mitch. A photo of Mitch and an elderly woman everyone called Granny shows him leaning over with his head touching hers so that their joint silhouette is that of a heart. It is the image being used on a new line of T-shirts being sold to raise money for the shelter. By the last year of his life, Mitch's lectures all over the country were raising about $100,000 a year.

She devoted two bookshelves to books, many of them inspirational in nature, such as *Mahatma Ghandi and His Apostles, The Wycliffe Bible Commentary,* and *The Autobiography of St. Therese of Lisieux.* She likes to cook and there are several cook books, including what counts as her one indisputably yuppie possession, *The Silver Palate Dinner Menu Cookbook.*

She decided to use a third shelf for her dishes—plates and bowls and pots and pottery she had accumulated over the years, some of it broken, all of it treasured.

Throughout she placed her several potpourris, a category of gift she receives with enough frequency to prompt her to think there's some kind of etiquette book that recommends these tasteful little baskets filled with scented petals as perfect for the lady activist.

On top of her bureau she placed a glass jar containing the gallstone that killed her friend Big John: a small brown thing like a marble that never should have had that much power. It was given to her by Mitch; she doesn't quite count it as a present. She also placed there an old juice bottle that she and Mitch had filled with water from the Sacramento River in California. They wanted to have a baby together, and the water was for its baptismal ceremony.

"Sacramento," she says softly, "means blessed."

Mitch had two children from a previous marriage, whom he abandoned when they were very young. Now they are in their twenties; the last Carol heard, Rick was looking for work as an accountant and Dean was in the military. "It was a painful subject for him," she now says. His absences as a father echoed the absence of his own father during childhood. He did not send his former wife any support money. "No one at the shelter has private money," says Carol. "He had none to send." He used to believe children should be little radicals, and tried to get Carol to feed hers on the soup line. As time went on, his ideas about how to rear children became more tolerant.

On the wall she hung up her artwork, message-laden reminders of the existence of ghettos and of pain, of moons and Madonnas.

She put up the crucifix that was made by a homeless man while he was in detox. She put up the crucifix that was made by her son, Shamus, when he was seven.

She hung two small rosaries that were left by anonymous

mourners on Mitch's coffin during the service. Next to her
bed is a wooden rosary from Italy, about five feet long. It is
near an icon of a birthing scene that she bought during a trip to
the Soviet Union last spring.

In one corner she placed a life-size papier-mâché statue of a
homeless woman dressed in rags, donated to the community
by an art student. Carol calls the statue Frances, after a homeless woman whom she once knew and who was very dear and
who has since disappeared.

By the side of her bed she placed a box left on Mitch's coffin
by a Vietnam veteran. It contains the vet's Bronze Star and a
typewritten note. By the side of her bed she also keeps one of
her favorite books, a collection of poetry that includes the
poem by Edna St. Vincent Millay that she read at his funeral:

> My candle burns at both ends;
> It will not last the night.
> But, ah, my foes, and, oh, my friends—
> It gives a lovely light.

Pinned to a board above her desk like an old corsage is a
nostalgic cluster of plastic identification bands from the times
their political actions led them to the hospital or jail. On her
desk is a wedding album that will remain empty. There is also
the bill from the funeral home that charged $275 for the oak
urn with a cross that contains his ashes.

Carol Fennelly believes in the corporal works of mercy, in
feeding the hungry, clothing the naked. She also believes in
the mortification of the flesh and at times gives up food and
drink, except for sips of water. She converted to Catholicism
a few years back, and in her room next to her bed there is even
a kneeler, a dark imposing railing where she sometimes bows
her head and prays for inner peace.

But she is not a nun.

In the closet she hung her pretty clothes, almost all secondhand, the swankiest from her friend Suzie Goldman. Mitch

disapproved of abundance; he always wore the same jeans and the same boots and the same army jacket to the point that when it began to disintegrate she would steal it in his sleep and replace it with another for him to also wear into oblivion. "Excess is theft," he always used to say, but she could never quite match the depth of his material abnegation. He was a true ascetic; he felt rich in proportion to what he could do without: "You only need one pair of shoes."

Her attitude has always been that there is no reason to add to the drabness of an already too drab world. Carol Fennelly even has a jewelry box, though it does not contain precious gems so much as fanciful engaging baubles. She has her hair done in a stylish bob about once a month at the upscale Okyo salon by Bernard Portelli, a fan of the shelter who donates his services to her. She likes pretty things, and one of the most common adjectives used by friends to describe her is feminine.

Maneuvering in the small space, flushed with exertion, relieved to be so busy, gladly auditioning the placement of the large dining table that she likes to point out is solid oak, and the TV, and the trunk she inherited from her grandmother, placing on the high bureau some old political pins that Mitch had kept as well as a little tray with his toiletries, she kept reciting like a mantra her favorite saying. "I think it's from Dostoyevsky, who I think was a famous Russian philosopher," she says. "Anyway, what he supposedly said was: 'Beauty will save the world.' "

For a long time, of course, she thought the burden of universal redemption belonged not to beauty but to her and Mitch Snyder. "We were," she says, "addicted to changing the world."

They had been a movement couple since the second time she saw him, leafleting at a rally on January 7, 1977. She'd been in town for four months, living at a left-wing community called Sojourners, running a free day-care center for inner-city children. By then her own children were in public school. Mitch had been with CCNV since 1973; he had heard about the community from an antiwar activist he had met in prison.

She bummed a cigarette even though she did not smoke. In their faded jeans and shirts embroidered with flowers, they embodied an old-fashioned sixties' idealism, a power-to-the-people sense of the world that today seems quaint.

"We courted," she says, "by going out to the heat grates to pick up people."

Sometimes when sleep comes slow, she pores through a little basket on the bureau filled with Mitch's old political pins: "John Wayne Needs Sensitivity Training" . . . "Dump Watts" . . . "Jesse!" . . . "300 More Today" . . . "Free the 99th Congress" . . . "Vote for 17" . . . "If the People Lead Eventually the Leaders Will Follow."

Her favorite novel is in this room, James Carroll's *Mortal Friends,* which is about the fictional lives of people who are just like her and Mitch. She has only to glance at the title to feel that it is her story, their story, about not just the hardship of a life dedicated to sweeping social change, but also about the intoxication, the romance. Oh, their struggles changed, from the fight against the war in Vietnam to the fight for the ERA to the more recent triumph of actually getting the government to fork over a huge empty building on Second Street to shelter the homeless, but their ardor did not. Together they adored the highs and lows of a life filled with political action. She giggles sometimes, just remembering the kinds of ideas Mitch came up with. He would plan what he called happenings, or events. Her personal favorite, the one that serves as the absolute model of peaceful yet antic disruption, was back in, when was it, '84? Yes, '84. Mitch found out that a group called the American Conservative Union had baked the world's largest pie, seventeen feet of crust and fruit, and as a demonstration of the "trickle-down" theory it was going to give out slices: under Republicanism, everyone can have a piece of the pie. Mitch Snyder served as chauffeur to Carol and others who dressed up as businesspeople and jumped into the pie, splattering apples everywhere.

"We were charged," she says, her face shining with merriment, "with unlawful trespass of a pie."

"Don't you see?" she says, trying to sum up what made them different from other people.

"We always did what we dreamed."

It took genius to be that daring, that nettlesome. In her eyes, Mitch was a brilliant maverick.

The former Maytag appliance salesman from Brooklyn who passed bad checks and did time in the Danbury, Connecticut, federal prison, which is where he met the Berrigan brothers and found his true path, was more than a mere mortal; he was a spellbinder, hero, saint. She never expects to meet a man like him again. He was an original; except for the nightgown and a garish three-dimensional plaster of paris rendition of the Last Supper that hangs on a fake gold chain next to the shelf with the dishes, and, well, Big John's gallstone, he did not shower her with the gifts that might be expected from a normal suitor. His finest offering was in fact abstract, the wonderful edgy, almost contagious passion of someone who insists on leading life to a feverish hilt. It is only now, looking back, that she realizes with a shiver of fear the kind of hold he had on her. It was not mere influence; it was, she says, "absolute power."

They also courted by courting death.

"All right now," he would sometimes say, especially right before he was about to embark on a fast that might kill him, "what do I want?"

She would flash her trademark smile, a large lopsided grin, and then the list of specifications would begin:

"You want gospel music.

"And the song 'Vincent.'

"Dick Gregory.

"Both Berrigans."

And then, in more recent years: "Martin Sheen."

Always, he wanted:

"Lots of people.

"It should be outdoors in a public place.

"And civil disobedience."

When she said it right his face would light up with pleasure, and it was always his face that drew her to him, that long bony mustachioed face with the big sad eyes.

"When I die," he always used to tell her, "you're going to have a really interesting funeral."

It seems curious now the way he phrased it: Why you? Why not I?

It was while she was with Mitch that she undertook a fast that came close to killing her. Two years ago, for forty-eight days she subsisted on Evian water. Toward the end, her blood pressure was measured at eighty over nothing. Her two children opposed what she was doing. Her son, Shamus, now twenty and a shoe salesman at Lord & Taylor, asked her to please eat. Her twenty-one-year-old daughter, Carrie Sunshine, a teacher of aerobics, was puzzled because in the past all the fasts were geared toward a certain goal, like when Mitch stopped eating in order to get Reagan to hand over the old Federal City College building, which became the nation's largest shelter for the homeless ("180,000 square feet!" as Carol is fond of saying), but this one seemed to be for its own consciousness-raising sake. At first their mother handled her hunger by reading cookbooks and preparing huge feasts for other people, but slowly her energy waned and by the end she did not even have the strength to stand up and weigh herself. In her room there is a photograph of her toward the end of the fast, just a head shot as she lay in her hospital bed. Her face is colorless and gaunt, all deep hollows and dulled eyes. When she is asked how she could justify a gesture of this magnitude given the still tender years of her children, her response is quick and oddly sanguine: "Oh, I always knew I would never die."

He sent her a booster note:

"I still love you," he wrote, "Even though you don't have potassium and electrolytes. Thanks for being you."

When he died, Mitch Snyder had two two-dollar bills tucked away in his wallet; they had become thin and melty from having been folded for so long. They sit on her desk now, next to a jar of peanut butter a stranger thrust upon her when she was out shopping recently, and she wants her children to have those bills as keepsakes and as amulets. Now that he is gone they can see more clearly the role he played as their honorary stepfather.

Their relationship with their father, a painting contractor who now lives in Hawaii, is spotty at best. "Let's put it this way. I call him on my birthday," says Shamus, a handsome and outgoing young man who shows his humor with a telephone tape of a flushing toilet and his recorded voice asking callers to leave a message because he is busy at the moment.

He and his sister grew up in shelters and in apartments in neighborhoods where they were often the only white people. "In one place where we lived," their mother says with a touch of something in her voice that sounds like pride, "their playmates were all the children of prostitutes." Carrie Sunshine, petite and pretty with a high-pitched happy voice, says they never had keys to the places where they lived because the door was always open. They do not remember much about their early years in California, where their mother says she went through a super homemaker stage but that her relationship with their father, whom she eventually married, was never great and reached its ebb at a department store when she did something that displeased him and he turned to her and said, "Why can't you just be more obedient?" Seething, she turned to him and said, "Dogs are obedient!" and promptly deposited herself on all fours and started barking and tugging on his pant cuffs with her teeth. Soon after that she saw a light and heard a voice urging her to leave: "I have something special for you and your children."

Carol remembers a middle-class childhood outside Los Angeles; she has two brothers who had more trouble with her father's nasty temper than she did. In fact, she thinks her young life in a male-dominated house is curiously echoed by her life in the shelter, filled as it mostly is with men. "For a long time," she says, "my parents kept hoping I'd be normal." They blame her crusading nature on a car accident she had when she was seventeen; she hurt her head and has never been, in their view, the same since. Carol's children find her to be so different from her parents that they often ask her, "Are you sure you weren't adopted?"

When the children get to talking about Mitch, their reminiscences trip over each other and they both try to convey at once the precise experience of hearing this musically impaired man sing. He not only had no idea how to carry a tune, but he could never remember any words anyway, so his impromptu concerts consisted mostly of crooning, loudly, with a kind of dumb happiness, da da da da over and over. He also had a habit of making the same awful jokes again and again, and when they heard one for the millionth time, they would groan, "Oh, God," and he would take that as his golden opportunity to raise his hands in mock protest: "Please, please, that's too formal. Just call me Mitch." He also had the world's worst eating habits; when he wasn't starving himself to death, he would prepare huge, utterly unappetizing basins of things like Rice-A-Roni or five pounds of steamed clams and then he would wonder why no one wanted to join him at the table. His jeans were sometimes so tight he could barely walk in them, but Carrie's warning that he was probably ruining his sperm made no difference. He used to say that he wasn't really a person, he was really just a cat.

The final months mirrored, almost mockingly, Mitch's and Carol's lives as activists: They were filled with highs and lows, tortured partings and ecstatic reunions.

In the end his transformation was a swift downward plunge

from being someone tormented beyond endurance by the cruelties of the world to someone who is in turn a cruel tormentor. In January 1990 they were going to get married, then they weren't. In April Carol went to the Soviet Union to look at alcohol treatment centers and while traveling she had an epiphany not unlike the one that sent her to Washington in the first place: they were meant to be together as inevitably as stars and sky, dust and desert. She had a vision of them as a couple on a grand, almost historic mission: they must marry, they should even have a baby. She bought the icon of the birthing scene. And she went wild buying Russian linens, beautiful fabric that she brought back as a kind of dowry, cloth that was fresh and unsullied for both of them to admire. Samples are now draped around her room.

They even set a date: September 9. He would wear his army jacket, naturally, but she would go full throttle and dress in white. The ceremony would be held outdoors, in public, and they would invite thousands of witnesses.

But by late spring his agony made him impossible to be around. For a while Carol moved down to the first floor near the infirmary, ostensibly to keep a closer watch on that part of the shelter's operation. She started spending more time with friends outside the shelter, including a jazz musician she remains close to today. She started to fear Mitch, and at night the worst sound she could imagine was his distinctive, heavy, heel-first footstep in the hall, coming closer and closer.

By June she was staying with friends away from the shelter on a routine basis. She would not tell him where she was going and she always took care to park her car, an easy-to-recognize, well-traveled silver Honda, blocks and blocks away from wherever she was. She won't talk about whether he hit her, but she will say that she was terrified of sudden rages, the way his face would twist itself and become unrecognizable with anger. Their last exchange was an ugly fight when she came back to the shelter to pick up a few of her things and he stalked her down the hall, accusing her of being with someone else, showering her with epithets of which she can remember one in particular: "Trash, trash, trash," over and over.

That was Monday, July 2. At that moment she had no thoughts of saving him: "All I could think about was my survival."

After that he went to his room and apparently sat by the phone, waiting for her to call. The next evening, most likely, was when he killed himself by hanging. He looped an electrical cord over a pipe along the ceiling.

"He had this incredible power over me," she says. "The ability to turn my head around. You see, the same rage he directed at injustice he directed at me. His incredible manipulation of public officials was the same as his incredible manipulation of me."

When she speaks about this, her voice tends to lower and she bows her head slightly: what was once thrilling seems now almost shameful.

Her eyes have a sudden shine.

"He needed to own me. I had allowed him to own me. In the end, there wasn't anybody else. It was that I no longer wanted to be owned. I wanted to love him and be with him.

"That wasn't enough."

Now, if she has her way, she will soon own him. The lawyers have said there is a good chance she can become his legal widow. He had a girlfriend named Mary Ellen Hombs before he met Carol, and for years and years, even though they both worked at the shelter, Carol refused to speak to her. Why not? "She was rotten to me. She wouldn't leave me alone. She harassed me. I'm sure she'd say I harassed her. That's all I have to say on the subject. Right now, we speak through our attorneys."

Mitch's 1984 will made Carol and Mary Ellen joint legal representatives of his estate. The reason she wants to become his legal spouse is a point of personal pride: "I will never love any man as much as I loved Mitch, but I don't want to be known as his longtime companion when I would have been his wife if his mental illness had not intervened. I want not just the legal but also the social standing." One of her consolations on sleepless nights is to summon those times of closeness in both public and private, to close her eyes against the shifting shadows and to recall the ways in which they were spouses, the exchange of rings, the actual references to being husband and wife, most frequently at hospitals when in defeat and panic one of them was rushing toward the other for what might be the final time.

Mitch's ashes now occupy a small table with a candle next to her bed; soot and bone, soft and hard, like silk and pearl.

But that's not really him. He is elsewhere, maybe everywhere. The horror of the last year has shown up in her dreams. One time she had a vision of something oozing through the vents in the ceiling, something ugly and molten and throbbing, that seemed to be evil itself, evil vents, evil events. Another time she saw while she slept a mansion next to a sunlit meadow filled with happy people. Inside she saw Mitch laid out on what looked like an operating table and a medical team working on him, but what was so odd was that they seemed to be doing some kind of heart surgery, so Carol spoke to the people in the dream: "You don't understand—he hung himself, he did not have a heart attack." And the voices in the dream answered back: "We're not healing him from what others did to him but from what he did to others." It was a relief to dream that, to be able to wake up the next day and look at his rugged image on her walls and say, "Damn you, Mitch, for dumping all this on me!"

He was cremated with a copy of his favorite movie, "It's a Wonderful Life." She thought he might want the medal left on his coffin by the nameless vet to join his ashes, but she was told that the medal would outlast the flame, and so she kept it out, and when she wants to think of all the good he did for so many, she reads the note that came with it:

"You gave shelter to those who fought when the country turned its back."

No, those ashes are not him. Mitch to her is enthusiasm and action and one less hungry person, one more person on a clean cot for the night. Mitch is all the money that he brought in personally to the shelter and that she must find a way to bring in now. He is the reminder that there's always more work to be done: you can never do it right, never do enough. She will carry on. The last thing she wants is for anyone to think of her as weak. Here she is, health itself, filled with potassium and electrolytes, and her blood pressure is perfectly respectable. His goals are hers. She is his true bride.

❧ ❧ ❧

Shortly after the piece on Carol Fennelly appeared in the *Washington Post,* she received a check for the shelter from a family-run foundation for twenty-five thousand dollars. There has been interest from several movie companies in making a sequel to the *Samaritan,* with a major emphasis on her love affair with activist Mitch Snyder, including overtures from a company run by Diane Keaton.

"Just imagine," she says, "Diane Keaton playing me!"

ZEPP'S
LAST STAND

There was indeed one of us who hesitated and did not want to fall into line. That was Joseph Behm, a plump, homely fellow. But he did allow himself to be persuaded, otherwise he would have been ostracized. And perhaps more of us thought as he did, but no one could very well stand out, because at that time even one's parents were ready with the word "coward."
ERICH MARIA REMARQUE, *All Quiet on the Western Front*

All his life Edward Zepp has wanted nothing so much as to go to the next world with a clear conscience. So on September 11, the old man, carrying a borrowed briefcase filled with papers, boarded the Amtrak train in Deerfield Beach and headed north on the Silver Meteor to our nation's capital. As the porter showed him to his roomette, Ed Zepp kept saying, "I'm eighty-three years old. Eighty-three."

At 9 A.M. the next day, Zepp was to appear at the Pentagon for a hearing before the Board for Corrections of Military Records. This was, he said, "the supreme effort, the final fight" in the private battle of Private Zepp, Company D, 323rd Machine Gun Battalion, veteran of World War I, discharged on November 9, 1919—with dishonor.

Something happens to people after a certain age, and the distinctions of youth disappear. The wrinkles conquer, like an army. In his old age, Zepp is bald. He wears fragile glasses. His shoulders are rounded. His pace is stooped and slow. It is hard, in a way, to remove sixty years, and picture him tall, lanky, a rebel.

The old man, wearing a carefully chosen business suit which he hoped would be appropriately subdued for the Pentagon, sat in the chair of the roomette as the train pulled out of

Deerfield Beach. With a certain palsied eagerness he foraged his briefcase. Before the train reached full speed, he arranged on his lap the relics from his days at war. There were the dog tags and draft card, even his Department of War Risk life insurance policy. There was a letter to his mother written in 1919 in France, explaining why he was in the stockade. His fingers, curled with arthritis and in pain, attacked several documents. He unfurled the pages of a copy of the original court-martial proceedings which found him in violation of the sixty-forth Article of War: failure to obey the command of a superior officer. There was also a copy of the rule book for Fort Leavenworth, where Zepp had been sentenced to ten years at hard labor.

· When Ed Zepp was drafted in 1917, he told his draft board that he had conscientious objections to fighting overseas. The draft board told him his objections did not count; at the time only Quakers and Mennonites were routinely granted C.O. (conscientious objector) status. "As a Lutheran, I didn't cut any ice," he said. Zepp was one of 20,873 men between the ages of twenty-one and thirty-one who were classified as C.O.s but inducted nonetheless. Of those, only 3,999 made formal claims once they were in camp. Zepp's claim occurred on June 10, 1918, at Fort Merritt, New Jersey, the day before his battalion was scheduled for shipment overseas. Earlier, Zepp had tried to explain his position to a commanding officer, who told him he had a "damn fool belief." On June 10, Zepp was ordered to pack his barracks bag. When he refused, a sergeant— "Sgt. Hitchcock, a real hard-boiled guy, a Regular Army man"—held a gun to his head: "Pack that bag or I'll shoot."

"Shoot," said Zepp, "you son of a bitch."

Conscientious objection has always been a difficult issue for the military, but perhaps less difficult in 1917 than in recent time. Men who refused to fight were called "slackers" and "cowards." By the time the United States entered the war, the public had been subjected to a steady onslaught of "blatant

Photo by John Doman

propaganda," according to Raymond O'Connor, professor of American history at the University of Miami.

The government found ways to erode the spirit of isolationism felt by many Americans and replace it with a feeling of jubilant hostility against the Germans. It was patriotic to despise the kaiser. It was patriotic to sing: "Over There," "Oh, I Hate To Get Up in The Morning," and "It's a Long Way to Tipperary." A new recruiting poster pointed out that "Uncle Sam Wants You." The war's most important hero was Sergeant York, a conscientious objector who was later decorated for capturing Germans. They made a movie of Sgt. Alvin York's heroics.

They made an example of Pvt. Edward Zepp, a kid from Cleveland.

Zepp was formally released from the army sixty years and two days ago.

But Zepp has never released the army.

At his upcoming hearing at the Pentagon, Zepp was after a subtle distinction, two words really, "honorable discharge," meaningless to anybody but him. It would be a victory that couldn't even be shared with the most important person in his life, his wife Christine, who died in 1977.

In 1952, Zepp appeared before the same military board. At that time the army agreed that he was a sincere C.O. His discharge was upgraded to a "general discharge with honor." He became entitled to the same benefits as any other veteran, but he has never taken any money: "I have lived without their benefits all my life." The board refused to hear his case again; only a bureaucratic snafu and the intercession of Rep. Daniel Mica (D., Palm Beach) paved the way to the hearing scheduled for September 12.

For forty-one years Zepp worked as the money raiser for the Community Chest, now called The United Way, in Cleveland. He learned how to get things done, to get things from people.

For years, he has sought his due from the Pentagon. His persistence was not only heroic, but also a touch ornery. Here is a man who refused to fight in World War I but who takes a blackjack with him to ward off potential punks every time he leaves his Margate condominium at night. He talks about how there are just wars, and maybe we should have gone all out in Vietnam, "just like we did in Hiroshima, killing the whole city" and in the next breath he talks about the problems that occur when "the Church starts waving a Flag."

It is impossible to tell how much of his fight is hobby and how much the passion of a man who says he cannot die—he literally cannot leave this earth—until his honor is fully restored.

To some, his refusal to fight meant cowardice; to Zepp, it represented heroism. It is an ethical no-man's-land. War leaves no room for subtle distinctions.

For his day in court, Ed Zepp was not taking any chances. His health is failing; he is at the age of illness and eulogy. He has an understandable preoccupation with his own debilities (proximal atrial fibrillations, coronary heart disease, pernicious anemia). Many of his references, especially his war stories, are to people now gone. At $270 for a round-trip train ticket, the plane would have been cheaper, but Zepp thought flying would be too risky; it might bring on a seizure, a blackout, something worse.

On the train the old man talked obsessively about what happened during the war. He told his story over and over and over—clack clack clack, like the train on the rails. Except for this constant talk, there was nothing about him that revealed his mission. As he hesitantly walked the narrow, shaking corridors, making his way from car to car, he did not have the air of a man headed for the crucial confrontation of his life. He looked like a nicely dressed elderly man who might be taking the train out of a preference for gravity or perhaps in sentimental memory of the glory days of railroading.

"This was the war to end war," Zepp said on the way to the dining car. "The war to make the world safe for democracy. *Democracy.* They gave me a kangaroo court-martial."

All his life, Zepp has believed he was denied the very freedoms he had been recruited to defend. He has nursed his grievances like an old war injury, which, on one level, is exactly what they are. "They murdered me, you know. They tried to, in a way."

His refusal to fight turned him into a fighter: "I was cursed," he said. "It made a killer out of me almost."

He said he was seeking only one thing: "My honor. My good name. I don't see how a great nation can stigmatize as dishonorable a person who was following the dictates of his conscience. When I die, I want it said of me, 'Well done, thou good and faithful servant.' "

Ed Zepp turned to the young waiter, in his starched white mess coat, who had been patiently waiting for him to order lunch. He ordered a turkey sandwich: "I can't eat much. My doctor says I should eat lightly. I take enzyme pills to help me digest."

September 1979, Sebring, Florida: Ed Zepp's light lunch has just been placed before him. September 1917, Cleveland, Ohio: Ed Zepp's appeals to the draft board have been rejected twice.

During any long trip, there is a distortion of landscape and time; the old man's talk echoed the feeling of suspension that comes with being on the road. The closer he got to the Pentagon, the closer he got to 1917.

Before he was drafted at the age of twenty-one, Zepp had already earned a business degree and worked as a clerk at Johns Manville. At the time, his native Cleveland was heavily industrialized, with much social and political unrest. Socialist Eugene Debs was a frequent visitor; Zepp says the man was "fire." He remembers listening to his speeches and once joined a Debs march, clear across town, to a large hall on the west side. Debs preached workers' rights and counseled against war. So did Zepp's pastor, who was censured by the Lutheran church for his outspoken views against the war. "War," says Ed Zepp, "was an ocean away."

Zepp's parents were Polish immigrants, Michael and Louise Czepieus. His father was a blacksmith, "not the kind who made shoes for horses, but rather he made all the ironwork pertaining to a wagon." There were five children and all of them were sent to business school and ended up, says Zepp, "in the office world."

"I was a top-notch office man all my life," he says. In any family there is talk about somebody's lost promise, failed opportunity, and in the Zepp family, there was talk, principally among his sisters, about how, with his meticulous mind, he would have been a great lawyer but for the war, but for what happened over there.

The waiter removed the empty plate from Zepp's table, and the next group of hungry passengers was seated.

Three P.M. Waldo, Florida, in the club car. Ed Zepp was nursing a soda, and on the table in front of him, like a deck of marked cards, were the original court-martial proceedings.

Eighty miles an hour.

The train was moving almost as fast as Edward Zepp is old, and he seemed impressed by that. "It is," he said, "a wonderful way to see the countryside." The world passed by in a blur.

Despite his ailments, there is something energetic and alert about Zepp; for two months before the hearing, he swam every day for half an hour to build stamina. Sipping his soda, he wondered whether he had chosen the correct clothes. His suit was brown and orange. He had a color-coordinated, clip-on tie and a beige shirt. "I have another suit that my wife, Christine, picked out for me, but it has all the colors of the rainbow, and I didn't want to show up at the Pentagon looking like a sport in front of all those monkeys. Oops. I'd better be careful. They probably wouldn't like if it I called them monkeys, would they?"

This trip was partly in memory of Christine, Zepp's third wife, whom he married in 1962, shortly before he retired to Florida. His first marriage was brief; during the second marriage he had two children, a son who died in his early thirties ("He served in Korea and he was a teacher") and a daughter, now forty-six years old, a psychiatric social worker who lives near Boston.

"Christine would want me to do this. She was a fighter, she was a real person. She was the only one I cared about. And what happened? She died. All the guys in my condominium thought I would be the first to go but she passed away on May

1, 1977, two days before my eighty-first birthday. Do you know what she said to me before she died? 'I want to be buried with my wedding ring on.' I meet other women at the square dances at the senior center. One of them said, 'Ed let's go to the Bahamas for a week. Get your mind off this. It's too much pressure.' But I couldn't go away. Christine and I are married, even in death."

When Ed Zepp speaks of his third wife, his face sometimes gets an odd look; there is a dreamlike minute or so. The voice catches, the blue eyes become rheumy, his words come out in a higher pitch. Just as it seems as if he will break down and sob, composure returns. The same thing often happens when he speaks of what happened during the war.

"Anyone who reads this court-martial," said Zepp, "will acquaint himself with all the vital points of my case: how the draft board refused to listen; how the army loused it up in Camp Sherman when they failed to inform me of General Order Number 28; how, at Fort Merritt, Sergeant Hitchcock held the gun to my head and forced me to pack, and then they Shanghaied me out of the country on the SS *Carmania,* and in France they gave me a kangaroo court-martial."

General Order Number 28, issued by the War Department on March 23, 1918, was an effort by the government in midwar to expand the definition of those who qualified for C.O. status. Men who had already been drafted, but had sought C.O. status were supposed to be informed by a "tactful and considerate" officer of their right to choose noncombatant service.

"General Order Number 28 was never read or posted during the time I was at boot camp at Camp Sherman in Chillicothe, Ohio," Zepp maintains. "This was how it was done—gospel truth: 250 of us were lined up in retreat. Lt. Paul Herbert went through the ranks, asking each man, 'Any objections to fighting the Germans?' Well, I thought they were looking for pro-German sympathizers. I wasn't a pro-German sympathizer. My parents were Polish. I did not speak up.

"Then at Fort Merritt, Sergeant Hitchcock, he was a hard-boiled sergeant, put the gun on me. He never told the court-martial about that. He approached me in a belligerent manner; there was no kindly and courteous officer informing me of my rights as specified in General Order Number 28.

"They shipped me overseas against my will, and for two months in France I still didn't know what action would be taken against me for defying Sergeant Hitchcock and Captain Faxon. They kept me busy with regular military work. I helped erect a machine-gun range, I had rifle practice, I learned how to break a person's arm in close combat.

"During that time, Lieutenant Herbert propositioned me with a nice soft easy job. He came up to me and he said, 'Zepp, how about calling the whole thing off? I'll get you a nice soft easy job in the quartermaster.' " Zepp repeated Herbert's words. "He tried to make a deal. But I had no confidence. I smelled a rat. And to prove to you beyond a shadow of a doubt it was not a sincere offer, find one word in the court-martial proceedings that he offered me a job. He was trying to make a deal. It was a trap.

"And then they Shanghaied me out of the country and gave me a kangaroo court-martial. I wasn't even allowed to face my accusers." During Zepp's court-martial many of the basic facts which are part of his litany are mentioned. The sergeant who held a gun to his head testified, but no mention was made of that action. Capt. C. W. Faxon said he believed Zepp had "sincere religious objections." Sgt. Steve Kozman admitted to giving the defendant "a few kicks in the behind" on his way to the SS *Carmania*.

In his testimony, Zepp told about how, the same evening he refused to pack his barracks bag. "Lt. Paul Herbert came up to me and spoke in a general way about my views and called them pro-German. He also asked me if I had a mother and I said, 'Yes,' and he asked me if I had a sister and I said, 'Yes,' and he said, 'Would you disgrace them by having your picture in the paper?' "

Zepp argued that in light of General Order Number 28 the army had no right to ship him overseas without first offering noncombatant service. The heart of Zepp's case, as he spoke it before that tribunal long ago, showed his instinct for fine, if quixotic, distinctions:

"I did not willfully disobey two lawful orders, but I was compelled to willfully disobey two alleged lawful orders."

Savannah, Georgia 7 P.M. The train had crossed state lines, and Zepp had just entered the dining car for an evening meal of fish and vegetables. His conversation once again crossed the borders of geography and time.

Even at dinner, it was impossible for him to abandon his topic.

"Let me tell you about what happened after the court-martial. They put me in a dungeon; there were rats running over me, the floor was wet, it was just a place to throw potatoes, except they'd all rot. It was later condemned as unfit for human habitation by the psychiatrist who interviewed me. That was a perfect opportunity to act crazy and get out of the whole thing. But I stuck by my conscience. I was not a coward. It's easier to take a chance with a bullet than stand up on your own two feet and defy."

He talked about how the army discovered he had "office skills" and he spent much of his time as a clerk—"sergeant's work, or at least corporal's."

He said he was transferred to army bases all over France during 1919; the best time was under Capt. John Evans: "I had my own desk, and Captain Evans put a box of chocolates on it, which he shouldn't have, because it turned me into a 250-pounder. I had the liberty of the city, and Captain Evans gave me an unsolicited recommendation." Zepp quoted it by heart: "Private Zepp has worked for me since Jan 3, 1919. During this time he has been my personal clerk, and anyone desiring a stenographer will find him trustworthy and with no mean ability."

In August of 1919, as part of his clerical duties, Zepp was

"making out service records for boys to return home to the United States, and finally the time came for me to make one out for myself."

In September he arrived in Fort Leavenworth where once again he served as a clerk: "They made me secretary to the chaplain, and I taught the boys how to operate a typewriter.

"Finally on November 9, 1919, they released me. I still don't know why I didn't serve the complete sentence. I never asked for their mercy. I think it must have been my mother, she must have gone to our pastor, and he intervened."

Zepp paused, and his look became distant. There was that catch in his voice; he cried without tears.

Dinner was over.

10:00 P.M. Florence, South Carolina. After nursing one beer in the club car, Zepp decided it was time to get some sleep. As he prepared to leave for his roomette, he said, "They tried to make Martin Luther recant, but he wouldn't. Remember: 'If they put you to shame or call you faithless, it is better that God call you faithful and honorable than that the world call you faithful and honorable.' Those are Luther's own words. 1526."

It was hard to sleep on the train; it rocked at high speeds and it made a number of jerking stops and churning starts in the middle of the night in small towns in North Carolina.

Ed Zepp asked the porter to wake him an hour before the 6 A.M. arrival in Washington, but his sleep was light and he awoke on his own at 4. He shaved, dressed, and then sat in the roomette, briefcase beside him. The train pulled in on time, before sunrise.

Wandering the almost-empty station, Zepp had a tall dignity, eyeglasses adding to his air of alertness. He sat by himself on a bench, waiting for his lawyer who was due at 7. Zepp's lawyer was a young fellow who had read about his client in *Liberty Magazine*. Thirty-four years old, John St. Landau works at the Center for Conscientious Objection in Philadelphia. Landau called the old man in Florida and volunteered his services. They made plans to meet at Union Station, and Zepp told the lawyer, "Don't worry. You'll recognize me. I'll be the decrepit old man creeping down the platform."

Landau, himself a C.O. during the Vietnam War, arrived at the appointed hour. The two men found an empty coffee shop where they huddled at a table for about an hour. Zepp told his lawyer he had not brought his blackjack to Washington, and the lawyer said, smiling, "I take it you are no longer a C.O."

At 8:30 they left to take the Metro, Washington's eerily modern subway system with computerized "farecards," to the Pentagon.

Zepp was easily the oldest person on the commuter-filled subway. He did not try to speak above the roar. His was a vigil of silence. When the doors sliced open at the "Pentagon" stop, the hour of judgment was upon him.

"The gates of hell," he said, "shall not prevail."

It would be hard to surmise, given the enthusiasm of his recital, that Zepp was in Washington on not much more than a wing and a prayer. In April, the Pentagon had mistakenly promised him a hearing; it was a bureaucratic bungle. On May 9, he was told there had been an error; there was no new evidence in his case; therefore there should be no new hearing. On May 31, Representative Mica wrote to the review board requesting a new hearing on the strength of his office. It was granted for September 12, but Zepp had been forewarned in a letter from the Pentagon that just because he was getting his hearing, he should not conclude from this concession that "the department" admits "any error or injustice now . . . in your records."

Just before Zepp was ushered into the small hearing room at 11, he gave himself a pep talk: "I am going to be real nice. Getting even doesn't do anything, punching someone around. I want to do things the Christian way. And I'll use the oil can. When I was at the Community Chest, I called all the women 'darlings' and I would polka with them at the parties. I used the oil can profusely."

Zepp departed for the hearing room.

The fate of the World War I veteran, defended by a Vietnam-era lawyer, was to be decided by a panel of five—four veterans of World War II, one veteran of the Korean War. The chairman was Charles Woodside, who also served on the panel that heard the appeal of the widow of Pvt. Eddie Slovik, the first deserter since the Civil War to be executed. Less than a week before Zepp's hearing, newspapers carried a story about how Slovik's widow, denied a pension by the army, had finally died, penniless, in a nursing home.

Landau stated Zepp's case, saying that the defendant accepted the findings of the 1952 hearing, the findings which concluded Zepp had in fact been sincere: "The reason we're here is that we believe the general discharge ought to be upgraded to an honorable discharge. . . . What we see as the critical issue is the quality of [Mr. Zepp's] service."

The first witness was Martin Sovik, a member of the staff of the Office for Governmental Affairs of the Lutheran Church Council. Like Landau, Sovik had also been a C.O. during Vietnam.

He confirmed that in 1969 the Lutheran Church in America supported individual members of the church, following their consciences, to oppose participation in war. One member of the panel asked Sovik how you can determine whether a person is in fact a C.O.

"That decision is made within a person's mind—obviously you can't know whether a person is a C.O. anymore than whether he is a Yankees' fan or an Orioles' fan except by his own affirmation."

Next, the old man took his turn. The panel urged him to remain seated during the testimony. The old man marshalled the highlights of his military experience: *"Shanghaied"; "nice soft easy job"; "tactful and courteous officer"; "hard-boiled ser-*

geant"; "gun at my head"; "face my accusers"; "unfit for human habitation"; "unsolicited recommendation." The words tumbled out, a litany.

Every now and then Zepp's composure cracked, stalling the proceedings. "I'm sure it's hard to recall," said Woodside.

"It's not that," said the defendant. "I'm just living it. This was indelibly impressed, it is vivid on my mind, like something that happened yesterday."

At 1, a luncheon recess was called. Woodside promised that he would continue to listen with sympathy when the hearing resumed.

"Govern yourself by the facts," said Zepp. "Then we'll both be happy."

As they were leaving the hearing room, Zepp turned to Landau and Sovik and apologized for breaking down. "You're doing all right, you're doing just fine," said Sovik.

"I can't help it. Every now and then my voice breaks," said Zepp. "It touches me."

Sovik, putting his hand on the old man's arms, said: "It touches us all."

The afternoon was more of the same: "Lieutenant Herbert was not making me a sincere offer"; "German sympathizer"; "disgrace your sisters"; "sincere religious objections."

Finally the executive secretary of the Corrections Board, Ray Williams, the man most familiar with Zepp's case, asked the defendant:

"Mr. Zepp, since you received your general discharge under honorable conditions back in 1953 as a result of a recommendation of this board, have you ever applied to the V.A. for any benefits?"

Zepp: "No, I haven't."

Williams: "You understand you are entitled to all the benefits of an honorably discharged soldier."

Zepp: "That's right. The one thing that bothers me is my conscience, my allegiance to the Almighty. I have to see this thing through. . . . I don't think that a person who follows the dictates of his conscience and is a true Christian should be stigmatized as a dishonorable person. And I think he shouldn't even get a second-rate discharge."

Williams: "In all good conscience you can say that your discharge is under honorable conditions."

Zepp: "I personally feel it would behoove the United States of America, who believes in freedom of conscience, religion, or the Bill of Rights, that a person who follows, truthfully follows, the dictates of his conscience, and you are obligated to follow it because you've got a relationship with God, and I don't think that we should stigmatize anybody like that as being a dishonorable person.

"And the reason I'm here at my advanced age—eighty-three, arthritis and all that—my inner self, my conscience, says, 'Now here. You go to the board and make one last effort.'" Zepp paused, He hunched forward and made ready to sling one final arrow: "In view of the fact, Mr. Williams, that there's not much difference, then why not make it honorable? There isn't much difference. Let's make it honorable and we'll all be happy."

Zepp's lawyer closed with this plea:

"The military has come a long way since 1918 in their dealing with these individuals who have religious scruples about continued military service. . . . I would contend that it's in part because of individuals like Mr. Zepp who were willing to put their principles on the line many years ago . . . that it took individuals like that to finally work out a good system of dealing with conscientious objection. And that's what the military has now after many, many years. That, in its own right, is a very important service to the military."

The panel closed the proceedings. A decision was promised sometime within the next month.

Back at Union Station, waiting for the return trip: gone now the derelict emptiness of the early morning hours. In the evening the station was smart with purpose: well-dressed men and women, toting briefcases and newspapers, in long lines waiting for trains. The old man sat on a chair and reviewed the day. He smiled and his eyes were bright.

"I feel very confident. I sensed victory. I put all my cards on the table and I called a spade a spade. Did you see how I went up afterwards and I shook all their hands, just like they were my friends. I even shook the hands of Williams, my enemy, and I leaned over and said to him, 'I love you, darling.' I acted as if I expected victory and I did not accept defeat. I used the oil can profusely."

He paused. Zepp looked up, seeming to study the ceiling. He cupped his chin with his left hand. The old man was silent. A college-aged girl across from him watched him in his reverie, and she smiled a young smile.

Finally, the old man spoke. He seemed shaken. His voice was soft, filled with fear, the earlier confidence gone. The thought had come, like a traitor, jabbing him in the heart:

"What next?"

"I'll be lonesome without this. Here's my problem. Now that I don't have anything to battle for, what will I do? There's nothing I know of in the horizon to compete with that."

He paused. His face brightened. "Well, I can go swimming. And I can keep square dancing. Something happens to me when I square dance; it's the—what do they call it—the adrenalin. I am a top-form dancer. Maybe I can go back to being the treasurer of the Broward Community Senior Center. I did that before my wife became sick, but I quit to take care of her. I always was a fine office man. Maybe I'll become active in the Hope Lutheran Church. In other words, keep moving. Keep moving. That's the secret.

"All I know is that I could not face my departure from this earth if I had failed to put up this fight."

At 7:20, there came the boom of an announcement over the loudspeaker; the voice was anonymous and businesslike:

"The Silver Meteor, bound for Miami, Florida, scheduled

to depart at 7:40, is ready for boarding. All passengers may now board the Silver Meteor, with stops in Alexandria . . . Richmond . . . Petersburg . . . Fayetteville . . . Florence . . . Charleston . . . Savannah . . . Jacksonville . . . Waldo . . . Ocala . . . Wildwood . . . Winter Haven . . . Serbing . . . West Palm Beach . . . Deerfield Beach . . . Fort Lauderdale . . . Hollywood . . . Miami."

Edward Zepp boarded the train, located his roomette and departed for home. Within minutes of leaving the station, exhausted by the day's excitement, he fell asleep.

On Tuesday, October 2, 1979, the Pentagon issued the following statement: "Having considered the additional findings, conclusions and recommendation of the Army Board for Correction of Military Records and under the provisions of 10 U.S.C. 1552, the action of the Secretary of the Army on 4 December 1952 is hereby amended insofar as the character of discharge is concerned, and it is directed: (1) That all Department of the Army records of Edward Zepp be corrected to show that he was separated from the Army of the United States on a Certificate of Honorable Discharge in November 1919. (2) That the Department of the Army issue to Edward Zepp a Certificate of Honorable Discharge from the Army of the United States dated 9 November 1919 in lieu of the General Discharge Certificate of the same date now held by him."

"In other words," said Edward Zepp, "I was right all along."

A week later, a copy of the Pentagon's decision arrived at Zepp's Margate condominium. He discovered the decision was not unanimous. One member, James Hise, had voted against him.

"I'm so mad I could kick the hell out of him. A guy like that shouldn't be sitting on the Board. I am going to write to the Pentagon and tell them he should be thrown off the panel. It would be better to have just a head up there loaded with concrete or sawdust than this guy Hise, who doesn't know the first thing about justice. If he can't judge better that that, he should be kicked off. He's a menace to justice in this world. "I'd like to go up there and bust his head wide open."

🐭 🐭 🐭

If Mr. Zepp is still alive, he is well into his nineties. A check of the death notices of the *Miami Herald* turned up no mention of him, but there is a gap in time because these were not computerized until 1983. Somehow there is a spiritual correctness in not being able to account for his whereabouts because what really matters is the indisputable knowledge that wherever he is he is still telling his story to anyone who will listen: "Those monkeys at the Pentagon, you know what their heads are filled with? I'll tell you what their heads are filled with. Concrete and sawdust, that's what."

LETHAL
WEAPON

Wendy Blankenship walks funny. The expectation is
that a prostitute would have mastered a seductive
swagger. But Wendy, nineteen and a half years old,
enters the lobby of the Dade County Women's Detention
Center with the awkward, jerky stride of a careening child.
The color of her skin is a little flat, probably because on the
street she lives on crack, on the orange drink called Sunny
Delight, on Mounds and Reese's. She is tall, about five feet
eight inches, and while in jail she tries to gain as much weight
as she can, adding up to fifteen, twenty pounds, so as to have
reserves to draw on when she goes back out. The weight she
gains has a disconcerting way of gathering at her stomach,
and she sometimes grabs at the swelling folds of flesh and
complains about how she looks pregnant, but—and then the
grin, with its lopsided revelation of a badly chipped front
tooth—she isn't. The tooth just kind of fell apart one day
while she was eating ice cream.

"Got any cigarettes? Got any matches? Got money for the
candy machine?"

She is used to only one form of human interaction, and that
is the kind in which trades are made. Nothing is free, and
everything is for sale or barter. M & Ms for quotes.

"Well, I'm from California, a California girl. I can't remember too much about my mother. She disowned me because she said I raped my little sister, which I don't agree with. I really don't think I ever did that. My name Wendy, it comes from a Beach Boy song that was popular when I was born.

"On the street they call me Turnpike because that's the way I run. You pay before you get on, and the longer you ride the more it costs."

"We who labor here seek only the truth."

This slogan, which appears in many of the courtrooms at the Metro Justice Building, has a lulling effect. The intent is noble, but is it accurate? Truth only?

Never revenge? Never vindication?

Never freedom from certain fears?

Wendy Blankenship has become a legal cause, a quandary. The woman who on the streets has a diseased waifish anonymity, who is urban and invisible, has suddenly become an object of burning concern in the world most opposite her own—the nine-to-five world of men and women in suits at court. The attention to Wendy is not because she has been arrested seventeen times since hitching a ride to Miami two years ago, always on charges relating to her life as a prostitute. It is not because she, and hundreds, maybe thousands like her, live brutishly in the midst of affluence, reduced to selling their sex or trading it for drugs.

Wendy Blankenship has demanded our attention because she has the AIDS virus, and she is indifferent about it. At the end of her inevitably short rest stops in prison, she is back out on the street plying the only trade she knows. The degree of her contagiousness is in the province of medical speculation. But what is known is that it is possible for Wendy to infect a sex partner after a single contact, and that on the street she is likely to have sex with an average of five men a night. "Ten," she says, "if things are hopping."

Miami Herald photo by Al Diaz

If she were the only prostitute in the world with the AIDS virus, her existence would still be a cause of great official concern. But there are many others like her, especially in Miami, and the fear, of course, is that the men who pay for her favors have wives and lovers, and that the deadly disease will be communicated beyond the alleys and byways of the Little

River area, with its sad daily scenario of hollow-eyed women parading shopworn wares to men cruising in their cars, men curiously undeterred by the shame in all this, or the danger.

So now everyone's interested, "20/20" is interested; "60 Minutes" cares.

At the Dade County Women's Detention Center, Turnpike has a new nickname.

Movie Star.

Dade Judge Morton Perry: "Every time Wendy comes into court a television camera comes with her and I always give the same speech. Ten years ago prostitution was considered to be a victimless crime. Today, prostitution is a crime that carries with it the possibility of death, and yet it still carries the same penalty as that of a second-degree misdemeanor, namely a sentence of sixty days. Normally it takes that long to come to trial.

"Is it necessary for prostitutes to carry machine guns with AIDS written on them for the legislature to increase the penalty for prostitution in Dade County, which has the second-highest AIDS rate among prostitutes in the nation, besting every city in this country with the exception of Newark? Forty-one percent of Miami's inner-city prostitutes have the AIDS virus and 16 percent of all prostitutes in Dade County.

"These days a man who visits a prostitute can become a victim of AIDS, and not just him but his family, his wife, his lover, his unborn children.

"AIDS is a tragedy, but Wendy's behavior is criminal and carries with it a possible death penalty.

"What's the answer? Counseling? How is a crack addict controlled by a pimp who has been living on the streets for years going to be affected by counseling?"

"I know I should tell my tricks to use condoms," Wendy says, "but a lot of them don't want to, and if they don't want to, I'm still going to date them because business is business. I need the money and when I'm high, I don't think of nothing but another hit."

Prostitution is famous for its persistence, its resistance to remedies and alternatives. To listen to Wendy is to glimpse the reason, the deep and tangled roots that make reformation seem an impossibility:

"Nights I'm tricking, OK, here's what I do to get ready. I work the graveyard shift, see. I leave the house around eleven or twelve at night. I can't stand the sun. It's just too hot here to work in Miami during the day. What I do is I might change what I'm wearing, and usually I splash some perfume on my blouse. The kind of perfume I use is called John Nady and it costs two or three dollars for a big bottle.

"I like to get high right before I go out. What I charge depends on whether I am high or not.

"There are some weird people out there. There are men who want you to urine on them. One time a guy paid me good money to let him lick my feet clean and I'd been wearing flip-flops all day in the rain. . . . There's guys that like bondage, like fighting, like pain.

"I have rules, like pay first and if they don't get off in a hour, that means they've been drinking and doing coke, and that's all the chance they get."

She always demands cash up front, and if she is performing oral sex, she keeps the money in her hand and one reason she prefers regular sex is that way she can fold the bill up real small and hide it in her mouth.

"OK," says the television man, "It really is up to you. If you decide to go with the silhouette, that's fine. But you should know there is a down side. There have been studies that show that the person at home sees the silhouette, and says, 'What's this person got to hide' and they tend not to listen as seriously."

In preparation for this interview, the lobby of the detention center has been cleaned by a trusty who is standing guard over it, proprietary in that way that only people with a mop can be. The institution takes pride in the attention to Wendy; the sense of importance is catching.

Wendy is very torn. She looks at her lawyer, beseeching his advice, and the expression on her face is almost distraught. She had gotten her hair cut and curled, which was a big deal because some girls are real snobs and they won't touch other girls with the AIDS virus, but Wendy found one who was nice and didn't mind. Someone even loaned her some makeup, a really good kind, Maybelline. Wendy stood in front of the dimly lit prison mirror in the rest room of the lobby and tried to figure out how to put color on her cheeks. She does not know how to put on makeup, and does not intend to learn. "If a trick doesn't want to date me just because I'm not wearing makeup, then he doesn't have to date me."

The television reporter had finished his spiel. He made his point; he did not badger. The freckles in his face created an impression of wholesome, healthy sincerity.

When it was over, he said to her attorney to please make sure she understands that with luck her interview might occupy up to fifteen seconds of air time.

He also asked the lawyer to make sure she understood the story was about AIDS and not about Wendy.

She stood and stretched, lumbering and graceless. The care she had taken in choosing her outfit, a brown suit aching with a wish for respectability, was undercut by the discordant presence on her feet of fluffy pink, soft-soled slippers, a fashion note dictated by her jailers in the well-founded fear that among some inmates everything, even a shoe, is a possible weapon.

"When I go to court, maybe the judge will give me a ticket home. It would be great to go back to California and live a normal life."

Her contact with her family boils down to phone conversations with a great-aunt who lets her call collect from time to time. As for her mother, she says, "Me and her don't talk." She has a much younger stepbrother and stepsister (the sibling she has been accused of molesting) and a full sister, Lisa, twenty months older. Wendy says she likes her sister Lisa all right and would not like it if Lisa ever found out that Wendy often gives her name as an alias when she is arrested. She says Lisa is a Goody-Two-Shoes-type girl and works as some kind of secretary, "Lisa don't do no drugs, don't drink, and makes boo-coo bucks."

She says her father is John Blankenship of "someplace in Indiana," but she has not seen him for years. She has vague memories of stepfathers from when she was a child, men who went out with her mother, but she "didn't really have a fatherlike man in the house until my mother met a guy who let me call him Dad and helped me with my homework."

She grew up in southern California. "I was raised right there at Disneyland. Really. I even knew a fence near the freeway you could climb over to sneak in." The best home-cooked meal she can remember is called chicken divine, and the recipe consists of chicken, frozen broccoli, cream of mushroom soup, cheese on top, let it melt.

Both her great-aunt Corrine and her aunt Denise noticed tension between Wendy and her mother from the earliest days of childhood.

Corrine: "It's fear she never had. I remember her at age five climbing a high trestle. She should have had help long ago."

Denise: "Wendy was always the black sheep. Me and her have that in common because I was always the kid who did everything wrong. My sister Phyllis, Wendy's mother, would always accuse Wendy, 'I got me a Denise for a kid.' Wendy was always being locked in her room for the day, not getting fed dinner, never being let in on privileges.

"Wendy was one of those real hyperactive kids everyone called the monkey."

Wendy remembers a stint in a psychiatric hospital, but she

says, "I wasn't no crazy one. They never tied me down to a bed and gave me shots. Not me. I was there because my stepfather raped me."

Her aunt remembers that Wendy's real father had her taken out of the hospital and took her home with him. Wendy ended up throwing boiling water on a neighbor's child and attempting to burn down someone's trailer. When she left her father, she pretty much hit the streets.

She was only twelve years old, and she took the money from her first trick and went to a neat place right near Disneyland where you could ride boats under a what's it called, that dancing water. Oh yeah, a waterfall.

If she weren't a prostitute, Wendy has only one other notion about what she would like to be and that's a truck driver. She has been hitchhiking rides with them since she was twelve. It's easy. You get on the CB and ask if anyone needs a beaver to ride with them, or if you're working, you say commercial beaver. Even if she's not working, she usually offers them a little something but not all the time. She doesn't like stopping by the side of the road every hour.

From what she has heard, truck drivers can get really rich. They make between four and five hundred dollars a week, and they can live in their trucks if they want and that way they don't have to be bothered with rent.

Wendy imagines owning an eighteen-wheeler International with a bunk bed, a two-story truck.

"When I was raped by my stepfather," says Wendy, "something happened. Inside I don't get the feelings . . . what's it called, orgasm."

Aunt Coco: "He tried it with Lisa, but she was a sharpie. In other words, he picked the weak one. But that's, you know, life. . . ."

Lisa: "I knew it was going on, but I was too scared to tell anybody. I sensed it, I walked in on them once when they were in the living room. He tried to press against me once, but

I walked away. I remember being confused. But after that I just didn't trust him. I was a lot more independent than Wendy. Plus, I remember, he acted like he really believed in her, helped her with her homework all the time, and I guess she just figured if she didn't do what he wanted her to do, she wouldn't get all that attention.

"Then Wendy left home but once when she was back, at about age fifteen, my little sister came out with this story that Wendy's doing sexual things with her. I never heard none of the details, but that's when my mother really disowned Wendy.

"She shocks me, she really does. But I wish something good would happen to her. It just seems the news gets worse and worse."

MY LIFE by Wendy Blankenship

Well my stepfather used to take me everywhere with him.

On every saterday we went and cut the grass then take it to the dump then we would go watch the bike races and then we sit in the camper and watch the citty lights that's when he start to feel on me and kiss all over me.

One day my mom went to washington state for the wekend my little sister and brother went to their fathers house. And Lisa went to her friend house and it was just me and him.

He asked me to take a shower with him, then we had dinner then he filtt me all over.

Well the next day my sister came home when my sister went to bed he came up behind me with lights off when I was watching T.V. and started to rub himself on my behind then my sister went to the bathroom and I jump up and went to bed so she wouldn't think anything then in the middle of the night I was woken to him playing with me with my sister sleeping next to me.

Shortly after composing this essay, Wendy sighed and admitted:

"I liked that man, I really did. If I seed him now, you know what I think? I think we'd fall in love. My mom says the reason it happened is I flaunted in front of him, wearing my T-shirt and underpants at age eight. Didn't have nothing, don't know why he wanted me.

"Sometimes I wish I never told anybody what he did. If I didn't say anything, we would still be a good family."

Normally Wendy is against books because "they got all them long words," but recently one of the church ladies gave her an inspirational volume about a prostitute junkie. These are the same church ladies who came around at Christmas with cookies and sang la la la la la outside the cells and Wendy clapped, just to be polite. But this time they really came through with something worthwhile. The main character in the book gets into lots of dangerous tricks, guys knifing her and all. That reminded Wendy of the time one of her own tricks tried to kill her, explaining that his dead father talked to him in a dream and said he wanted someone like Wendy in heaven with him. Wendy was surprised the book was so good. In the end the girl meets the Lord in jail.

Wendy has no symptoms of AIDS, at least not yet, and she doesn't understand why the hoopla, why everyone's talking about it all the time.

"I feel fine," she says, shrugging. "I'm not sick." She acts as if the AIDS virus is an extreme annoyance, on the order of a flat tire.

Wendy on AIDS:

"OK, it's a virus, just like the flu, only worse. It runs through your body like a sniffle. AIDS virus is something that has been through your body but not hit you yet because so far you have enough antibody to fight it off.

"When the sickness hits bad things happen, like holes in your tongue."

Judge Perry has sentenced Wendy to serve a year for violating her probation. After she is released, she will be on probation for six months. That's the maximum for her offenses.

Wendy is not displeased by her sentence. If anything, her attitude is one of gratitude and relief.

She hopes she will be sent to a psychiatric facility.

"I like mental hospitals, I really do."

When she is asked why, she flashes a look of pure scorn, marveling at the naivete of someone so ill versed in the ways of the world. And then, she softens; the voice is kinder, almost confidential.

"Because," she says, leaning forward, speaking with the patience of a teacher coaching a slow student, "on Tuesdays they have bowling."

❦ ❦ ❦

Wendy Blankenship died of AIDS-related complications at the age of twenty on October 15, 1988. The obituary in the *Miami Herald* spoke of how she started hitchhiking with truckers at the age of twelve. She said her favorite stop was Seattle. "I loved living on the water and picking strawberries and cherries."

Lee Cohn, her attorney, told a *Herald* reporter, "Everyone treated Wendy as a landmark case—and they meant well. Everyone was just so uneducated about AIDS. Wendy put on this brave face, but she was helpless.

"She was just a kid. Just a poor kid."

THE TWISTING
OF KENNY WHITE

There were four shots in all, one accidental, one test shot, and then the shots for the two victims.

Neighbors recollected hearing the gunfire, but they mistook it for something else. They heard the sound and they tamed it. It was the busy time of the day in a nice part of town, the time when mothers call to their children to come in for dinner, when there is the clatter of garage doors opening and closing while bicycles and other equipment are stored for the night, or that unmistakable thump!—one last toss of the ball into the hoop. The report from the gun was automatically, unconsciously processed into the expected reasons for such a sound in such a neighborhood.

Firecrackers.

Or, a car backfiring.

Or, the Jacksons must be working hard on their gazebo.

Kenny White sits on a bench in the windswept courtyard of Youth Hall, dressed in the standard-issue gym shorts and T-shirt, studying his gnawed nails, and trying to summon the exact mood of the day when at the age of twelve he shot and killed his brother and his mother with a Colt Python handgun.

A year has passed.

Miami Herald photo

"Have you," he says, "ever been in a fight?" He appraises his audience, and something about her, something she's wearing perhaps, the look around the eyes, a hesitancy in her manner, makes him shake his head violently and quickly conclude: "No you probably haven't. As soon as you start to move forward everything goes real fast. Every time you see a face you swing at it. That's the way the day went by, in a blur."

On October 19, 1983 Kenny White woke up late.

He took a new shortcut to school that turned out to be even longer than the regular way. Grades were issued and he got his first F for the year.

He had girlfriend problems.

An extra-credit report got messed up in the rain.

He deliberately economized on lunch and bought just milk so he could buy an Astro Pop from the ice-cream man on his way home from school.

The ice-cream man wasn't there.

When he got home it was his job to put supper in the oven: every night it was pour-a-quiche or chicken, chicken or pour-a-quiche, one or the other. That afternoon he forgot to check the temperature of the oven and soon the odor of charred poultry overtook the whole house.

That afternoon, in the living room of their tract house in the suburbs, he sat watching television, and waited for his mother, and waited, and when he heard the door he thought: here she is. But no such luck. His younger brother, nine-year-old Kevin, came home first.

"It was," says Kenny, "a bad day all around."

"We are not the kind of people to have a tragedy like this," says Richard White, Kenny's father, a small balding man of forty-eight.

He speaks in a quiet, even voice; it has the shy keep-the-peace tone of someone who wants very much to avoid a scolding. The words often have a formal flavor, as in a speech.

"We were a happy family. If there had been alcohol, or drugs, or child abuse, if there had been internal strife, or jealousy, or the belittling of one child versus another, well then what happened might have been if not something you could understand, well at least you could expect it. But there was nothing like that."

Richard White is in his office at Rosen Management, where he supervises condominiums. Born in Atlanta, a graduate of The Citadel ("the West Point of the South"), a member of the air force's Strategic Air Command before his marriage to June August in 1967, he is the son of a boxer, and there is a hint in Richard White that if he had followed less sedentary pursuits, his frame—which now conveys an overall softness—might have possessed a measure of stocky pugnacity.

His most startling feature is the near-dazzling blueness of his eyes. It is a handicap of eyes like that, and an unfair burden to their possessor, the way they convey an impression of reflecting more than they absorb, as if their purpose is to be looked at rather than to look. He shakes his head, back and forth, sadly. He says there are two events in his life bonded by mystery and sorrow and he doesn't understand them and never hopes to: why Kenny did what he did and why his own father walked out on his mother when he was one year old.

"To me, there is no point in looking for an answer to either of these questions because there is no answer I can accept."

West Kendall resonates with upward mobility and easy living. There is an air of come-on and of carnival in the signs that beckon prospective buyers like those signs on highways that advertise tourist traps: fifty miles, then ten, and finally last chance to see whatever wonder is being proclaimed. The signs are propped up in empty lots, poking out from above the saw grass: ten thousand down and this life style can be yours!

The Whites lived in the Calusa section in a four-bedroom house, built almost ten years ago. The facades are all the same. The uniformity of the dwellings is experienced less as suffocating than reassuring. The neighborhood is so new that there are few trees, and the shade is grudging, like a fake smile, meager and ineffective.

The Whites were pioneers in that part of town. There was a shortage of classrooms. Richard and June White organized the first meeting of the homeowners association to fight for more schools. They were featured more than once in news stories in the late seventies.

Calusa Elementary School opened in 1981; located less than five minutes from the Whites' house, this is where the younger boy attended grades one through three and where Kenny spent the fifth and sixth grade.

James Gould, principal at Calusa, says the calm of the area belies its true tension: more than half the children come from single-parent families. "You know what's missing from this area? Grandparents. Not for our children, but for our children's parents. They are on their own; they don't have that sense of heritage, of continuity."

A point of pride at his school are three bulging scrapbooks filled with school memorabilia, writings by the children, class photos, and spontaneous pictures of students at play. The scrapbooks are a touching attempt at legacy in a school which, like the community it serves, has an atmosphere of unrelieved newness.

Gould likes to claim he runs the safest day-care program in Dade County: more than 150 students stay after school every day. Kevin stayed in this program every day. The school had on file a letter signed by his father: "Kevin, our son, may walk home from day-care by himself at 6 P.M. each day. If we are unable to sign him out by this hour, he has been instructed to walk home in any weather."

The Whites were very busy, often changing jobs but always working hard. Neighbors say both parents were gone from morning until evening. The principal remembers a time when Kenneth had misbehaved and he asked June White to leave her work and come sit with Kenneth in the office while her son was made to eat lunch alone there every day for a week. She came and stationed herself behind the boy, not across from him, and they barely exchanged a word. "She acted," he said, "like this was her punishment too."

The Whites' involvement in the daily life of the neighborhood was minimal. It boiled down to donating their gas grill to the annual block party. When Linda Riser, who lived next door, adopted her daughter, June White did something that suggested she was unusually touched by this event—perhaps because both her sons were adopted as well. "She brought over a pink dress, and the woman's face was just glowing." It was, in all the years of living next door the only time Linda Riser could recall a moment of real connection with her neighbor. June White and Paula Conger, from across the street, collaborated briefly on a beauty and color analysis business, counseling women on how to obtain, through the meticulous orchestration of hue and cosmetics and the cut of one's clothes, A Certain Look. When the partnership dissolved, June White refused to acknowledge her neighbor, and even the children were ordered not to say hello.

Kevin was extremely quiet. "He never talked," said one neighbor, "and he never showed emotion." In general, people familiar with both boys expressed more concern about Kevin than Kenneth, who had bounce and vitality and, in many respects, a very winning style.

Kenneth's parents often punished him for his poor academic performance and his bad attitude. "Kenny was always grounded," says his friend Brett. Kenny told one psychiatrist he used to like to put firecrackers in the mouths of lizards and watch them explode, but he knew lots of other kids who did lots worse to much nicer animals. The worse mischief in his life occurred when he and some friends went into a trailer and were accused of vandalism. His father had to pay seventy-five dollars in damages. When he was allowed out, Kenneth liked to hang around the golf course and collect lost balls to sell to the players, or hide in the bushes far away with a BB gun, and when one of the players bent over to concentrate on a shot, he took aim on the broad targets and squeezed the trigger. He and his friends would laugh. He never got caught.

His favorite place was Kendall Lakes Mall; he was known among his friends for always being "up for the mall." He and Brett would eat pizza, play with the computers at K mart, bang on the miniature pianos at Lucia's, steal candy bars and sometimes put Vaseline on the handles of car doors. But usually, Kenneth had orders to stay inside the house.

"Grounded," says Andy Jackson, Kenneth's friend from across the street, "was the most famous word in Kenny's house."

"Friendship," an essay by Kenneth White, age eleven, preserved in the scrapbooks at Calusa Elementary, accompanied by a snapshot of Kenneth playing tug-of-war:

> The dictionary deffination of friendship—The state of being friends. My deffination of friendship. A friend should be trust worthy, loile, a friend would be able to take some insults and know when to fight back. A friend to talk to a sholder to cry on but most of all someone who under stands you. He should be like you he should like most of the things that you do. He should a little crazy but make sure he doesn't like the same girl as you do. So far I have never found a friend like that but Im still looking.

There are many theories about rage. One favors the notion that rage has its catalyst, if not its roots, in the first home, the first relationships; and if that is so, most violence in society is the result of the child's postponed violent urges. By that rationale, violence by a child has, if nothing else, the flimsy merit of having occurred pretty much on schedule.

On the day of the murders, Andrew's mother, Elizabeth Jackson, a psychologist with the Dade County School system, remembers seeing Kenneth walking home from school by himself. There was a peculiar loneliness in the sight—a child, unattended, on his own. Elizabeth Jackson did not stop that day; twice earlier in the week she had offered Kenneth rides, and with the customary polite respect he always showed adults, he had refused.

But the picture of him that day lives in the memory of Elizabeth Jackson: in Kenneth's hand was a willow stick, and as he moved through the whipping saw grass, he seemed to be threshing a path. Her mind never summons that picture without also summoning the misgiving: if only she had stopped. Maybe she could have helped.

Later, that evening, when the murders became public, meteoric fame, quick lived and crashing, befell the otherwise quiet area. The house was cordoned off and ambulances and police cruisers and media vehicles jammed the street in front. At one point, someone counted nineteen cars out front. Residents of the neighborhood remember this scene as a vulturous assault on the zealously maintained serenity of the neighborhood. Reporters tried to take children aside and interview them without the permission of parents: the sight of these adults interrogating the children came to symbolize, almost as much as the murders themselves, the feeling of absolute violation that overtook Calusa on that day.

Kenny was watching television while the police conducted the investigation from the Risers' house next door. Linda Riser, a nurse, interpreted the mildness in his manner as testimony to the shock.

After midnight, Richard White went to stay with a relative. One of the police officers offered to drive Kenny to the same place, but first he wanted Kenny to point out a few of the neighborhood sights. The officer had noticed that Kenny's accounts of the afternoon contained some inconsistencies. As they drove past Andy and Jeremy's house, past Shane's, past Brett's, the officer pursued the accident theory of the crime: Were you showing your brother the gun? Did it go off by mistake?

"Remember how we powdered your hands earlier today? The results of that test will tell us whether or not you handled a weapon today."

It was that easy.

Kenny confessed. He told the police that he and his mother had never gotten along. He said his parents were always sending him away, like to survival camp in the summers. His birthday was coming up in less than a week, and he was supposed to have a Bar Mitzvah, but his mother had canceled it months before. She'd told him the money for the party already had been spent on military school.

He had had birthday parties canceled in the past, but no previous cancellation disturbed him as much as the Bar Mitzvah.

Later, in the Youth Hall courtyard: "It's something you get to do if you're Jewish and you're male. To do it you have to study Hebrew, a whole other language. It's a big party, a little like Sweet Sixteen for a girl, you get presents and stuff. The Rabbi gives a sermon, and you get admitted into manhood. It's fun. It's not like Seder, which is this celebration, sort of, where you just sit and look at food for three hours. After you're Bar Mitzvahed, you get to sit with the men and wear this special thing, the tallis, when you go to Temple. She said she wasn't going to let me have it. She cut it off right there."

He expected to enter seventh grade with his friends, but his parents decided in the summer of his twelfth year that he should go to Riverside Military Academy in Gainesville, Georgia.

Kenny had a plan. If military school didn't work out, he would kill his mother and then himself.

"Me and her were the problems. So, get rid of the problems."

He saw his scheme as an act of altruism: he would end the

constant fighting and dissension and at the same time provide his father and brother with a chance at a decent life.

He was back in Miami in less than two weeks: "Before he even had time to dirty his uniforms," went the whispered talk.

When he came back to Miami he had bruises. He told everyone he had been hazed and tortured by the school officials.

Everyone believed him.

Actually, much later he admitted that what happened was that there was hazing and the older boys all had an apparent obsession with the shine of the younger ones' shoes and they'd step on Kenny's shoes and then say they were scuffed and make him do fifty push-ups, and when he asked permission to get up, they'd say sure and then they'd kick his arms out from under.

But the black-and-blue marks that bought Kenneth his freedom were courted quite deliberately: he asked a buddy to punch him out in the middle of the night, and then he pretended he had been attacked in the dark by an anonymous gang.

After a year at Youth Hall, Kenny not only learned how to pick locks (comb for the school door, shoelace for the gym, brute strength for the cafeteria), but also how to express himself in jailhouse jive. When he describes his leavetaking from military school he thinks of it as escape: "My dad came up and broke me out." Neighbors said taking Kenny out of school was one of the few times Richard White ever defied the wishes of his wife.

"This is what I don't understand," says Richard White. "When Kenny came home from military school, he actually had more freedom than he'd ever had in his life. We told him: you are on your own now. We're not going to bail you out or chaperon or escort you everywhere any more. It's all up to you to take care of yourself. We actually backed off from him:

"See what I mean," says Richard White, in that almost benumbed voice. "The pressure was off."

On the night of the murders, most of the men in Calusa, for some reason, were able to fall asleep, but most of the women stayed awake. By then, Kenny had confessed to the crime and been arrested.

Linda Riser, from next door, remembers a feeling of gratitude at finding out Kenny committed the crimes: She was terrified to think a madman might be loose at 6:15 going around killing women and children.

Paula Conger, from across the street, felt the opposite.

"It would have been easier to accept a madman. I was terrified to think it was Kenny."

As for Kenny, his first night in Youth Hall was spent in wariness. Small, slim, with dark curly hair, and dark eyes, he looked every bit as young as he was: a week shy of thirteen. The sense at Youth Hall of barracks and deprivation was not entirely unfamiliar to Kenneth; he was reminded immediately of summers at survival camp and those two weeks at military school. That morning, he did at Youth Hall what he would have done at those other places. He spent half an hour making his bed: "You know, military style, corners on the sheets, real tight, you can bounce a dime. I thought Youth Hall was going to be real strict."

That same morning, when word reached Calusa Elementary that Kevin had been slain, his first-grade teacher thought: at least before he died, Kevin had finally learned how to smile, at least in her classroom.

When Kevin, an intense child whose face showed no emotion, entered her class, she could think of only one word to describe the constriction that characterizes his every gesture: tight. By the end of the year he was, she says, "joking with his neighbors, and I actually had to chastise him." To her it was as great a triumph as any academic accomplishment.

Shortly after nine that morning, Principal James Gould was

told that Mr. White was on the phone and would like to speak to him.

"I am calling," said Richard White, speaking in that precise way, "to tell you Kevin won't be in school today."

The principal was speechless: "Mr. White," he stuttered, barely able to complete a sentence. "I know . . . I'm so sorry, Mr. White."

"I just wanted," said the boy's father, "to be sure I followed procedure."

Whenever an event this appalling occurs, an event that so undermines the established sense of rightful order, images from the life of the family, fair and unfair, overwhelm the papers and the broadcasts.

The inquest into the linens is frantic.

We lie in wait for information, we decode it, hoping for the detail that is drenched in omen, something that sets these people apart, that makes them different and more likely candidates for this kind of grotesque mishap. "We are not the kind of people to have a tragedy like this."

The Whites defied such obvious demonology.

The first media reports were of a model boy. Kenny was called a typical kid, all American. "*A little gentleman.*" He was very bright: His IQ is 131. The affluence of the family was appealing; the murders had occurred, after all, in the game room, and something about the repeated use of this term in all the stories created an impression of an emporium for kids, a kind of well-equipped arcade. These were people with all the advantages.

Then, inevitably, a few rips in the seamless idyll.

The family had had financial pressures. A real estate venture started by the Whites had failed. Lately, June White had taken up one of those pursuits with a slightly dubious ring: she was studying futurology. Neighbors say they never once observed the entire family getting into a car together. As a sideline, the Whites once tried to sell neighbors on a food plan for when the big war came. Years ago, June White stopped cooking for the family because she perceived her efforts were unappreciated.

Both boys were adopted, and that fact alone was enough to make many people cease their wondering. It feeds a common, if unkind, prejudice about adopted children: the lineage is mysterious; who knows what kind of genetic endowment these children brought with them to the Whites, what unknown freight?

Both children had problems in school. Kevin had to repeat first grade, and for a year and a half Kenneth had gone to a private school dedicated to helping children overcome dyslexia, a perception problem which impedes reading. The initial news stories created an impression, not really accurate, of a long list of psychiatric referrals and extensive therapy for the boy, all obviously to no avail. He was tested and evaluated, often, but never treated on a long-term basis.

After the murders, no one in this boy's family wanted anything to do with him. The father told authorities: "How can I? He killed the wife that I love, the son that I love. He has taken everything from me."

An uncle who is married to June White's sister, told a reporter: "Ever since he was a little boy he would walk up, shake your hand and punch you in the belly."

And the attitude of the mother's family was best summed up in the opinion they expressed to a police officer shortly after Kenny's confession:

"Hang him."

Richard White says he met June August through relatives.

Their first date was spent at the Playboy Club, a choice that to this day he regrets as possibly "inappropriate."

"I know it wasn't really the right thing to do."

He was in the service, and she worked for Jordan Marsh, as a buyer.

They were married six months after they met. From the

moment he saw her, he says, "There was a concept there, she was the girl for me."

Her family is prominent locally. She was part of the August Brothers' Bakery. There was talk that her family wished Richard could be more of a go-getter, and June White suffered from comparisons to her sister, Francine, whose husband, Peter, matched the August dynasty in entrepreneurial prominence. His was the East Coast Fisheries family. "The marriage," people used to say of Francine and Peter Swartz, of "the bagels and the lox." There was no such jovial slogan for June's union with Richard.

June White was always proud that in her family of two brothers and one sister she was the only one to graduate from college: the University of Miami. Shortly after they were married, Richard White resigned from the air force; he says he didn't think the hazardous missions he flew as part of his work were right for a family man.

Richard White said he and his wife were tested frequently to determine why they could not have children, but he cannot recall whether doctors were able to pinpoint the problem. He told one psychiatrist who had evaluated Kenneth there was a possibility his "semen was allergic to his wife's juices" or perhaps he had been affected by radiation while in the service. They decided they would adopt and applied at the Children's Home Society.

"We had a tragic situation occur just before we got Kenneth. Our social worker was inexperienced, and we were her first clients at the Children's Home Society. We received a call from her saying there was a little girl for us, and then she called back and said the mother had changed her mind, she did not want to give her up. It was a tremendous up, and down. I felt as though I had lost a child. It was one of the few times in my life I ever passed out from drinking.

"When the call came for Kenneth, we went right down. Both boys came from the same agency, and I tend to get the information mixed up. Both their mothers were young, one was eighteen and one was sixteen, and they assured us the mothers hadn't taken drugs or anything like that. One of the fathers was a student, I believe, and the other was a policeman.

"I'll never forget what happens. They sit you down and talk to you for about thirty minutes and tell you a little about the background of the child, and then they ask, 'Do you want to see the child?' They leave you sitting in a room for about ten or fifteen minutes and then they come and take you down a hall into the nursery. I still remember looking at that bassinet, and it was the most magnificent feeling in the world.

"I changed the diapers and fed both boys; it didn't scare me to get in there and clean up the messes. I enjoyed rocking the boys to sleep. Both boys. Kevin was special to hug; he was hard and skinny, but when you hugged him he went soft, every muscle in his body relaxed. But there was never any love differential between the two boys. Sometimes I'd crawl into bed with them and hold them and kiss them. I didn't have what I consider a male resentment when I held them. It's all part of life and makes for a better bond."

She felt a drive to get out of the house, to seek work.

The conflict could sometimes be overwhelming: she got the call to come and adopt Kevin the day before she was supposed to take her real estate test.

A small woman, not much over five feet tall, about 103 pounds, tidy and boyish in her appearance, she had a pretty face and dark black hair. She favored, in her dress, a subdued, noncontroversial style; Linda Riser remembers thinking that it was almost odd how someone who liked to counsel others to express their personal style and inner being in their outward appearance would "give away nothing about herself in the way she dressed." Her style was strict and devoid of flourishes.

Paula Conger said June was so bitter when the partnership

in their beauty business dissolved that when she started getting harassing phone calls shortly afterward, she suspected her
neighbor. After a time, the calls stopped, but they had started
up again about a month before the murders.

Kenneth:

"My mother was short, she had short black hair, dark eyes,
and milky white skin. She wore lots of makeup. Her perfume
costs thirty-two dollars an ounce. I know that because if I ever
squirted it at my brother she yelled at me, 'Stop. That cost
thirty-two dollars an ounce.' She was greedy, power hungry,
cold. Once I asked her for a quarter, I was at this video arcade
with my friends and she was there to pick me up and she
actually gave it to me. I thanked her and gave her a hug and
she looked at me like 'What's that?' So I said, 'Somebody
showed me how. My girlfriend.' And then we had an argument about how I was too young to have a girlfriend. She
said, 'You're still a little boy.' I hated that more than anything,
being called a little boy."

Belva White, Richard's mother, worked hard all her life. "I
was," she says, "a waitress in the best of clubs. I made good."

She speaks with one of those gossamer Southern accents;
every word is nearly sung. Even at seventy-two, there is a
trim, energetic nimbleness in the way she moves. These days
she spends one day a week at her son's new townhouse,
cleaning it for him, doing his laundry.

When Kenneth was four years old and Kevin an infant, she
started living at the White household to supervise the children
while her son and his wife worked, but she kept her own place
and went home once a week to pick up her mail.

Her view of June White:

"You could not ask for a better daughter-in-law. If she
wanted to buy a necklace, she'd buy two, one for me and
sometimes three, one for her mother too. June treated me like
a child instead of a mother-in-law. She would tell me how to

spell words, help me pick out makeup, and she told me the colors I should wear. Mostly light colors.

"Kenneth hit me once. Yes he did. He didn't like it when I told him to watch television in another room and he stood up and here come Kenny with his fist. . . .

"You know, he's offered to kill his brother lots of times. Now I never heard him say that about his mother though.

"You know what I think? It all goes back to that real mother. You never know what she was thinking. Maybe she took dope or something. She marked him some way."

She leans forward, and there is a passion in her voice. The slow Southern speech, with its molasses momentum picks up ever so slightly: "Most of it was borned in him."

Kenneth White always knew he was adopted, and he says he didn't have any fantasies about meeting his biological mother. "She probably wouldn't recognize me now because I looked different when I was born. I probably didn't even have hair then or anything."

The Children's Home Society supplied this picture of the woman who gave birth to the child who became Kenneth Louis White:

"Kenneth is the child of single parents. His mother was eighteen years of age at the time of his birth. His putative father was age twenty. His mother came to Miami from another state for the purpose of completing the pregnancy. The mother came to C.H.S. in the fifth month of her pregnancy and had medical care from then until the time of birth.

"The baby was the product of a forty-weeks pregnancy, delivery was spontaneous and his physical development while in the care of the agency was normal.

"Mother had no communicable illnesses, injuries, accidents, drug usage or abortion attempts. Rh negative.

"The mother is an attractive young lady who presents a picture of neatness and confidence. She is a high-school graduate. . . . She's taken part-time college courses in English, composition, speech, and psychology."

"What we noticed was a rebelliousness, where we thought he had developed an attitude where he thought women were inferior."

Richard White was trying to pinpoint the nature of Kenneth's problems. "Later, though, he started to show disrespect for men too so we were never sure about that."

It was in the second grade that a teacher noticed Kenneth's inability to read on grade level. When she brought this to June White's attention her response was to place him immediately in a special school. She chose McGlannan, which specializes in helping overcome dyslexia. One of the boys' counselors at Calusa and at Arvida said she showed a peculiar eagerness to have both boys tested frequently for learning disabilities.

"The warnings, the warnings, the warnings."

Frances McGlannan, the headmistress and founder of the private South Dade school, is speaking.

She said she had noticed in Kenneth an odd resistance to punishment, a coldness and stoicism in the face of criticism. Rather than plead or weep, the child would withdraw.

She suggested to the Whites that their child be evaluated.

Dr. Michael Hughes examined him in May of 1979. When the family said they did not have any money, or the time, for the boy to continue treatment, Dr. Hughes took it upon himself to recruit the family pediatrician to persuade the family, and he found low-cost public treatment for the boy. But the Whites did not cooperate.

Kenneth was eight and a half at the time; the complaints were that he was hyperactive, had trouble controlling himself and sitting still.

Dr. Hughes consulted his case notes. "The parents," he said, "described their son as always having been bright and verbal, but that in the second grade it was discovered he was not learning. They said no matter what they did to punish him the only time he would break into tears was when he was right. The father's punishments included a strap on the rear and isolation. The mother's punishment usually consisted of silence and cold scorn.

"Kenneth complained terribly about their working. His parents would say that they wouldn't have to work if he didn't require special schooling. His parents said that six weeks before they adopted Kenneth they almost adopted a girl and that psychologically they had prepared for a daughter. The mother said that she never felt as if Kenneth belonged to her until he was six months old. He wet the bed until he was almost seven, despite a system of buzzers and alarms, and the mother resented it and seemed ashamed. She seemed bleak and distant, angry and competitive with her husband. She expressed little involvement except anger with the boys and showed a great desire to get away from home."

Dr. Hughes asked Kenneth to draw a person, and he had trouble sitting still to do it. When he was done, he wanted to tear up the paper. He had drawn a very scribbly clown with silly ears. When he was asked to tell a story about his clown, Kenneth said:

"He couldn't get a job at the circus."

When he was asked what his father did for fun, he said work.

His mother?

Work.

He said the family hadn't gotten together to do anything fun for three months: "They just want money."

Dr. Hughes: "He was a very driven kid. He wouldn't let up in his demands that things could be better."

"What," asked the doctor, "do you like about yourself?"

"Nothing."

Richard White is now living in Dadeland Walk, a townhouse development. It is, like Calusa, in its exterior at least, a calm and restful place, and the dwellings all have Calusa's consoling sameness. He has all new furniture; his color scheme is muted, with a strong emphasis on dusky mauves. "Some people might find this feminine, but to me it's just soft."

He has thrown away most of the artifacts from his old life; they are not important to his new phase.

He has kept a photo of his wife and Kevin taken during the summer before their deaths. It shows her closely cropped hair, cut in the style that some people called severe, and an intelligent look to her face. Kevin is beautiful, and in an uncanny way, obviously just one of those accidental things—he was after all, adopted—his looks favored his mother greatly; he had the same strong, good bones. Both of them are looking off to the left, away from the camera, and there is an expression of a strange listlessness.

They are seated next to each other, and there is a physical contact. Her arm is hanging over his shoulder. But the hand is limp, and the touch is not what could be called, with any precision, an embrace.

Richard White treasures the picture. It is one of his favorites.

"You have to have met June to believe what I'm going to say, but she could have been president of the United States. She was that kind of woman.

"After she died, I called an open house in our house to tell the neighbors how much pride I had in my wife, how it was a pleasure to hold June and touch her. I was proud of the emotional closeness we had and I wanted everybody to know. I also told them I was sorry to create a situation like this in the neighborhood, but this was a phase in my life, and now it's over, and I would be moving on to a new phase, and I didn't want people looking at me with pity and they shouldn't whisper behind my back.

"Throughout our married career June and I were real loners, we had no real close friends. June and I were enough for each other.

"She was constantly trying to make me do a better job. She

would critique me. She was a superb shopper, and she helped me with my spelling, and she would tell me if something was not a good way of saying something. I always went to her for guidance.

"It is true, right before her death, she was under pressure from her new job at the bank. It was a difficult job. She spent all day listening to people make complaints, and when she came home, yes, we sat down and she told me about her day and yes, sometimes she got emotional, but to me this was what marriage is all about. Now Kenneth might have felt she was attacking me, but I knew she wasn't. Her job was a hard job. When she poured all those things out at night, to me there was only one word for it. This was communication.

"I'm not sure Kenneth understood why I would just sit there and listen. I think he might have felt as if June was trying to destroy me. He couldn't see that I was always trying to take advantage of June's tremendous capabilities."

Because the family kept to itself, there were not many friends or acquaintances he could recommend who might be able to speak about his wife, about her good points. In the end, he suggested two former colleagues. Patting his pocket he reached for his glasses so he could read the entries in his address book.

"Do you want to know one of the results of this tragedy?

"For years my eyes were fine. I never needed glasses, and a month after this tragedy I had to get these. I have double vision, and I've been to the eye doctor three times."

He looks up. The eyes, as always, are overpoweringly light.

He shakes his head slowly and copies out two numbers.

"I can't see."

The two people Richard White recommended had little to say. One said: "A computer married to a computer." And the other, "She was the most disturbing woman I ever met."

There were few father-son outings. Kenneth White remem-

bers, with overwhelming fondness, the couple of occasions
when Richard White took him to the firing range, a rare time
of closeness. Richard White always has liked guns and has had
an extensive collection of firearms. "I was an expert shot with
a pistol as well as a rifle. I never dwelled upon the records, all
the newspaper articles they wrote about me when I was in
high school, how I held the highest score in competitive rifle
shooting in the city, I usually led the city, all those articles
were put away, and certainly all the guns were secured."

All but one: the Colt Python .45 behind the nightstand in
his father's bedroom, placed there for the family's protection.
To this day, Kenneth speaks of it with admiration:

"A fine gun, the best."

There was in the White household a certain preoccupation
with defect, or at least with its opposite, perfection. Of all the
possessions in the White household, Richard White was
proudest of his and his wife's collection of books about financial status and physical appearance. The shelves were crowded
with volumes: *Restoring the American Dream, Winning Through
Intimidation, Pathfinders, Nothing Down, You Can Negotiate Anything, How You Can Use Inflation to Beat the I.R.S., Color Me
Beautiful, Dress for Success, Short Chic, Looking Terrific, Complete Dress Thin System.* "My wife and I had the most extensive
library in self-improvement, I would say, in Dade County.

"No," he says, correcting himself, striving, as usual, for
exactitude, "I would even say in Florida."

These books provided the sole sense of bounty or plenitude
in the entire house.

It was on the whole a bare, contained place; airtight, with
few moments of spontaneity. The color scheme was unyield-
ing: browns and creams and beiges, concertedly neutral, no
embarrassing revelations. There was very little on the walls.
The game room consisted of a carpet with a game theme, a
sofa, and not much else. There were a couple of books in each
of the boy's rooms, *The Cat in the Hat Comes Back* for Kevin

and *A Light in the Attic* for Kenneth, and a ball or two but the rooms were almost eerie in their startling absence of the usual, cheerful, endlessly proliferating clutter of kids. "I was proud," Kenneth says. "I didn't have a lot of toys. My mom said toys were for babies, and I didn't want to be a baby."

"The thing I want to do most of all is . . . a rifel."

Less than a month before the slayings, Kenneth White was asked by the Dade County school system to take a sentence completion test.

Here are some other responses:

"If I could have three wishes come true, I'd like one million dollars, the whole earth to have peace forever, and an infinity more wishes."

"I know it's silly but . . . I am afraid of nothing."

"When I was a baby . . . I liked to eat everything."

"I think most girls are . . . pretty but I only like a few."

"My mother . . . doesn't cook so well."

"I would do anything to forget the time I . . . got cought busting a trailer."

"I sure wish my father would . . . take me to the rifel range."

"When I think of my brother I . . . think of a fish."

"I am not so good at . . . school, or staying on task."

"I like my father but . . . he can be a pain."

"My family treats me like . . . a son."

"The other kids in school are . . . smarter."

"The thing that makes girls different from boys is . . . hair and muscel."

"Whenever I try to do something . . . I usualy mess up."

"Sometimes I'd really like to clobber (smash) . . . my brother."

"When I get worried . . . when something out of the ordinary happens."

"My family is . . . the best family in the world."

"When I see my mother and father together . . . I think of a postcard."

"When I grow up I . . . want to live alone."

"I'd be really happy if . . . my parents would calm down."

"When I can't do what I want to I . . . punch my bed."

"What I want the most . . . me to get my own rifel."

"The thing that's most fun is . . . shooting."

"The thing I do best is . . . shoot."

"Tardy again, White."

These were the first words to greet Kenneth upon his arrival at school on the day of the murders.

"My patience span right now, I'd have cussed that teacher out, but back then I was respectful."

The early morning hours in the White household had been the normal rush to get out and launch the day. At six June White had awakened, and she was out of the house by seven to beat the traffic to her downtown job. She was dressed in a typically tasteful outfit: a maroon blouse; navy skirt; sensible pumps. Kevin arrived for his first class at Calusa Elementary shortly before eight. Richard White went to the post office and then to work at Rosen Associates near Dadeland.

Kenneth's grades that day were a disaster. He got an F in English; no great surprise. He got a D in math; how he always hated math. That day, as he sat in class trying to puzzle through a problem, he turned to a girl sitting near him: I wish I could kill my mother, he said. She barely paid attention.

He went to science and got the one and only good mark of the day. Not that it mattered. His parents had a favorite saying: you're only as good as your lowest grade. Their other famous saying was: if you mess up once, you have to be an angel for the rest of your life.

And then, on the way home from school, complete betrayal: no ice cream man.

He couldn't even get an Astro Pop.

The thing about an Astro Pop is it's not ice cream, it's a sucker and it lasts all day.

He took a willow stick and began beating the brush.

Dinner was his responsibility that night. He took out some chicken and put it in the oven but forgot to check the temperature, which was on broil.

It burned.

He was upset; and he remembered that when his father gets upset sometimes he fixes a drink, so Kenneth fixed one: cranapple and vodka, in a tall tumbler. It was working; soon there was a spin in his head, just like at that wedding he went to, when the bartender snuck him a drink: Long Island iced tea; five kinds of something, Kenneth wasn't sure what, but he thought it was five kinds of rum. He played the plan in his head.

He went into his parents' room. He looked for his father's Colt Python in its secret place, on a hook, behind the nightstand.

The first shot went off accidently, inside the house, blowing a hole in the floorboards of one of the bedrooms.

Carrying the gun, Kenneth went outside to see if the exterior of the house had been damaged as well.

Then, just to make sure the gun was working OK, he aimed it at a tree: shot number two. A sizable chunk of bark splayed itself across the lawn.

At five o'clock, June White left for home; she would be a little later than usual because she planned to pick up some dry cleaning and was supposed to get a snack to bring to Kevin's Cub Scout meeting later that evening. Richard White had a meeting with a client scheduled for late in the day, and then he was planning to teach a class. Kevin stayed at the after-school care program until it closed; the sign-out sheet shows his child's scrawl and indicates he left at 6 P.M.

Kenneth was seated on the living room sofa. "M★A★S★H" was on the television. The Colt Python was at Kenneth's side, hidden beneath a pillow.

6:05 P.M. Kevin White enters his home.

Kenneth thought: "Oh, no, I'm going to have to abandon the mission."

"Where's Mom?"

"She's not home yet."

"Oh."

"Why don't you go out and play?"

"I don't want to."

"Mommy said it would be OK."

"I don't want to."

He was following his brother. The gun was behind his back.

"Here, would you put this toy away, right there in that closet?"

It was the walk-in type, a utility closet, used to store paint and other household items.

"As soon as you start to move forward everything goes real fast. Everytime you see a face you swing at it." Kevin obeyed. He walked into the big closet, his back to his brother. Kenneth, coming from behind, lifted the hidden gun; he raised it level with the head of his brother, whose back was still turned.

The third shot of the day.

Kenneth closed the door of the closet and went back to watching "M★A★S★H." Over the sound of the set he thought he could detect words mixed with the sounds of his brother's final breathing: he thought Kevin was urging him to keep up with his plan.

6:15: June White walks through the door.

"Attempt At A History":

That's what Kenneth White called an odd and disturbing document, a sort of fantasy essay he wrote while at Youth Hall, a disjointed piece that one wishes to find urgent with allegory, to read and then be able to declare: this is it, this contains the key, the confession, the apologia.

The hero is Sir Dane, a gladiator of "uncomparable hero-ism." Sir Dane had only one fault, a little-known secret:

"His one and only flaw that could overthrow his great deffences was, for all he tried, he couldn't bring himself to harm a lady.

"Once the great wisard Daggermor heard this, he started conjuring. After days of conception he came up with a 'Blueprint' for the perfect feminine body. The eyes were white as the first snow of the season. With a hint of red to show the tiresome sole. In the center was eyes of blue as the bluest streams of heaven.

"Her skin was as soft as a doney pillow. . . . Her lips were as red as the flames of Hell. All this was so beautiful the prince forgot to look into her heart. After all her heart was black as night and filled with hatred and grief."

Sir Dane fell deeply in love with the lady. This distressed the wizard, who began to see the woman returning Sir Dane's love: he detected "small readings filled with 'emotions?' Emotions like love, affection and careing. Which he didn't programe in."

With his sword Sir Dane killed the wizard who was standing in front of the lady and it was with great shock that Sir Dane realized both had been stabbed. In her dying breath the princess said, " 'I love you with all my heart. But I must die, for I am evil.' Now only wispering she said, 'But my soul and heart will live on forever in the heart of the shiest chambermaid.' Then with a smile on her face and a shine in her heart, she died.

"She layed there limp and lifeless."

The prince sat beside her, half-crying and half-laughing over the princess.

"When morning came they barried the body in a mahgany casket covered with foral designs. After the funeral the prince met a beatiful chambermaid, but she wouldn't talk to him. She ran away but the prince ran after her and of coures cought her (BECAUSE BOYES ARE BETTER THAN GIRLS.) She had a hood over her head when the prince had grabbed her he knocked it off.

"She was the most beatiful woman the prince had ever seen. Her eyes prenetrated all his deffences and melted him to nothing. Right there on the spot the prince proposed. And the first word he ever heard out of her mouth was 'I do.' (CLEASHAY TIME.) And they lived happily ever after. THE END!"

It is a puzzlement.
    In it a boy wants desperately to hurt a girl.
    But he can't.
    He finally does, after hurting a boy first.
    The death of the first girl frees him to find another one.
    Miss Suzanne, his teacher at Youth Hall, gave the paper an "A." She called it very creative but warned her pupil to watch his spelling.

There's one aspect to all this that continues to trouble Kenneth White. He doesn't understand why he didn't kill himself. He really was planning on it. It's just that right then, after the murders, when he tried to bring the gun to his temple, he couldn't. He wanted to, but he could not. He fled from the house. A friend saw him running toward the canal and asked him why he was crying. Kenneth said he had pinkeye. At the canal, he shot at some fish. Later he would tell police that was "pretty neat." Then he threw the gun in the water.

When he got back home he avoided the game room. At around 7 P.M., he called his father at his office, interrupting him in the middle of his real estate class.

"Daddy, I'm scared. Kevin is gone and Mom is gone and there's nobody in the house." He said he could not leave the class, but he arranged to call the scoutmaster and asked him to come by and check out the house. When the scoutmaster arrived he discovered June White, her shoes partially kicked off.

Later, the father expressed the fear that the boy was trying to lure him home to face the same fate.

When Richard White arrived home that evening, the paraphernalia of emergency, barricades and ambulances, greeted him. Crime technicians and reporters swarmed in front of his house, modern-day harpies.

He was immediately ushered into the Risers' house next door.

He knew the body of his wife had been found. When the police told him that Kevin had also been killed he began to sob.

It was then that he suggested to the police that they check to see if the gun he kept behind the nightstand was in its place. The neighbors stood about and decried the horror of life in a city that routinely hosts acts of violence, and they reviewed the day for any unusual traffic in the vicinity, for any frightening strangers. Richard White's mind was not on a stranger. He had already formed a suspicion as to who the killer might be: Kenneth.

When Kenneth White first arrived at Youth Hall, he did not speak with anyone. He was convinced that Doris Capri, the director, disliked him intensely even though she had virtually nothing to do with him. The aloofness of his manner, combined with knowledge of what he had done, kept other children, and workers, at a distance. Child-care workers recall that Kenneth was different from most children arrested for murder: usually at night they curl up and wrap their arms around themselves and rock back and forth and cry themselves to sleep.

Not Kenneth. He was composed.

At first his father found it impossible to visit the boy, and their communication consisted of short letters about the Dolphins and the logistics in Richard White's life, how he wanted to find a nice place to live and soon he wanted to start dating. In the end, he did visit a few times.

"Do you know what it means to plead guilty?"

Circuit Court Judge David Gersten, ceremonial in his black robes, hunched forward and addressed the boy.

"Yes." Kenny was dwarfed by the stern majesty of the

judicial chambers, the oversized furniture and high ceilings. He had shaved twice in his life, and this was one of those times.

"How do you plead?"

"Guilty."

Something about him, actually a combination of things, the nice background, his pleasant looks, the high IQ, and, most notably, his extreme youth, conspired on his behalf. Defense attorneys and prosecutors huddled to devise a sentence that combined confinement with some small sliver of hope.

"What we have here," said the judge, "is a child killer, and this sentence represents a noble effort to prevent a child killer from turning into an adult killer, if it is possible to do so.

"Our approach today is a unique and especially important one.

"Perhaps now Kenneth can get the help he truly needs and was never able to obtain.

"I can't say I have the confidence but I have the hope."

The lawyers on both sides of this case, Michael Cornely and Shay Bilchik for the state, and Steve Levine for the defense, worked out an agreement where Kenny pleaded guilty to two counts of homicide and was sentenced to twenty years probation. He would begin with an indeterminate commitment to a psychiatric facility, St. Alban's Hospital in Virginia. He is unlikely to be free before he is eighteen. Before sentencing, Judge Gersten ordered the child evaluated by almost a dozen psychiatrists, psychologists and social workers.

Kenneth hated it:

"They ask stupid stuff, all sorts of first-grade questions, and they repeat themselves, like they'll ask, 'What's your favorite sport?' and 'What sport to do like to play most?' If you are smart enough, after a while, you catch onto their tricks. Like they show you an inkblot and ask, 'What's it look like?' turn it around and ask them, 'What's it look like to you?' Or if they want you to draw people, like your family, they're always watching which one you draw first, and to see if the ladies are, you know, developed. Next time I'll draw myself bigger than everyone else in the family. I'll really fool them. I'll draw all the heads first, then the necks . . . really freak them out."

The judge and lawyers in the case relied most heavily on the recommendations of Dr. Alan Zients, of Washington, D.C.

Dr. Zients:

"He's striking in that I think he does have some difficulties in differentiating his own fantasy life from the reality of the world. Kenneth, I think, at the time that he murdered his mother and brother, was trying very hard to get his mother's respect and was feeling put down by her in every area.

"One of the unique aspects, and I found it very very disturbing, was the length of time that passed."

Kenneth had had the plan for at least six weeks before he executed it. But what troubled Zients at least as much was "the period of time between the death of the brother and the death of the mother. I see the passage of that time as very significant. I've been involved in other situations where a youngster would, at that point, be shocked, would become maybe even physically sick at what he had done and would not be able to go any further."

Dr. Zients said Kenneth's future depends upon whether he is able to experience empathy. It is not considered something a person is born with, but rather it is a learned ability, demonstrated by children at an early age. Usually, by the age two and a half or three, a child who missed his mother should be able to summon a picture of her and be consoled even if she is not present. People who can't feel empathy, who can't imagine what another person is going through, usually have missed this stage somehow.

Can he do this? Can Kenny feel? Dr. Zients did not know.

"It was fair," Kenneth said, speaking of his sentence. "I thought the judge was real open-minded about my case."

At times when Kenneth speaks he brings a boggling mildness to the discussion; one might think, from his tone, that what was under discussion was not his sentence for homicide but something blander and less pressing, the weather or the time of day. His face also lacks a certain animation. It has, sometimes, a tightness like Kevin's did.

"I gotta always watch it," he said, motioning toward some very small boys in a lackluster lineup in the distance, marching from the intake unit to the cafeteria. "All I gotta do is beat the s—— out of one of them little shorties and they'll send me away for thirty years."

Kenneth was looking forward to St. Alban's: "There's a lake, nice scenery. It snows."

By the end of his stay at Youth Hall, which lasted a little more that a year ("I'm lucky," said Kenneth, "They waited to send me until after my birthday . . . and Halloween!") he was universally acclaimed "the sweetest kid here."

At Youth Hall, he says, he learned how to fight: "Most white people don't have to fight to stay alive, but black people are used to fighting. A lot of the black kids here dropped out of the seventh grade, and they've been stealing ever since. They had trouble understanding what I did. Usually all they have is their parents, usually just their mothers, and they have the highest respect and love for her. All they understand is being beaten. Some of those kids have marks all over their bodies from extension cords. I told them what I did, but I said it was a foster home, and my foster mother and brother were f—ing me over, they sent me to military school and told people to beat me up and made me hike twenty miles a day and I got bit by a raccoon. They were really messing me over, so I messed with them right back.

"The counselors here, I told the truth, like Roundtree and my teacher Miss Suzanne, and I guess they understood. At least they still like me."

Miss Suzanne had a nickname for him, and she meant it: "Sunshine."

At rare intervals, Kenneth hears from old friends in Calusa. Andrew Jackson wrote him a letter and said the "neighborhood just isn't what it used to be."

Andy's younger brother wrote:

"Dear Kenny,

"I hope you are haveing a good time because I haven't. I just got over a broken ankle. This years block party wasn't good.

There wasn't even a bon-fire."

It was signed: "Your life-time friend, Jeremy."

The house at 13260 S.W. 96th Terrace has been rented. At first, the new people were shocked to think that murder had occurred there, but they told neighbors they were able to rout the negative energy, and the realtor was very apologetic, claiming she had no idea it was *that house* but also aware that even if she had known there really is no ethical obligation to inform tenants because, technically speaking, homicide is "not a fault of the house."

Kevin is memorialized at Calusa Elementary: more than a thousand dollars was collected for a tribute. The money was used to retile a portion of the art room, to buy a globe for the media center, and to plant some trees.

Kenneth is said to be doing well in St. Alban's. Richard White has visited his son in Virginia once. On the few visits he made to Youth Hall, child-care workers observed that father and son spoke little, with the father looking around the room and the boy looking at his nails.

The child who could not read now reads all the time, and he wanted very much to take his books up there but he thought better of it. They're precious, and he had no idea what St. Alban would be like, "how bad the thieves would be."

He says that if all goes well, when he gets out he would like to join a branch of the military. He hopes someday to marry and would like to have one child, a boy. He would love a career as a manager of one of the lands at Disney World, and his favorite land is Frontierland, with the old wooden houses and muskets and pioneer stuff. To him, "Disney World is the only place in the world where it's peaceful."

He says he missed his brother and will never be able to fully repent for what he did to him. "He got on my nerves, as all brothers do, but he was OK. My brother didn't deserve that."

He thinks he killed his mother because:

"I wanted her love so bad it hurt me inside."

He does not miss her:

"How can I? She was never there."

Today if he could have three wishes they would be:

"To get my *real* parents back.

"To understand my emotions better.

"To travel through time."

The clock said 6:15. The calendar said October 19.

Appearing as smart and put-together and in place when she returned from work as she had when she left, June White, burdened with the dry cleaning, saw Kenneth and asked:

"Where's Kevin?"

"I don't know."

"Didn't he come home?"

"Yeah, but he went out."

"What's burning?"

"Dinner."

She put down her purse and started for the game room, looking for Kevin. When she failed to see him, she turned around to reenter the kitchen.

Her oldest son was waiting for her.

In the instant before he shot her, he recalled something he learned at military school: it is less painful if you shoot someone in the head.

He aimed for her eyes.

She staggered, slumped and fell.

The fourth and final shot.

He felt, he would say later, like the whole world was lifted off his shoulders.

🐝 🐝 🐝

Kenny White is a university student in Virginia, living in the same town as the hospital where he spent his high school years as a patient. He is short, wirey, with long curly dark hair which he pats from time to time, with pride. When he arrived at the hospital for a sort of massive psychological retooling, he was frightened. His doctor gave his usual speech: "I'd like to develop a lot of ways of dealing with you, but if you choose to limit my choices and I have to be either a sap or a son of a bitch. . . ." Kenny was asked if he had any questions. He wanted to know how much stealing went on at the hospital, how bad the fights got.

Today he rents a room in the house of a former teacher. He works at a local mall; the shopkeepers there have become his extended family. Sometimes when the mall closes he and other young workers hang out in the parking lot, under the dawn-to-dusk light, driving their cars in circles, making do-nuts. His doctors believe their radical intervention at such a young age has probably saved Kenny, and he agrees: "The question of course is would this work on a grand scale? Would four years of saturation therapy save other children who are like me? I don't know. Has it even worked for me? Well, it didn't turn me into a rocket scientist, but also I'm not rotting in prison. I'm financially independent. I have a job at the mall and I make about $225 a week. I pay back society by paying taxes. My grade point average is okay. I don't know what I want to be yet, though several of my teachers say I have a flair for writing.

"I look back on those days when I lived in Miami and I realize I was on the way to becoming a perfect little android. There was practically no affection in that house. Whenever I hugged my mother, she became stiff. She herself wasn't just obsessive or just a perfectionist; she was obsessively perfec-tionistic. The only things she liked to eat were brown rice and vitamins. It took her fifteen to twenty minutes to brush her teeth. She had very dark hair which she dyed every morning because she didn't want a milliliter of gray to show through.

"Lots of times I ran away and I'd sleep on the roof of my school. That was so the cockroaches and the snakes wouldn't get you. Sometimes my parents wouldn't even bother to look for me. The rules were always changing. Some days you'd come home and it would be mandatory reading for three hours and some days none at all. Sometimes you could watch TV and other days there would be a lock on the end of the cord.

"My father worshipped my mother. He did anything she said. He hid the bills from her so she wouldn't be upset about money.

"The physical abuse was not all the time. Say if you were crying and they said 'Stop, or I'll give you something to cry about,' well you did stop. I remember once I didn't and my father slapped me really hard. He had this big jumbo Citadel class ring and by mistake it was turned so that the stone hit me hard. Afterward he felt really bad. In the end he always told you when he was sorry. To be blatantly bluntly honest that's probably why he's still living. Even now he cares. He sends me one hundred dollars a month.

"When it happened I wonder if I wasn't a psychopath in the sense that I had a goal here and I was there and absolutely nothing was going to get in my way. I think that's why my brother died. I kept telling him to leave the house and he kept thinking I was kidding. It was as if he thought he was going to be missing something fun, like I was going to have my girlfriend over or something.

"I am on probation for twenty years from the day of my sentencing on March 21, 1984. I could drive recklessly or even spit on the sidewalk and I risk going to prison for the rest of my life.

"This will color the rest of my life. I could win the Nobel Prize every day until the day I died and I would still be the boy who killed his mother and his brother. No matter what, I have that label. I think about my brother a lot, not every day, but on special days. On his most recent birthday he would have turned sixteen. On a charisma scale of one to twenty, he was twenty plus. He was going to be a real winner. I took that.

"There have been studies done on babies, how if they don't get touched and played with they die.

"Not only babies.

"A real big part of me was dead, the part that separates us from animals."

THE
BABYSITTER

Christine Falling, the baby killer:
"I love young 'uns. I don't know why I done what I done. Young 'uns is real cute. They don't really give you no problem. They sleep most of the time. They is affection and you can cuddle them. Little girls is fun because their clothes is prettier than boys and you can dress them up more fancier. I always give young 'uns candy, or a cookie, get on my hands and knees and chase a truck with them. I've been babysitting since I was fourteen. I never hit a young 'un. I always left that up to the parents.

"Everybody asks me, why you done it, why you done it. I keep askin' myself. I could a seen it if it was a grown-up, could take up for itself, but a little one ain't gonna hurt a grown-up. If it was a grown-up I could have hollered self-defense. The way I done it, I seen it done on TV shows. Only way I ever thought to do it. The simplest and the easiest. No one could hear them scream.

"Sometimes I think I done it 'cause I got bad nerves and all them crying, pitchin' fits, throwing stuff, all the time messin' on you, peein' on you, burpin' up on you. Make my nerves go haywire. Only thing I want to do is shut them up. I go to any extreme. I went too far.

"Maybe it was a seizure. I have them grand mal seizures. They is the worse seizures they are.

"Maybe it's 'cause I cain't have young 'uns. Cain't carry them. Something's wrong with my uterus, deformed, retarded, somethin'. When my sisters have one I'm jealous. Maybe that's why I did Geneva's the way I did. I never did touch Carol's young 'uns though. Cain't say why not.

"Maybe it's 'cause I didn't get paid half the time. Geneva never paid me but she was kin. Now some of them parents owed me and owed me and owed me. They was gonna pay me and it kept doubling up and doubling up. Fifteen dollars a day times three months. I don't know how much that is. Cain't add that good.

"Sometimes I want to blame the way I was raised up.

"Sometimes I think I have a streak of mean.

"A streak of mental illness.

"Undoubtfully you don't do somethin' for nothin'.

"Got to have a reason somewhere.

"I keep having these dreams, seein' all the babies in a row, all the same as they was only they can talk and they're sayin' all this junk. 'You killed us: now we're gonna kill you.' I want to get rid of those dreams and go back to normal life.

"I don't understand.

"I brought it all out in the open.

"Why I still have dreams about it, I'll never know.

"I remember when we was little my stepmother, Aunt Dolly, she would take me to church Sunday nights and while the services was goin' on, me and some other girls used to sneak out back. We was mean when we was little. We used to take cats, much as I love cats, throwed 'em up in the air and wringed their necks just to see if a cat had nine lives.

"That what we done it for.

"A cat does not have nine lives.

"I found that out.

"You kill it one time, it ain't gonna come back eight more times."

Miami Herald photo by Keith Graham

For two and a half years she made headlines: Christine Falling, the babysitter of northern Florida, presumed carrier of a mysterious virus that infected and then killed first one then two, three, four, and finally five children left in her care from early 1980 until July of 1982. She was famous, ("I got letters from Hawaii,") a modern-day Typhoid Mary, a one-person epidemic of Sudden Infant Death Syndrome. "They put me in all them Enquirers and them Mirrors and them Globes. TV, too." She told reporters that the "awful weird coincidence" of the deaths was not enough to keep her from babysitting. Her comments were bizarre, so offhand:

"I'm not scared to babysit. Nobody knows if a young 'un is going to die. You can babysit for a young 'un who has never been sick a day in her life and they'll just drop dead on you.

"In a way, I'm glad I never had no young 'uns 'cause if I had one die on me like that, why, they might just bury me along with it.

"Sometimes I wonder if I don't have some kind of spell over me when I get around young 'uns."

Christine's case was as wild and peculiar as the countryside of the Panhandle where the sad drama took place, the portable horror show traveling from one town to another: Lakeland, Perry, Blountstown. It is a rural area known as South Georgia, something out of *Deliverance*. It is God-fearing country with billboards to show it: "Heaven or Hell—You determine it." Logging country, the land is covered with tall pines and great oaks. The close-by rivers have noble names: the Suwannee, the Steinhatchee, Apalachicola. They move past the small towns as slow as time, and they are just as old.

The people are poor; without education, without prospects. Carol Phillips, Christine's sister, says the best jobs in Perry are at Buckeye, the paper plant, and after that Winn Dixie and K mart. Those are the jobs people would kill for. Housing is rundown and often not clean; as Christine would say, "It's hard to keep your personal hygienes up and all." Inside one trailer, one evening, dinnertime: a bowl of greens, huge servings of mashed potatoes with gravy, a single piece of gristle tossed back and forth among three young children, one shouting, "I hate fat meat." The offending morsel lands on the plate of the youngest, powerless to toss it elsewhere. The television is on. No one is talking. Parents and children glumly fill their mouths. The husband will be leaving soon on a run; he drives a truck. He likes it: it's hard to think about going to work after the freedom of a truck. The man is in his late twenties, sick with stomach ulcers, doctor says he's dying. The man thinks he got the ulcers from too much Pepsi. He wants an open casket. Outside tethered dogs bark at the moon.

Under such conditions there is not much margin for grace. Mortality is a presence and a reality. A portion of the cemetery in Perry is called Babyland. Crude metal markers honor the passing of about thirty children. "Another angel before the

Heavens," says one of the markers. Carol Phillips, Christine's older sister, has a baby in the cemetery. "They say that at Woodlawn there are two children to every adult. Half my junior high school class is here because of some foolishness they was into: car wreck, a dare." Carol bends over, pulling up the weeds and uprighting the fallen baskets of flowers, not just at her daughter's grave, but also at Jennifer Daniels's grave and at the graves of strangers.

When the children in Christine Falling's care died, it was assumed they were like everybody else: life's victims. No one thought "smotheration." Everyone figured it was that disease that keeps the young 'uns from breathing; a touch of that.

No one would accept that she was a murderer. Not her family, not the townspeople, not the doctors, not the parents of her victims.

Reporters wrote that her "babysitting business" was suffering because of the bad publicity. The phrase conveys a wildly false reputability. It implies a facility, some kind of licensing, the keeping of books, a cheerful decor of dancing animals. This picture parodies the reality of a gang of kids in the custody of an epileptic teenaged girl, of low intelligence, in trailers and shacks, tended for hours on end. These people were poor: the parents of Jeffrey and the parents of Joe-Boy were out fishbaiting; driving worms from the earth, vibrating them up through the use of crude tools, collecting them into buckets and selling them. Each bucket, containing about five hundred, earns between seventeen and twenty-eight dollars, depending on the time of year; it's a common side income for pregnant women to get up extra money for a nursery.

They accepted their victimization. Jeffrey's death was blamed on the water. It was contaminated: young 'uns couldn't handle it. Joe-Boy's parents were attending Jeffrey's funeral when Joe-Boy took ill suddenly. The talk again turned to the water.

The mother of the final victim was out at night. She was

seventeen years old, celebrating the release of her two-month-old son Travis from the hospital after a week's bout with what was said to be "yemonia." The child was saved after he developed breathing difficulties in Christine's care. A week later, Travis was returned to Christine's care and died.

Jennifer's mother had left Christine for a matter of minutes when the death occurred. She was inside a Winn Dixie buying some diapers while Christine watched her daughter when she took ill and turned purple and stopped breathing. When she came out Christine waited until they started driving to tell the mother something was wrong. "I knowed I could put on a cover-up story." Her cover-up story: "This baby ain't breathing." The mother: "Babies don't breathe hard, Christine." She looked over. Her child was blue. "There was no spond." "Spond" is Christine's word for "response." They raced to the hospital. Christine dropped the child's glass bottle on the way in. As always Christine was in shock when questioned by the authorities; the tears came easily. At the funeral when "Precious Memories" was played, Christine fled.

Despite the deaths, families of the victims and friends continued to offer tributes to Christine's skills as a sitter: she was nice to young 'uns, she brought them presents, she let them take sips of her iced tea. Also, there were dozens and dozens of children who had survived her caretaking, a statistic intended to demonstrate that Christine could hardly have killed those five in the light of the multitude she didn't kill.

"I tried," she said, "never to go under a dollar an hour." Sometimes she did, exchanging her services for food and a place to sleep.

Buddy Smith, Calhoun County sheriff: "It was a sad case on both sides." Baya Harrison, defense attorney: "The full horror of this story has yet to come out." Dr. Robert Wray, psychiatrist: "Mass adolescent female murderers are extremely rare." Jerry Blair, prosecutor: "Falling is the victim of her environment. She couldn't handle stress very well. I probably have more sympathy for Christine Falling than anyone I've ever prosecuted for a criminal offense."

At the time, no one would believe it was murder. From the *Perry News-Herald,* July 29, 1982:

> Some of Christine Falling's "family" in Perry say they're glad she has been charged with the murder of two infants in her care because, this way, she'll eventually be brought to trial where she'll be found innocent of all charges.
>
> Then, maybe then, Falling's life will get back to normal and people will leave her and her family alone. Falling was charged with the murder of two Blountstown children last Thursday. The charges were another chapter in a long nightmare for the nineteen-year-old former Perry resident whose babysitting jobs were her sole means of support.

Geneva Burnette Daniels, Christine's stepsister, the mother of Joe-Boy and Jennifer, was sure at the time that the children were killed by illness, not by Christine. She said Christine's epilepsy made her sensitive to sick children. "She knew what the kids were going through."

Carol: "She must be a very sick person if she did what they said she did. I won't believe it. I can't. If God came down and stood on that sidewalk and said to me, 'Your sister did it,' I'd have to say, 'You're crazy. Not Chris.'"

When Christine was arrested, police tried to link her with the death of Carol's daughter. Christine had visited when the baby was a couple of weeks old. "It makes me really mad," says Carol, "that they tried to blame that on her."

Jesse Falling, adoptive father: "Maybe she's got her nerves crossed."

Dolly Falling, adoptive mother: "Like our friend, his two

nerves was crossed in the back of his head. All he could do was sit and cry all day, yes ma'am, tears coming down all day and then he went to Chattahoochee for a year and had that operation to get his two nerves uncrossed and he's been his old self ever since."

In Christine's world:
   It is the nineteenth century.
   Russia bombed Pearl Harbor.
   Columbus rode the *Mayflower* and discovered Florida.
   Wallace and Carter are former presidents.
   Elephants gestate for two years and their offspring weigh twenty tons.
   It was either George Washington, or maybe Abraham Lincoln, who discovered electricity. In any case, it happened before she was born. She doesn't understand why she has to know things from before she was born.
   The psychiatrists keep giving her tests. She thinks they are stupid, suitable for "a three-year-old young 'un."
   "They ask you about your sex life, what age was you when you lost your virge . . . virge . . . virginity. Silly questions: if you had a sex life would you want to be spreading your personal sex life all around. They ask are you a homosex or a bisex, which at that time I put no.
   "On the tests they want you to tell them what kind of picture you see in this paint spattered, most of it's just butterflies and bats. They do that to see if you got any brains. They like to play with what's up here."
   A psychological evaluation conducted on October 25, 1982, revealed that Christine's IQ was eighty-five, in the low average range of intellectual ability.
   Christine listed her hobbies as watching Saturday morning cartoons.
   Some of the fevered curiosity that greeted the case of Christine Falling diminished because of how she looked: Christine, Christine, beauty queen, went the chant in her hometown of

Perry. Christine was obese, over two hundred pounds. The long straight hair fell flat, untended. The wide forehead was a ledge, overhanging sunken eyes. There was a lack of differentiation to her features; the cheeks were chubby. She was a mockery of someone younger; a giant baby.

She certainly did not fit the clichéd cheerleader image of pretty, young babysitters dressed in the latest outlandish style, trusted element of society, absolutely essential to the sanity of the burgher marriage, girls who think everything worthwhile is either cute or really cute. They arrive to babysit with their textbooks in virtuous if ostentatious tow. They are given a nervous little lesson in 911, offered the bounty of the refrigerator and the cable and all in all rather elaborately courted. For their part the girls are expected to convey an air of reassuring normality. In the newspaper pictures and on television, she never looked normal. Nor reassuring.

Carol Phillips is tall and thin, with curly hair, freckles, and two chipped front teeth. Like Christine, her sister, she has a country drawl, yet not the same flat monotone.

Carol and her husband, Mike, live in Jacksonville. He earns six something an hour at a plant that manufactures shingles. The work is difficult, and a man can be standing there laughing one minute and wrapped up in a machine the next. He would like to get on the day shift and hopes to join the credit union so he and Carol can buy a 1980 Plymouth Scamp. Carol spends her time keeping their one-bedroom apartment clean and neat, getting groceries, going to the laundromat. The apartment is sparsely furnished. There are some photos from Mike and Carol's wedding on display. The visual centerpiece is Carol's high-school diploma, earned at the vocational school in Perry, four years of study compressed into seven months.

Carol gestures with diffident pride at the framed document, "I always said it was nothing but a piece of paper, but. . . ."

Carol dreams of going to college, studying modeling and merchandising. She likes to make summer tops so maybe she'll go into the summer line of clothes. She remains Christine's only faithful correspondent. She writes her a letter at least once a week, and sometimes tries to send her a card that says "Smile" or "Been Thinking of You." Sometimes Carol will be in the midst of something totally unrelated to her sister, and she'll start thinking of Christine and for no reason start to cry. Carol often says she doesn't want to live through her purpose on earth too quickly: her purpose is to see that Christine has a home if she ever leaves prison, to keep in touch with her.

Prison life:

"Lots of girls in here on check charges. Some of them murdered people they don't even know. At least half a dozen's in here for the same thing as me."

"Two things they don't like here. If you killed a cop or you killed a young 'un. After a while the nagging stops, but there's them years when they won't let it go."

When Christine Falling first arrived at Broward Correctional Institute she received some notes filled with vituperation and threatening her life. Prison officials reacted quickly: prolonging her orientation, keeping her out of the main compound until it was discovered that these notes were scrawled in Christine's own handwriting. When she tried to burn down her cell, on March 11, the evening before her twentieth birthday, other women rescued her, suffering smoke inhalation and burns. Christine wasn't hurt; they were.

"Grossest thing I heard since I been here, they was one girl killed her baby, put it in the oven and cooked it and fed it to her husband. According to what everybody say, her husband asked, where's the baby and she said, you're eating it." Christine places full credence in this story, even though officials say it never happened.

"They asked me if I want to meet her. No, I don't think me and her would get along. Least it wasn't my young 'un. Least I didn't feed them to nobody. Least I called the ambulance and carried them to the hospital."

Even when she confessed, her confession was not readily believed; from United Press International: "Was the confession a matter of Falling, a poor, overweight, poorly educated teenager, who has spent her life being shuttled from family member to family member and who may have been a victim of child abuse herself, finally submitting to pressures, however subtle, exerted on her at the hospital?"

In the end Christine owned up to the deaths of three of "them innocent children" and she has been linked with the deaths of two more children and one old man. The old man, she says, doesn't count, because the cause of death was never determined: "It's not my fault his family didn't run an autopsy." Although she confessed to Joe-Boy's and Jeffrey's deaths to a psychiatrist, she was never formally charged, and she prefers to stand by the death certificates: "Myocarditis," or, as she says, "exploding hearts." When she confessed to the murder of Muffin Johnson, Jennifer Daniels, and Travis Coleman, she ended a mystery that probably should never have existed. Joseph Sapala, the medical examiner who broke the case with the Coleman baby, accused his colleagues of traveling the "primrose path of statistics," ascribing to Sudden Infant Death Syndrome what should have been diagnosed as strangulation. SIDS, he said, is a "wastebasket term; if you don't know what the hell you have, it's crib death." What tripped up the examiners was the presence of disease in the children. They found a debility, myocarditis for instance, an inflammation of the muscle of the heart not uncommon and not necessarily fatal; and in a place where the death of babies is commonplace, where such things are often given biblical interpretations, where God is said to take nursing babies from the mother's breasts to serve his purpose, in such a place the passing of these children was seen to be routine. Not only by townspeople, but also by medical examiners.

Christine:

"It was too perfect. There was no way for them to know I

done it unless I said so. They was no homicide evidence, no trauma. Joe-Boy and Jeffrey, their hearts exploded. They said Muffin had brain fever which collapsed her brain. The brain waves froze and all. Jennifer they said had this SIDS, this crib death. Jennifer just upped and died which that's popular with young 'uns. Travis, same thing."

By plea bargaining, Christine avoided a trial and received a twenty-five-year mandatory prison term. In December she was transferred from Calhoun Country Jail to the Broward Correctional Institute in the western corner of the county where Pines Boulevard and State Road 27 intersect, a monotony of canals and roadbed and roadbed and canals inhabited by truckers, alligators, and insects. Not visible from the road, the prison arises from the saw grass about a mile in. It has the air of an industrial complex, a grim mirage, growing out of nowhere. It is a place of near absolute isolation, barren under too much sun.

With her confession to crimes as odious as can be imagined, Christine Falling receded from public view: the horrid force, the bad seed, retarded and monstrous, was now contained. Jailed. Never a figure of sympathy, she ceased to be one of curiosity.

Before her arrest her dealings with the press consisted entirely of issuing bizarre remarks. After her arrest, a gag order prohibited her from speaking with the press before the scheduled trial.

In prison, Carol has been her only visitor from home. On Christmas Day she was disappointed to call home at the very minute her adoptive parents were fixing to leave the house.

She decided to tell her story for one reason.

"I got to the point," she said, "where reporters is better than nothing."

Christine Laverne Slaughter Falling was born on March 12, 1963, the second child of Ann Omans Moore Slaughter Adkins, a sixteen-year-old. Ann's first child, Carol, is a year and a half older than Christine. Ann's husband, Tom Slaughter, was an old man even then. Today he is eighty-five, going deaf, and the victim of numerous accidents in the log woods where he used to work. He still stands tall, and spends his time puttering around the front yard outside the shack where he lives. It is one of those yards not uncommon in the deep country, totally covered with cans, car parts, broken furniture. Tom Slaughter takes pieces of debris and puts them together. These are his inventions. He is not much of a historian when it comes to Christine's early days. He knows he's not Christine's father, nor Carol's, nor the next one's—what was his name, he got adopted out, Michael Wayne. He gave all three his last name because it was only right. "They was caught in my trap. Weren't the daddy of but one of the four, Edward Earl; he might be mine." That one died, though; something was wrong with his muscles when he was born. He wasted away, turned to bone. The four children were born within four years of each other. Carol remembers her mother leaving and coming back pregnant, not with Christine, she doesn't remember back that far, but with Michael Wayne, and then leaving again for a time, and coming back and having Edward Earl. The extent of Tom Slaughter's baby stories is an account of his daughters' first meals: "Carol, she weren't a day old, born Friday night and at noon the next day she ate lima beans and mullet fish for dinner" and Christine ate yolk of egg and butter and grits in equally good time. The menu at baby's first meal is frequently recited in the county, as if there is something quite signal and gratifying about this event.

Some memories:

Carol: "I never did miss Mama. I guess she was never around long enough to get attached."

Carol remembers having to take charge of Christine and the baby. She was about four. Neighbors dropped in now and then. Once Carol was trying to keep Christine from wetting her pants, and she and a slightly older child hung Christine by her shirt on the clothesline to dry out. Carol says Christine cried, but Christine has no recollection. The two sisters give varying accounts of their childhood. They agree on basic matters, but frequently one will have an elaborate memory of an event, and the other sister will be nearly blank on the happening. The broadest view, of course, is that no event is ever lost. Something not recalled, at least not openly, goes underground and is transformed into an outlook, maybe a compulsion or a fear, perhaps a way of behaving that has no obvious roots.

Carol's first memory: "A kitten died."

Christine's: "I was in the hospital, I had a seizure, or when I fell, and they give me IV to keep my nutrition up, and I remember they sticked it in the wrong place, and all the fluid come up my arm and it turned all purple, and they kept trying to restick and I kept jerking it out everytime they restick it."

When Ann was away on one of her frequent trips, which usually took her one hundred miles away to her home town of Blountstown, the children often accompanied Tom Slaughter to the woods on his job, staying all day in a big playpen.

Christine: "Daddy had us out in the log woods in a playpen with a net on top against the mosquitos the day he got in his accident. Me and Carol was laying in it, when a log fell, busted his head open, busted his intestines, three-fourths of his stomach is plastic intestines. Right or left side of his face, I forget which, ain't nothin but cotton. He has a metal plate in his head. Who come and got us I don't know. The foreman or somebody else, I don't know. All I know is, Daddy was in the hospital, and it weren't long after we went to Dolly and Jesse.

"Ann wouldn't take care of us.

"Tom couldn't."

Carol: "What happened was, after Daddy's accident Mom took all us kids, and carried us to a store or a shopping center, it was somewhere in Perry and she put all the young 'uns on a bench outside the store and she told us to just sit there and she walked away. I yelled after her, 'When are you coming back?' and she wouldn't answer me. She never turned around to answer her own daughter. She throwed us away like we was garbage, can you imagine doing that to your young 'uns? She throwed us away. My own Mama doesn't want us. Felt like an outcast for sure."

Christine: "I don't remember that. If Carol says so, I'm sure it's true, but I cain't memory it."

Carol: "I love Ann as far as her bearing us. That's the only kind of connection I have."

Christine says that for the nine years with Jesse and Dolly Falling, the two sisters never saw their mother. Carol disagrees. She says they saw her three times at three funerals. Uncle Archie's, Uncle Willie's, and Grandmom's.

Aunt Dolly: "I had this hunger in my heart to have me a baby. I went to five doctors, but no one could help me. One day I was at church and the preacher brung in Carol and Christine and my husband said, 'Do you want those children?' 'Well, somebody has to take them.' They was relations of Jesse.

"We never abused those young 'uns, no sir. No one has ever actually seen it with their own eyes. He never drank alcohol in front of them, never beat them unmerciful, never took in another woman in front of those two children. I blame myself for spoiling the children when they were young. They had the cutest little dresses you could buy in Perry. I brought them up to fear God, to believe in the Bible. I went too many miles for that girl. She knows the ground I stand on. Things started to turn when the children proved old enough to know we wasn't their real parents. They would say it to our face and how would you feel, children you spent money on and raised?

"I'll tell you what Christine did one time. Me and my husband had a mind of building this house here, and I seen a picture in a magazine jes like the house I wanted and I cut it out. Children, I said, leave this here alone. This piece of paper. And what did Christine do? She took it and tore it right up. I took the pieces and copied a picture from them and locked it away in my footlocker.

"I think Christine's problem is that she absolutely growed from a child into a woman nearly overnight. That's what happened. She growed too fast. She got daresome.

"I don't trust that girl. She never did want me and Jesse to have anything for ourselves. She saw Jesse and me get on our feet and it looked like it near about killed her. I told them, we're building for them. One day every drape, every car, every well, every refrigerator, every mirror, every dresser, every commode, every fan will be yours. We're building for the children. Them children is grown. They don't belong to me no more. If they don't have a house of their own it's their own fault. We fulfilled our duty to our children.

"Christine called on Christmas Day. She's always ringing my number and expects me to accept the charges.

"I told her she was free to write to me anytime she wishes."

"She wants us to visit. We won't go this year. Not in 1983. This house is not finished, not finished, not finished. There are no baseboards in this house, not a bit. We have to fix that up. We don't have the money to make that trip with."

Carol has a memory of Dolly Falling's footlocker, filled with relics from her childhood, report cards, ribbons the girls won, a certificate saying that Carol has the aptitude to become a telephone operator. "Just junk but Dolly had kept it."

The junk is gone. Now it contains Christine's Bible that Dolly is prepared to return to her "once she's got a little bit of sense and acts like an human being ought to." There are some house papers, Jesse's army records in case he has to go to the hospital, some old Valentine boxes. Beyond that the only relics are some 45 rpm records that Dolly used to like and the children used to try to take and break. They remain in safe-keeping: "Satisfied Mind" by Red and Betty Foley, "Whirl-pool of Love" sung by Webb Price, and "Mother Prays Loud In Her Sleep" by Lester Flatt and Earl Scruggs.

"Them children," says Aunt Dolly, a frail stripped-down kind of a woman who is all eyeglasses and nervous, darting gestures, "fulfilled my mother hunger. I done got a square bite of it, don't want no more."

Jesse Falling, taller than his wife with tan weathered skin: "The past is the past. I never hurt those girls, never touched them. If I did, had to be drunk or ignorance. Now I did whup 'em when they rebelled and talked back to my wife; what kind of husband would let his adopted daughter talk to his wife like that.

"Even now if I could get my wife to agree I'd get me one and raise it."

Christine: "One day Uncle Jesse took us down to a housing project he was working on, jes me and Carol. Dolly had a hairdresser's appointment. Jesse told Carol to get out, and I started to get out, and he said, 'No, you stay in the car.' He took Carol in one of them buildings and when she came out, her pants wasn't even on right, her shirt was wrong side out, and when we went to pick up Dolly, I started running my big mouth, saying Carol's clothes was all messed up. I ain't seen Dolly give Jesse such a dirtiest look all her life.

"Weren't much later I come into Carol's room and Jesse's standing over her, and her pants was off, and she was crying, which I didn't know what hurt she had, so I tried to call the law to get her help, not to say he done something wrong. I didn't know what he done. The way the phone was I couldn't just pick it up; I was just tall enough I could hit the bottom of the phone and the ear part fell where I could catch it. That was the time Jesse tried to choke me, he put the cord around my neck. Dolly knowed about it. She was right there but she weren't going to do nothin' but preachin' and prayin'."

Carol tries hard not to think about that aspect of the past: "I made myself rise above it. It was nothing Jesse planned. I could be in the kitchen, in the yard, and he would start touching me. I try not to think about it. Dolly and Jesse did a lot for me. They kept me from going to an orphanage and staying there forever. When they adopted us, they weren't anyone else that wanted us, because of our age, and we was so many. And we was unruly. We had been let loose. We was plain and simple twenty-four hours a day unruly."

But she does remember the day Jesse tried to choke Christine. Jesse told her to go to her room and change her clothes. Which she did. Jesse came in the room. Carol remembers no sexual abuse that time: "He burnt some money, and was hollering about the prices of sex and stuff. I could see Christine in the hallway behind Daddy and I could see her run to the phone. When I come out, Daddy was choking Christine. I was so scared. I started screaming at Mama to help. She wasn't doing anything. It made me so mad at her. She should have been helping Christine. I tried to make Jesse stop and he popped me real hard and throwed me up against the breakfast bar, and I ran down to Jesse and Dolly's bedroom and I locked the door and picked up the phone.

"When the cops come around Jesse locked hisself in the bathroom. They broke his arm and three ribs.

"That day Daddy was a madman."

Upon advice of Dolly's minister, Carol and Christine were removed from the Falling home and placed in Great Oaks Village, a county-run children's refuge in Orlando. Carol remembers that Dolly and Jesse wanted to visit, and she did not want to see them, but Christine begged her to let them visit. The two girls had a pact that neither would see either of their adoptive parents without the other.

According to records from Great Oaks Village, Christine had trouble adjusting. She was a compulsive liar: she would steal other children's possessions—once, some playing cards, once some makeup—and then try to fix the blame on others. "She will try to do anything to get attention," one report reads, "even if she knows it means restriction. If she feels we are paying more attention to someone else, she will come and tell lies on them."

One evaluator was asked to indicate any "special interests the child exhibits." Answer: "None." "What would you single out for praise in the child's behavior?" Answer: "Nothing."

In another document, a social worker indicates that Jesse Falling had been arrested at least twice on charges of sexual abuse of Christine. The first time, the records say, there was a hung jury. The second time, Dolly had the charges dropped.

In a letter dated June 21, 1972, a social worker reports that Dolly "blames the childen for all her marital problems. Since she views the children as deterrents to her happiness with her husband, she is now relieved that the girls have been removed from their home."

But after a year the children were returned to the Fallings.

Christine and Carol remember Great Oaks Village with fondness. Christine liked it because it had a swimming pool, and every Friday night a movie was shown and the children were given Dr. Pepper and popcorn.

Christine: "There weren't no one constantly beatin on us."

Carol: "A vintage year."

Once home, Carol says, the molestation stopped. But not the beatings. Over the years Christine seemed to attract more beating than her sister: "Christine never understood that expression, 'Children is to be seen and not heard.' Christine didn't exactly understand the expression no matter how many whippings she got. For a long time I didn't talk. I swear, I'd have forgotten how if I hadn't been in school and forced to speak up there."

Christine: "One remark he'd always use: 'This hurts me more than it hurts you.' That's an old saying old folks have."

Carol's version of the final fight in the Falling household:

October 30, 1975, Christine comes home from school ten minutes late.

Jesse accuses her of not coming straight home. He starts

spanking her. He begins to spank her "where she is supposed to be spanked." Then he starts in on the legs, the back; the blood is at the point of breaking the skin.

"A man that's angry, a man that's been drinking, he's going to hurt a child. Dolly was just standing at the door. I tried to talk Mama into stopping him but she wouldn't. What kind of mother, what kind of Christian, what kind of human would just stand there?"

There is a knife on the kitchen counter. "I saw my opportunity; go for the gusto: 'Daddy, stop. I'll see you dead before you hurt Christine again.' "

She jumps on him with the knife. He slaps her across the face with the belt. He takes the knife away. He freezes; he just stands there and looks at her, and lets Carol hit him and hit him and hit him. "He started crying and he told me to leave.

"Christine was laying on the floor. She wouldn't move. She would not."

Later, Carol lifts her sister off the floor and carries her to the bedroom. "Chris," she whispers, "it'll all be over soon. We'll soon be gone."

"The next day Jesse made her go to school and he told her to wear shorts. To show off the justice.

"I packed a Winn Dixie bag with all our belongings and I told Chris she wouldn't have to bother to take the bus home from school that day, that she could leave with me."

Christine has no memory of the final beating.

"I cain't remember what urged me to leave. All I know is, I left."

The sister found an older girl willing to share her apartment. Carol entered a school program in which she worked half a day. "For two years," says Carol, "Jesse and Dolly didn't know if we was runaways or we was dead."

About six weeks after the two girls left home, Christine left Perry for Blountstown to find her real mother. She did, and for the next few years, the sisters were out of touch. Christine says her mother tried to turn her into a prostitute. "You shouldn't do your young 'uns like that," Christine says.

On September 19, 1977, Christine got married. She was fourteen.

For a long time the "most happiest" day of Christine's life had been her trip to Disney World, a "fancy-nating" place. She loved Cinderella's castle, the rides, and the souvenirs, "shirts and hats with pictures of the Disneyland players, Goofy and all them."

But Disney World got replaced as the happiest day by her wedding day, when she married Bobby Adkins, a city worker in Blountstown, a big man of few words, in his early twenties. He was the stepson of Christine's mother. "The ceremony was set for 5:30 because that's when Bobby got off work. We had a cake stacked three, and on top was a little man and woman with wedding suits on and all. I wore a white velvet dress, size 18. There was lace coming from the stomach all the way up to the neck. Preacher Nichols performed the ceremony between two funerals and he didn't charge nothin' but we gaved him thirty dollars for his troubles. After he left we spiked the punch with either Seagrams Seven or Lord Calvert.

"I got drunk. I woke up the next morning with blood all over me."

The marriage ended six weeks later. "I don't care who a man is, sooner or later he's going to run around on you," says Christine. She threw a stereo at Bobby. When the marriage ended, especially like that, Disney World went back to being her most happiest day.

Carol:

"People who have problems deal with them in different way. Daddy didn't deal with this real well. I graduated from high school for my mom and dad. They had told us that they wanted one of us to make it through, me or Christine, it didn't matter which one. They didn't even show up for the ceremony. I made the class speech and five minutes before it was supposed to begin, I kept looking out there and I couldn't see them so I called home, and Dolly told me the electrician has just come to fix something that was wrong with the wires. And they had to wait. I kept my eye on the door every minute. They never did show up. I can't forgive them for that. I wanted to make them proud."

On the weekend before Christine's twentieth birthday, Carol visited her in prison. The sisters spoke softly to each other, in that country way, giving everything the same drawling emphasis. Both were nervous. A little fearful. Christine borrowed a pretty blouse from another inmate.

"Really, Carol, it's just like college only they got a gate around it. You sleep in a dorm, and you got it guaranteed where's your next meal. If you're pregnant they got what they call prenatal planning, teach you how to be a mother. They teach college skills and culinary skills which that means kitchen."

"Well, Chris, I'm glad to see you're doing OK. Some day you're going to be a real lady. Your hair's always been so pretty. I was wondering: How long has it been since you wore feather bangs? You might not believe this, but sometimes I wish I was where you are. Sometimes the world can be a hard place. It's good to see you, looking good and to catch you up on the news, who's all had babies, how everybody is. Chris, I was wondering, if I talked to the lawyers, to Baya, and there was some way to get you into a place where you could get some help, I'm not saying there's anything wrong with your mind, but if I could get it so you could go somewhere else. . . ."

"Fine by me. Half of 'em here's crazy anyway, talking to theirselves, answering theirselves back."

Carol: "They gotta take care of her now, the taxpayers. It's their ballgame. Something should have been done a long time ago. Life's gave me a run for my money. It never gave Chris a run. It just took her over.

"I think it hurt her because of the fact of who she looked like. She was the spitting image of Ann. It must have hurt her to look in the mirror and see herself become an image of a woman you hate. I remember standing in front of the mirror, primping, and Christine would just be standing there, not looking at the mirror, but at the walls or the floor crying.

"Sometimes I think my grandmother was what gave me the punch to go on. Christine was too young to get her benefits. I told you my real mother sometimes carried us over to Blountstown, and my mother would go off somewhere and we would stay with her mother. My grandmother made me her pick. Seems like even before I was born she growed to love the baby my mama was about to have. My grandmother was always telling me how pretty I was, how much she loved me, what kind of person I was going to be.

"Me and her, we'd sit at the kitchen table, always talking about my hair, getting ribbons for it and how we was going to make some new dresses.

"Christine's my baby. I'm sorry but I love her more than I love myself."

Christine: "If they was something depended on my sister's life, if it meant for me being killed, I would save her. I'd rather be killed than her."

State where and how the accident occurred: Chest pains with pain in left arm.
Diagnosis: Psychoneurotic.
Treatment: Placebo. Two cc's.
Instructions to Patient: See her doctor in five days.

This was the routine at Calhoun General Hospital for Christine. She visited its emergency room more than fifty times between 1978 and 1980 with complaints of ailments and mishaps, some real, some not: seizures, snakebites, red spots, bleeding tonsils, dislocated bones, terrible falls, hot grease on left arm, stepping on wire, sharp pains, hit by crowbar while fishbaiting. Once she went to the hospital complaining of vaginal bleeding. The diagnosis: normal menses.

A crisis was building. These visits reached a crescendo in January 1980 when she complained that her period would not go away, the blood would not stop. She was admitted to the hospital but analysis of sample tissue scraped from her womb showed that she was all right. To this day she claims that she was pregnant and the doctors performed an abortion. A baby died in her imagination. Not much later, on February 25, 1980, a baby died in reality. Muffin Johnson, age two, would not stop crying.

Two and a half years later, she confessed, "I would be doing something simple, like pulling a blanket over me, and a voice would say, 'Kill the baby,' over and over and then I would come to and realize what had happened."

Christine is scheduled to be released from prison in the year 2007, at the age of forty-four. So far she has served eight months of her term at BCI.

In that time, she has had homosex. "That way you have somebody to look out for you."

She has lost almost fifty pounds; "I always heard prison food is better than outside world food. Well, it ain't."

She has plans to go to the prison beauty shop to get a curly perm.

The prison dentist is fixing her teeth.

She was sentenced to ninety days in disciplinary lock-up for igniting the mattress in her cell: "No cigarets, no potato chips, cain't watch TV, not allowed to talk to them compound girls."

She still has a habit of looking sideways when she speaks; the color of her eyes is tepid, watery: "They turn with what I got on. I got weird eyes." These days they tend toward blue, reflecting the prison issue. She wants to grow out her nails, but they are still short and raw, bitten to the quick.

Christine:

"If I hadn't admitted up to it I might not be in jail right now, or if I was in jail, it'd be on a bad check charge.

"I'm here on my own word.

"Sometimes it makes me feel stupid as hell.

"Obviously, if I hadn't said nothing about it, chances other ones would have happened. It got to be hard on me. Ones I could get my hands on, which ones dead. Ones I couldn't, I jes wished it.

"The reason I confessed was mainly people talking to me, telling me I was looking at a death penalty. No way I could get off on all three charges, and it would be stupid to go in front of twelve juries who want to do one thing and that's put you in a chair. If I plea bargain, then I can go to prison, get a college skill that'll help me get a job. The best part about it," and at this she shows a flutter of animation, the dullness of the gray-blue eyes lightening a bit, "is the day you get out they give you one hundred dollars and buy you a new suit and give you a bus ticket anywhere."

🍎 🍎 🍎

Christine Falling has served about a third of her mandatory twenty-five years in prison. "Every day here is pretty much the same," says Christine Falling, inmate number 151110 at the Broward Correctional Institution for Women, " 'cept on the Fourth of July you get a slice of watermelon and at Thanksgiving they give you sweet potatoes and pumpkin pie and at Christmas you can decorate the dorm with all them Tiny Tims and Baby Jesuses. The food isn't so bad, 'cept when it's meat in a puddle who knows what meat."

Physically, she has changed very little, although now she

has a tropical tan, deep and gold and even. She is still stocky at five feet five inches and 176. Her features remain blunt and expressionless, framed by longish blond hair. She is a hulking sort of woman, with vague distant eyes, one of which wanders, dooming her to a sideways look at the world. Clutching the soda purchased by her visitor, she looked down in dismay at her nails, which were bitten to the quick. "They only growed out long once in my life, and that was when I was in the hospital in 1986 with my hysterectomy. My total female organs: all that was just a disaster area."

She sighed, somewhat casually, when asked how it felt to know she would never have children. "To tell you the truth, it's a relief. Who's to say this mistake couldn't happen again to mine instead of somebody else's."

The words with their strange lightness reverberate in the locked-up air of the visitors' room: *this mistake.*

She sees herself as having changed: "I'm not the child who came here in 1982. If this place doesn't mature you, nothing will. Back then I had a kid's way of thinking: it's my way or no way. I tamed down a lot. I don't snap at everything people say."

Marta Villacorta, herself new as the superintendent at Christine's arrival, says that Christine has accommodated herself to prison life. The recent years have been ones of quiet deprivation. No one visits, not family, not media. Her case has lost the competition in what the public finds interesting; lately women on death row have been more likely to be the subject of journalistic interviews. She treated her one recent visit with a reporter as she had similar visits in the past: here was someone different to talk to even if all the person did was ask questions and here was the chance for a soda and some chips, all in all a not unwelcome bleep in the monotony of a life in which the main point is to push time forward.

"I'm settled down here for twenty-five years. As it stands now, people with mandatory sentences will be doing their mandatory sentences. I thought about applying for clemency, but I figured why not just wait until I'd been here ten years. It would be something to do, like a hobby, like painting.

"In some ways I blame myself for being here. To this day I don't know why I ever confessed. Killing the babies wasn't the point of wanting to get caught, it was the point of playing around with the sheriff's departments, making them work for a change, making them earn their living.

"They couldn't find no foul play evidence anywhere. It was fun, watching the cops squirm, them acting like it's this total mystery thing. But I'm not proud of the children's deaths. I never was. I guess I did it because like my stepmother Aunt Dolly says I always was just plain mean."

One of her biggest hardships has been the lack of mail and of money. "I can't afford all the hygienes I need, them neutragenas and all that. People are allowed to send you a certain amount in a box each month, but when I call Aunt Dolly collect she keeps on saying she'll send me my hygienes next month, but next month never comes. I stopped holding my breath waiting for her to send some; if I did I'd probably end up dead and blue."

Christine's one link to the outside world is when Aunt Dolly actually accepts a collect call. It was during a phone conversation with Aunt Dolly that Christine learned that both her mother and Tom Slaughter died. As far as the loss of her mother is concerned:

"Who cares? That old Ann was nothing but a two bit whore. She had sixteen kids, not one had the same daddy 'cept the twins."

The funeral of the man she called her father, Tom Slaughter, was another story. She felt bad about his passing, and she still feels bad because her sister Carol said she would write to Christine about the service and send her a picture of all the flowers but she never did.

"My mother was found shot dead by a riverbank. Tom Slaughter died in peace."

Christine has heard that Carol has moved back to Perry, and

that her first marriage ended and so did her second one, but from that union she had a son who is almost six years old.

For her part, Carol says she still thinks about her sister all the time and is glad she is leading a healthier, more protected life in prison:

"Not a day goes by I don't think about her. She was like my first young'un, my own baby. When she first went to prison, her letters were filled with all the bad things, like how scared she felt. But now when she writes it's about how she's not wasting her time, how she finished high school and she got a job and had her hair cut and she made a new outfit. Now she tells me the good news."

Carol works as a housekeeper at a local motel, and she says she and her son live "real good" in a rented trailer. "We don't live rich, but we don't want for anything. Even though it's a single parent family, my son has a good life." A good life means the bills are going to be paid, no one's going to just leave and never come back, and that there is a minimum of spanking. "If my son does something super major, like throwing a rock and breaking a window or hitting some other child on the face with a board, well, then I might hit him on the butt once or twice, but those things don't really happen. If he's having a bad day, he has a corner he might have to sit in for a few minutes or I might put him on what's called restriction and take his tricycle away for a day. But mostly he's very good, a typical all-American boy who wants to be everything when he grows up, from fireman to president.

"I've told him about Christine, but he doesn't know why she's in prison. I told him one thing she did wrong was she passed bad checks, which is true, that's what they caught her on. I don't lie to him. But I figure I can tell him the rest when he's older and has more understanding."

Her stepmother Dolly says, "We hear from her pretty regular. We can't visit her down where she is because my husband is not physically able to drive. He can't even crank up a lawnmower, no ma'am. What's wrong with him has to do with oxygen; he isn't getting enough into his lungs the regular way so he gets it from a special machine now. The disease he has, it got a big name."

The high point of Christine's first eight years in prison was a couple of courses she has taken. "These were," she says, pausing pointedly, almost theatrically, for effect, "college type courses." One was in apparel design: "I made an evening gown similar to Cinderella's: the sleeves was lace and it had a big bow in back."

The other was called Psychology 101; she says she got an "A."

"We got to learn all about human behavior and the different minds of different people. In particular, we studied this one man, who based this big theory on human and animal behavior, what was similar about them." At first she could not recall his name then it came to her, slowly, hesitantly. "Fraudman. Grogman. Something like that." She paused, stumped. She touched her forehead: "Now how do you call his name?" A quick squint and then, "Oh, yeah, now I remember. Frogman Frigmund."

If there's anything she hates about prison, it's "all them shorttimers with a year and a day crying about their time. I can't even stand hearing people who have only five years complain: I did that standing on my head." And then, pausing, without acknowledging any irony in her use of the colloquialism: "Boy, that makes me want to kill them."

Christine has one prize possession, a pair of tennis shoes that someone left behind in 1987.

She still smokes, and she explained how she got the money to purchase a pack from time to time.

"Well, everyone in the world has to earn a living somehow."

She earns hers on commission by standing in line in the heat outside the canteen, waiting to buy goods for other inmates, and these same clients often pay her to sit in the parched prison yard by the clothesline, preventing the theft of their individually owned clothing. For this particular service, Christine likes to charge a whole pack. Private enterprise of this sort is probably against the prison rules but so what? "Practically everything is: no running in the compound, even if it's pouring rain, and if you comb someone else's hair they write you up: bodily contact."

Her biggest hope: "Someday soon the world will forget about what I did."

Until then, her days go like this: wake-up is at 6:00. She has to get up then because she has to take her medications that control her paranoia, the voices that come out of walls and ceilings. Breakfast is at 7:00, the only meal of the day in which coffee is served. She wishes there were more coffee in her life; doesn't understand why they are so stingy with it. Work call is at 8:00; recall is at 11:45, lunch is between 12:00 and 12:30, work call again at 1:00, recall at 4:30, supper is at 5:00 followed by free time followed by recall to the dorm at 7:30, lights out at 11:00. Friday and Saturday nights are a little different with lights out at 2:00. One day a year the population is allowed to stay up all night and that is on the last day of full staff before Christmas; the fatigue is considered by the authorities a salubrious distraction from the tensions of the holiday. Christine Falling is under the impression that if she follows this schedule day in and day out, year in and year out, that in twenty-five years she will be free. She does not fully grasp that according to the law she is merely eligible to have her case reviewed for possible release and parole after twenty-five years. She doesn't read much, but she likes TV okay. She tries to show self-respect and shower every other day. The biggest claim on her free time is that little business of hers, watching clothes dry.

She does seem calmer. There must be some safety in the sameness, something warm and healing.

Lumbering, gawky, with dull-beaten eyes, she possesses only one characteristic gesture that can be said to embody fleeting grace and it occurs whenever she is almost done with a bag of chips. She has this smart way of crinkling open the bag, puffing it out and in a single practiced swallow she drains its contents. This is her specialty, her circus trick, the one small moment in her life that shows precision or delicacy; the deft consumption of crumbs.

Marta Villacorta says that since the mandatory twenty-five-year sentences went into effect for first-degree murder, no one has served the full length of time and so there is no precedent for how much longer a person usually stays in prison after the quarter of a century has passed or what kind of halfway program generally works in preparing someone to return to what Christine and the other inmates like to call the free world.

"At the moment I do not think that Christine has the skills to take care of herself in an apartment or a job, so if she ever is released, I would hope that she would go through a controlled environment, some kind of supervised community setting. It is possible, given the fact that she is a multiple murderer and that she could go back to babysitting at nearly any age, that she will not ever be released. She does not show any insight into her actions, and that's always a factor. In her case, she may be better off where she is. She gets a lot of attention, she is provided for, and she does sometimes seem happy enough."

Christine Falling's notion of the future always includes getting out:

"What I want to do is find a job that's going to use my mind. My old job, minding young 'uns, well forget that. I don't want to be just a waitress: there's nothing to do 'cept don't drop the tray. I do have that certificate in apparel design, so I might look for something in that line of work. I don't know for sure where I'm going to live but I do know it's not going to be in either of the two counties I was charged in. If I had enough money I would go on a trip to and visit my two favorite countries, Australia and North America."

"But then again," she pauses, shrugging her shoulders, "Who knows? I might not even be alive by the time I get out of here."

THREE SCENES FROM THE LIFE OF A TORMENTED PLAYWRIGHT

The scene: Tennessee Williams's house on Duncan Street in Key West, a small, simple, white-frame house with red shutters and a picket fence. The time is late February, day's end. The living room is dominated by books and art. Out back is a studio where Williams works every day, seven days a week, waking up about five in the morning and sometimes using a Bloody Mary, if need be, "to overcome the initial timidity." He has often said, "I work everywhere, but I work best here." Under a skylight, surrounded by empty wine bottles and paint-caked brushes, seated before a manual typewriter, he awaits sunrise and inspiration. On Key West, there is a great ethic about sunset, but the playwright stalks the dawn.

Williams is sitting on the patio adjoining the house. He has arisen late from an afternoon nap and his face is still puffy with sleep. In a few hours, he will attend the opening of one of his plays at a local theater. From where he sits, there is a view of the backyard, which is dominated by a swimming pool, strangled weeds, and trampled plants. Williams glances with dismay at the untended growth snaking toward the pool.

"My gardener was shot, you know."

Photo © 1991 John Pineda

Tennessee Williams's life now on Key West in a way resembles the plot of one of his plays: an injured innocent in a honky-tonk town pitted against unprovoked malice, deliberate cruelty. Since January, his gardener has been murdered, his house ransacked twice. He has been mugged twice on the street, once reported, once not. His dog has disappeared. One winter evening some kids stood outside his house and threw beer cans on the porch, yelling at America's greatest playwright, "Come on out, faggot." The only person home at the time was a houseguest, writer Dotson Rader, and when the kids set off some firecrackers, Rader remembers thinking: "This is it. They've resorted to guns."

Yet Williams has reacted with the resiliency of one of his heroines, dismissing it all as "ridiculous." He uses the same cliché to explain it away as does the Key West Police Department: "There is violence everywhere." What has happened is enough to "shatter faith in essential human goodness," as Williams himself once put it, but he has insisted on a brave front, as if through "enduring the devil, he will earn, if nothing else, its respect." After the first reported mugging on Duval Street, he told the local newspaper: "I've been here since '49, longer than they have. I'll be back." He joked about the incident, as if through humor he can defeat it: "Maybe they weren't punks at all, but instead New York drama critics." "That mugging," said Williams, sounding almost jealous, "received better and more extensive publicity than anything I ever wrote."

Williams may sound cavalier, but the problems on Key West are of increasing concern to natives and tourists alike. For years the island has had a substantial gay population, and there has always been a certain amount of hot, tropical tension among the gays, rich tourists, leftover hippies, local teenagers, the drifters, and the druggies. In the winter the population jumps from thirty-two to forty-five thousand. The visitors range from rich Northerners who arrive by private jet and pay $125 a night for a suite at the newly renovated Casa

Marina on South Beach to homeless men arriving by Greyhound from Miami with cardboard cartons or, sometimes, green garbage bags as luggage. In season, there are four hundred robberies a month in Key West. This year, the frequency of attacks on gays has accelerated, and as a result Police Chief Winston "Jimmy" James has dispatched a squad of men to Duval Street late each evening, rounding up the transients on charges such as sleeping in the street, possession of illegal drugs, failure to wear a shirt in public. Still, the attacks continue, and by midnight it is no longer safe to walk the Old Town area. Chief James says the troubles began in 1912 "when they put in the railroad and we got deprived of being an island."

Dick Chapman, managing editor of the *Key West Citizen,* believes "winter's got a lot to do with it."

Mayor Charles "Sonny" McCoy says there used to be problems "between the sailors and teenagers after World War II. Now it's gays and teenagers."

It is not as if Williams alone has been singled out for attack. But as the island's most prominent artist in winter residence and most prominent homosexual, the attacks against him are symbolic of something gone terribly awry in this otherwise peaceful fishing village: life is no longer a breeze anywhere, even in the Florida Keys.

Tennessee Williams at age sixty-eight is not in repose on Key West, island paradise at the southernmost tip of this country, the place where the United States runs out of East Coast, known as The Last Resort. Williams has been on the road ever since, as a young man, he quit his job at the same shoe warehouse where his father was employed (Red Goose shoes, Buster Brown's chief competitor). He has been a stranger passing through the world's most glittering places. Yet when a New Orleans cardiologist advised him to retire to Key West and live like an old crocodile thirty years ago, Williams bought his house on Duncan Street and despite his gypsy nature, it has served as home base ever since. This season he no longer walks alone on the island at night. He dismisses it as merely "unfortunate," and says it will pass in a year or two.

On January 5, Frank Fontis, a forty-nine-year-old landscape architect, was gunned down. The curator of the Key West Railroad Museum, Fontis, for almost a decade, had been Williams's gardener and the caretaker of his property whenever the playwright was out of town. The police officer dispatched to the scene of the murder filed this report:

"I walked inside the door and observed the victim, naked (except for a pair of white socks). Victim was lying on his back just inside the doorway, a small hole above right ear, and another small hole below left side of neck. A large amount of blood was coming out of the victim's nose, also victim was lying in a large pool of blood which was partially coagulated. Upon checking victim's pulse and breathing I found he was already dead."

Three weeks later, on January 28, Williams and Rader were walking down Duval Street at one in the morning, a little high, singing hymns:

> He walks with me
> And He talks with me
> And He tells me I am his own

From the Key West police blotter, January 28, 1979:

Mr. Williams and friend, Mr. Dotson Rader were accosted by four or five white males in the 500 block of Duval Street. The attackers advised they knew who Mr. Williams was. At this point the attackers punched Mr. Dotson Rader in the jaw. Mr. Williams advised that he was thrown to the ground. Mr. Dotson Rader and Mr. Williams were then kicked at by the attackers. I could not see any evident injury to Mr. Rader or Mr. Williams. Neither wanted to get any medical treatment. The only description available was that the attackers were between the ages of 18 and 25, two had beards and the one who struck Mr. Rader was blonde-headed, had a darker beard, and wore a turtleneck sweater. Mr. Williams and Mr. Rader took a cab and went to Mr. Williams' house.

One of the attackers told the playwright: "We know who you are." Does Williams think the muggers were the same people responsible for the Fontis murder? "On, no," says Williams, "They were just punks. It happened quickly. There was no injury sustained. A lens fell out of my glasses. The publicity is ridiculous." Nevertheless, doesn't it bother him? "Of course not."

Why not? He seems surprised by the question, and his answer is delivered regally, in his best Southern drawl, cadenced, liquid, honeyed. "Because, baby, I don't allow it to."

The effect is eerie. Throughout Williams's work there has been one underlying definition of gallantry: "The grace with which one survives appalling experiences." It is remarkable: Williams in his life is imitating his own art.

The playwright steps across the patio through the doors leading to the living room. It is 6 P.M. on opening night. *Suddenly, Last Summer,* one of Williams's more violent plays, will be presented, the second production of the Tennessee Williams Repertory Company's inaugural season. *The Glass Menagerie* opened on January 30. Williams did not attend; he had left town.

He pours a glass of Gallo red wine into a plain kitchen glass. "When they ransacked the house, for some reason, they broke all the wine glasses." It is unclear which burglary he is talking about, the one that occurred January 8 when both Williams's and Fontis's houses were broken into and torn apart or the one that occurred at Williams's place about a week later. From the police blotter, January 14, 1979: "Entry was gained by tearing a screen and breaking a side window. The entire house was ransacked."

Williams sits on the couch, nursing the wine, waiting for the 6:30 news, a ritual which daily prompts him to wonder whether the planet can make it through 1979 without another world war. Williams at sixty-eight is almost an old man, yet his face retains an atmosphere of lush, full-featured alertness, especially in profile. He calls himself the "most promising playwright on Key West" and he cringes whenever anyone refers to him as the world's greatest living playwright. "I don't like that phrase. It has a way, don't you think, of implying the opposite."

He is gracious, instinctively courtly, even when he is in a bad mood, as he is on this evening. He admits to "always being crazy on opening nights." But that may not be the reason he missed the opening of *The Glass Menagerie*. The rumor among the repertory troupe was that he was afraid his appearance might cause commotion, even violence. There was talk in some circles that he was going to sell the house and move away from Key West. But rumor on Key West is said to grow like fungus, and Williams dismisses this speculation as so much jungle rot.

"I am not in the habit of retreat." There is a long silence. "The fact is, I had been planning to be out of town anyway and I don't much care to see *The Glass Menagerie* anymore." Another thoughtful pause: "It reminds me rather painfully of my mother."

He holds the glass of wine in front of him, examining the blood red in the muted twilight. "She never understood how much of her was Amanda," he says, almost to himself, referring to the domineering mother of *The Glass Menagerie*. Amanda is a woman of false airs and true spirit who insists on arranging for a gentleman caller for her painfully shy daughter, Laura, a character based on Williams's sister, Rose. Tom, Laura's brother, a secret poet known as "Shakespeare" at the warehouse where he works, is forced by his mother to provide a suitable caller.

"My mother is ninety-four years old," says Williams. "Longevity is a family disease." He punctuates this statement, nervously, with a "little breathless laugh," reminiscent of Alma, the spinster in *Summer and Smoke*.

Williams is joined for the evening news by his two houseguests, writer Richard Zoerink and Rader. The two young men fulfill many roles: sons, valets, chauffeurs, audience, companions. After the news, Williams disappears into his bedroom off the living room to dress for the theater. Dotson Rader talks about the recent fear and loathing:

"It has been terrible. Tenn won't talk about it, but it has been really frightening what's happening in Key West, and what's happening in this house. The worst was the night they stood outside the front porch throwing beer cans and shouting, 'Come on out, faggot.' When they set off the firecrackers, I remember thinking, 'God, this is it. We're under attack; they've started shooting.' I refuse to go out alone at night. I don't need to have my head bashed in with a lead pipe on Duval Street.

"When they broke into the house, they were obviously looking for something. The screens on the windows were slashed, and things were stolen, weird things that don't make any sense: lawn chairs, the toaster. Wine glasses were broken and the rose bushes out back trampled. I am more frightened here than I am in New York. I lock the door of my bedroom at night and I've already decided that if they come back again, I'll jump out of the window. They slashed the screens. Go look: it's upstairs.

"The police don't have the manpower to protect Williams as they should. I have been with celebrities doing stories in small towns all over the United States. In most small towns, they realize that if a famous person is hurt there, there are worldwide repercussions: your town gets known as the place where so and so got hurt."

Rader is not sure why Williams has been singled out for attack but he has three theories. "These people are antigay, despite the substantial gay population on Key West. They are xenophobes: they don't like strangers, and no matter how many years Williams has been here, the natives don't really accept him. And they hate celebrity, fame.

"Tennessee Williams is one of the great tourist attractions in Key West. You would think the county or city would see that he is comfortable here, safe here, can work here."

Why, in the face of all this violence, has Williams affected an air of unconcern, like Blanche Dubois in *A Streetcar Named Desire,* calculatedly blinding himself to the unpleasantness?

"Oh, he won't say anything. He has to live here. This is, for better or for worse, his home."

Williams returns to the living room, dressed for the theater, worried about a hole in his shirt: "Oh well, the shirt is clean, anyway. It's a good idea to look poor. Otherwise you have too many indigent people on your trail."

Williams applies the final sartorial touch before his night on the town: a black Greek sailor's cap of which he is extremely fond. "It makes me look like a mean son of a bitch, don't you think," he says to no one in particular. It doesn't: the cap is festive, nautical, jaunty.

Thus suited, Williams leaves the house with Richard, who drives him to dinner at the Rose Tattoo, a restaurant named in honor of one of his plays. After dinner, Williams walks down Duval Street, past Smokey Joe's with its big lettering: "Hemingway's favorite bar."

Williams points out the Hotel La Concha, where he wrote what is widely considered his best play, *A Streetcar Named Desire.* Key West's greatest tourist attraction is recognized by the polite, early evening crowd of tourists on Duval. Williams refrains from the singing of hymns. Richard asks whether the cast is aware he will be in the audience this evening.

"I hope so, baby," Williams says, sounding cantankerous.

He draws a deep breath. "Maybe it will make them act better."

The verandah of a large tourist hotel, later the same evening. Royal palms move with the soft, hot breeze, and an older man, wearing a Greek sailor's cap, sipping piña coladas, is surrounded by young people like a patriarch. They are toasting him with champagne and the music of their laughter. It is the cast party for *Suddenly, Last Summer* and the author is ebullient: Tennessee Williams loved the production, thought it was wonderful, the acting just marvelous. As a gift to the troupe, he offers to sing the hymn that caused so much commotion on Duval Street a few weeks earlier.

The autobiographical nature of the play sets off a stream of reminiscences in the playwright. As in much of Williams's work, the theme of *Suddenly, Last Summer* is incest, this time about a young girl who has just returned from a trip to Europe where she was used by her male cousin as a pawn, procuring young boys as his sexual partners. Eventually, he was destroyed, devoured, cannibalized by a band of berserk urchins. The girl's aunt, Mrs. Venable, wants Catherine put away, punished, lobotomized when she persists in recounting the sordid story of the summer. Mrs. Venable, to a doctor from the local asylum: "Cut this hideous story out of her brain."

Williams speaks with compelling intimacy, alternately referring to the young woman as Catherine and "Miss Rose," his sister, who underwent one of the first lobotomies in the nation. In 1934, an operation to remove a portion of the brain was considered fashionable, almost chic: the latest in putting the deranged out of their misery. This is the central sorrow of Williams's life and for years he has paid his sister's bills at the New York sanitarium where she is confined. In his *Memoirs,* the playwright wrote that taking care of Miss Rose was "probably the best thing I have done with my life besides a few bits of work."

An important thing to know about Williams is that he has

two families, this one—the cast, his admiring public—and the one he was born into in Columbus, Mississippi, the family that moved to St. Louis when he was eight years old: mother (ill), father (dead), sister, Rose (institutionalized), brother, Dakin (lawyer in Illinois). It is this second family which dominates his art, and, when he is in an expansive mood, his conversation.

Sitting at a large round table on the deck of the Pier House, Williams is besieged by autograph seekers. At one point, a middle-aged woman of substantial girth stands a few feet from the table, theater program in hand trying to work up the nerve ("You never know whether it pleases a famous person or it turns them off") to ask him for an autograph. "Well, here's 'E' for effort," she says, barging ahead. When she bends over to hand him the program, a wooden pendant she is wearing crashes into his face.

"Oh, excuse me! My husband made that," she says. "He's eighty-two years old." The woman begins to talk about her husband, but Williams cuts her off. "My mother is ninety-four," he says. The woman looks abashed. "She's dying, you know." The autograph seeker now has the wide-eyed look of somebody who has been told more than she wants to know. "She thinks there is a horse in her living room." The woman flees. Williams keeps talking:

"I used to be kind, gentle. Now I hear terrible things and I don't care. Oh, objectively I care, but I can't feel anything. Here's a story. I was in California recently and a friend of mine had a stroke. He is paralyzed on the right side and on the left side and he has brain cancer. Someone asked me how he was doing and I explained all this and the person said, 'But otherwise is he all right?' I said, 'What do you want? A coroner's report?' I never used to react harshly, but I feel continually assaulted by tragedy. I can't go past the fact of the tragedy; I cannot comprehend these things emotionally. I can't understand my friend who is sick in California and who loved life so much he is willing to live it on any terms.

"Sometimes I dream about getting away from things, re-covering myself from the continual shocks. People are dying all around you and I feel almost anesthetized, feel like a zombie. I fear an induration of the heart and the heart is, after all, part of your instrument as a writer. If your heart fails you, you begin to write cynically, harshly. I would like to get away to some quiet place with some nice person and recover my goodness. I cannot, for instance, feel anything about my mother. I dream about her, but I can't feel anything. All my dreams concern earlier parts of my life. The other night I dreamt my father told me I could go on the road selling shoes. Back then that's what I wanted to do: go on the road. We remain children in our unconscious. I am happy my mother dreams there is a horse in her living room. Her father would never let her ride a horse, so it is a happy dream. I won't answer the phone on Key West. Every time it rings I am sure it is somebody telling me my mother is dead. I won't answer it myself.

"Right now, my brother, Dakin, lives near her and checks in on her. My brother gave her a copy of the *Memoirs*. He needn't have, you know." Williams discussed his homosexuality in his autobiography, but the potentially disturbing memoirs didn't bother his mother, "because she thought I'd made them up." Again, the nervous little laugh. "Still it was insensitive of him. He was my father's favorite, but he isn't like anyone else in the family. We've often wondered about that. He keeps running for public office and it's quite pathetic. He's rather a small-town lawyer and he keeps running for offices he can't win. He has threatened to change his name to Illinois Williams. Rather a bad idea, don't you think?

"I would like to invite my sister, Rose, down to Key West for a visit. I was in psychoanalysis once for about nine months, and the psychiatrist told me to quit writing and to break up with someone. I did neither, but the one thing that analysis showed me was that my father was a victim, too, and mother was the strong one. She is the one who approved the lobotomy. My sister had been away at a school for girls, All Saints School, and when she came home she talked about how the girls stole candles from the chapel and committed self-abuse. My mother wanted her to stop saying all those terrible things, just like Mrs. Venable, the aunt in *Suddenly, Last Summer*. My mother could not bear the idea of anything sexual. Every time she had sexual intercourse with my father she would scream. Rose and I would hear her and we would run out of the house, screaming, off to a neighbor's. My mother had three children, so I imagine she was raped rather frequently."

At midnight, Williams and Richard are the first to leave the party, the better for the playwright to greet the next sunrise. As they walk to the parking lot, they realize, suddenly, that a young man is following them. He opens his jacket, revealing a shining gun strapped to his chest and announces: "I'm security, from the Pier House." Williams would later joke that he was more frightened of this guard than the mean streets, but to the armed stranger he says, "We can take care of ourselves, baby."

Noon, the following day. The world's greatest not-yet-dead playwright has survived to greet another dawn: "Mornings," he once wrote. "I love them so much . . . their great triumph over night." He is dressed informally, wearing only a bathrobe, having just left his studio where he is working on a play, *Clothes for a Summer Hotel,* about Scott and Zelda Fitzgerald. He has celebrated his session at the typewriter with a swim in his pool. Ordinarily, Williams moves like an old lion, full of slow ceremony. But twice a day he does spirited laps, back and forth for twenty minutes, displaying the vitality of a man much younger.

This is to be a session of photographs and the playwright very carefully composes the setting. He arranges himself in his bedroom, next to what he calls "the shrine." Above him on the wall is a portrait Williams painted of his long-time lover, Frank Merlo, who died in the early sixties, heralding for Williams a period of depression that lasted seven years: his own grim battle with the "unlighted side" of his nature. Once, in describing this interval of drugs, booze, insomnia, and conversion to Catholicism, since abandoned, he told Gore Vidal, "I slept through the sixties." Vidal responded, "You didn't miss anything."

The shrine honors Miss Rose. There is a tall structure, like a dripping candelabra, an Indian symbol called the tree of life. There are votive candles and, when the rose bushes are in bloom, freshly cut flowers. In the center is a madonna, veiled to convey spirituality. It is like the shrine in *The Rose Tattoo* which the author says should not "inspire ridicule, but rather respect for the religious yearning" it represents. There is a small booklet that says "St. Jude's Shrine."

Why a shrine named for the patron saint of lost causes? "Well," Williams says, "what could be more of a lost cause than someone who has had a lobotomy?" He set up the shrine in 1970. "I think at that time I had a greater appreciation of Miss Rose's tragedy. I was just out of the bin myself."

Is it true his mother and his sister are the only pure women he has ever met? "Oh, no. My grandmother too. It shocks me when women are coarse. Women should preserve grace and femininity. Those are the things that attract me to women. Of course, a woman has to let it down during moments of desire in private; she can't always be the reserved lady. I proposed marriage twice in my life, once to a childhood sweetheart and once to a nymphomaniac. I am so glad I didn't get married. I would have no freedom, saddled with a family. Now I have nothing to tie me down, nothing except my sister Rose."

He changes the subject, pointing to the painting of Frank Merlo: "I had many more friends on Key West when he was alive. He was very popular. They say he could have been mayor of Key West. I've often wondered, if I concentrated on it, if I could become a great painter. I trained myself as a writer, in a way, learning stagecraft. But I never had any training as a painter. It comes from the same creative impulse. Sometimes I think of retiring to the Hotel de Cap on Cap

D'Antibes in the south of France. It is the most beautiful place I have ever been. I imagine setting an easel out there on the lawn. Monet painted well into his eighties, you know. I'd like to live until I am seventy-five unless I learn to paint very well. It's ridiculous to deny the creative powers don't ebb with age, and I don't delude myself that I will surpass my earlier writing because I don't think that's in the cards."

Are these thoughts of death, this desire to get away, a reaction to the troubles on Key West? "Oh, no. It really doesn't concern me. I do sleep with the door to my room locked at night. But there is violence everywhere. I was mugged once in New York City on my way back to my hotel on Madison and Fifty-fourth. A drunk black suddenly appeared alongside me and grabbed my right arm, saying, 'Give me your wallet.' I said I would as soon as he freed by arm so I could get it. He let go and I seized the moment to rush away from him. I'm lucky, you see."

How does he feel about the band of urchins yelling obscenities on his front porch? "Kids amuse themselves that way, you know."

What about Fontis? Isn't he worried the same people who murdered the gardener are after him? "It's peculiar the way they ransacked the two houses on the same night. They were obviously looking for something. Dope, probably. At least that was the first theory. I don't think there have been any alternative theories. The police called earlier today and told me that they had just opened the safe at the museum (the Railroad Museum where Fontis was curator) and found a stack of manuscripts this high." His gesture is as big as the tree of life. "He was a peculiar man. I guess he supposed the manuscripts would be worth a great deal some day and that he would outlive me." Alma's laugh. "He'd been systematically stealing papers over the course of the nine years he took care of my house. I never noticed any of them missing. It's very difficult to find somebody to occupy your house. He could be so freakish. He was a great, tall man, very burly, and I remember one day I heard a terrible shriek in the garden, somebody wailing 'I am a sick woman.' I called an ambulance, but the next time he started shouting like that, I didn't call one."

And again, perhaps to himself, Williams says, "I am not in the habit of retreat."

From *The Night of the Iguana:* "When the Mexican painter Siqueiros did his portrait of the American poet Hart Crane, he had to paint him with his eyes closed because he couldn't paint him with his eyes open—there was too much suffering in them and he couldn't paint it."

Tennessee Williams has fallen silent. Wearing only the robe, seated next to the shrine and the portrait of his dead lover who stares straight ahead, there is a nakedness about the playwright, except for one detail. He is wearing sunglasses in the dim room, as if to reveal his eyes, particularly in the final scene, is to reveal too much, to demand too little of his audience. Still silent, the playwright studies the shrine.

Miss Rose has been punished for her madness, diagnosed as lunacy. He has been honored for his, recognized as genius. Has he escaped?

"Oh, no," he says in that cadenced voice, "I have been punished, too, by her punishment, and by difficulties of my own."

❦ ❦ ❦

On February 25, 1983, Tennessee Williams was found dead at the Hotel Elysée in New York City. Even in death, he attracted the same kind of misinformation and controversy that dogged him in life. Erroneous news reports initially indicated that he had been stabbed on the streets of the city during a robbery attempt, and then later a report that he had choked on a bottle cap was also shown to be false. A long thin rubber medicine stopper was found in his mouth, but it was not considered by the medical examiner's office to be capable of obstructing breathing. The official cause of his death at the age of seventy-two was given as a combination overdose of alcohol and barbituates.

For a time, Williams's modest Bahamian-style house was on the market for $425,000. Some local islanders were hoping to encourage a group of investors to buy it as a tax deduction and turn it into a historical landmark. Eventually the three-bedroom cottage sold at fair market value for $235,000. According to an article in the *Miami Herald,* a deed restriction accompanied the sale which prohibits the new owners from using the name of Tennessee Williams in association with the property. The people who purchased the house, which had been empty since Williams's death, are from Hong Kong. Their last name is Paradise.

THE POPE
OF QUOTATIONS

"Yes to Zora Neale Hurston and Kate Chopin," Justin
Kaplan is saying. "Yes to Nelson Mandela and Alexander Dubcek. No to Liv Ullman and Jimmy Can-
non. More Woody Allen, less JFK, Ronald Reagan is wel-
come, as long as what he has to say is an accurate reflection of
him and his presidency. He shouldn't look too good. Dan
Quayle? Well, for this edition, anyway, I'll let him be a footnote. . . ."

And so it goes, the painstaking process of compiling the
sixteenth edition of Bartlett's *Familiar Quotations,* a process in
which its editor serves as both kingmaker and assassin to an
amazing variety of voices belonging to poets, crooks, movie
stars, politicians, songwriters, novelists, and others.

For two years, Kaplan has taken inventory of the culture in
every respect, from popular to literary and political, and he
has decided which snippets of whose words will be enshrined
in what is widely conceded to be the most famous and favored
reference book for quotes in the world, the book mined for
snatches of wisdom and foolishness by dinner speakers and
valedictorians and writers of term papers seeking to shore up
their rhetoric.

Photo © 1991 Daniel Sheehan/New York Newsday

"It's been fun," says Kaplan, sitting in his study at his house in Cambridge, Massachusetts. Harvard University is a short, tree-lined stroll in the distance, and his neighbors include John Kenneth Galbraith and Julia Child. The walls are decorated with likenesses of Freud (his wife's granduncle), Whitman (in his old age), and Baudelaire ("I like those empty eyes").

There is a beautiful photo of his wife, the novelist Anne Bernays, which he took at the hospital after the birth of the first of their three daughters, now grown. He calls her Annie and she calls him Joe. He apologizes, half-heartedly, for the flaking paint in his study. Although not from Cambridge, he has an adopted New Englander's disdain for external appointments. "I suppose it's ready for another paint job. The last one was in 1959.

"In fact, Bartlett's has been more than mere fun; it's been sinfully playful," says the writer, editor, and lecturer. Kaplan won a Pulitzer Prize in 1967 for his biography *Mr. Clemens and Mark Twain*. He has also written a biography of Lincoln Steffens, and his 1980 life of Walt Whitman won an American Book Award.

Tallish, sixty-five years old, Kaplan has youthful dark hair and an aura of thoughtfulness underscored by the eyeglasses resting on his most prominent feature—an impressive nose, which, viewed from one angle, seems to proceed in several directions at once and in that way to echo the habits of the author's mind.

He was chosen to revise "Bartlett's" by William Phillips, the editor-in-chief of Little, Brown, and Co., after one phone call: "I've known Joe for a number of years, and I called him for his advice on who to name for a new general editor, and when he offered himself for the task, the penny dropped. I thought: My God, what a brilliant suggestion. As soon as he put himself forward, there were no other candidates. The process of compiling a new 'Bartlett's' is different from a dictionary. It is not scholarly and objective in the same way. At the same time it aims to be inclusive, and I know of no one who rivals the breadth of his interests."

As playful as the work has been for the profoundly intellectual Kaplan, it has been serious as well, for the end result—published in the fall of 1992—will finally be a mirror of our culture and some of the changes that have taken place in how Americans experience the world since 1980, when the fifteenth edition was issued.

Emily Morrison Beck, editor of that edition as well as the one in 1968 and 1955, was proud to be able to include quotes from the astronauts (Neil Armstrong walking on the moon in

1969: "That's one small step for man, one giant leap for mankind") as well as from rock stars such as Bob Dylan and from cowboy songs, sea shanties, and spirituals, most of them for the first time. She was thrilled when she found out that Kaplan was her successor and she had two pieces of advice: "I called him up and I told him, whatever you do, don't have a collaborator. To do the job right you have to rely on personal taste."

What was her other bit of advice for the new editor? "Oh," she answers, in her lofty voice spiced with merriment, "be sure to ask for a lot of money."

The new "Bartlett's" will be a mirror of Kaplan's unique vision of our culture. "A book like this cannot be done by committee or consensus; it would be too unwieldy," he says. "Ultimately, I'm a one-man band." Under Kaplan the cultural base will be even broader, and of course the first step in adding newcomers entails kicking some people out. "About one-third of the book consists of references from Shakespeare and the Bible and Milton and certain standard romantic and Victorian poets," says Kaplan. "In that sense, 'Bartlett's' functions as a kind of home concordance. There were few trims possible or desirable in either category."

Kaplan deleted some modern authors (if you are quoted in "Bartlett's," you are automatically called an author) including John Ciardi, a poet of some popularity about twenty years ago, and also the actress and writer Liv Ullman, the height of whose popularity coincided with the publication of the 1980 edition. Spencer Tracy is no longer in the book, but that's at least in part because Kaplan believes in attributing lines spoken by movie actors to the screenwriter whenever possible. But an actor who says something witty on his own will be credited with the quote, as in Cary Grant's famous observation: "Everyone wants to be Cary Grant. Even I want to be Cary Grant." The main place where the new editor got to be Mr. Scissorhands on a large scale was with the abundant representation of flowery English poets whose words today seem a deadening combination of ornamentation for its own sake and irrelevancy.

Some aspects of "Bartlett's" will remain the same. One is the order of presentation of the quotations. The authors are presented chronologically by birthdate (there is also an index listing keywords from quotations). "Once you open up 'Bartlett's,' you can't help but hop around it for a while. It has a wonderful feel—a reading book as well as a reference book," Kaplan says.

One of Kaplan's goals was to move away from Beacon Hill and Harvard as primary sources of quotations. He keeps a list of an informal breakdown of the background of the 250 new names; at a recent count, there were four Native Americans, seventeen blacks, forty-four women, sixty sources who lived in the United Kingdom and its Commonwealth and eighty-seven "O.F.s"—code for "other foreigners." There has been in the past, he says, "a shameful absence of blacks, women, and other minorities."

As for who these new authors are, Kaplan says: "Some quotes I picked simply because I liked them. I have a fairly good memory, and often I could remember the circumstances of when they were said but everything is checked by myself or by one of my two researchers. An example of something that just sticks in your memory is what Everett Dirksen once said, 'A billion here, a billion there, and pretty soon you're talking about real money.' I liked that because it was so direct, so American. I can't imagine a Frenchman, for instance, expressing himself in exactly those words. This is essentially an American book, although it will be promoted in the United Kingdom and I tried to give the book a more transatlantic global flavor.

"In that same category, one could include Marshall Field, who said, 'Give the lady what she wants' and also, for its native flavor, the famous lines of Nelson Algren: 'Never play cards with any man named "Doc." Never eat at any place named "Mom's." And never, ever, no matter what else you do in your life, never sleep with anyone whose troubles are worse than your own.'

"Or how about this one from a Tammany Hall politician by the name of George Washington Plunkett: 'I seen my opportunities and I took'em.' Or Sgt. Dan Daly during World War I urging his troops to battle, 'Come on, you sons of bitches. Do you want to live forever?' Or Duke Ellington, 'It don't mean a thing if it ain't got that swing.'

"Another example of a very American-sounding quote came from Norman Mailer's *The Executioner's Song*. I was amazed to discover that Mailer was missing from the previous 'Bartlett's,' and I'm not sure why unless it's that he is a hard writer to quote from because his prose often consists of one extended riff after another. I knew I wanted him represented in the new edition and I ended up choosing something he wrote about Marilyn." What Mailer had written about Marilyn Monroe was that she was "every man's love affair with America, Marilyn Monroe who was blonde and beautiful and had a sweet little rinky-dink of a voice and all the cleanliness of all the clean American backyards. She was our angel, the sweet angel of sex, and the sugar of sex came up from her like a resonance of sound in the clearest grain of a violin."

Kaplan also quoted from Mailer's *The Armies of the Night*, but said the quotation that seemed absolutely American came from *The Executioner's Song*. It was from a scene in the book describing Gary Gilmore's execution: "Then the warden said, 'Do you have anything you'd like to say?' and Gary looked up at the ceiling and hesitated, then said, 'Let's do it.' That was it.

"What I liked was that expression, 'Let's do it.' So pure and laconic, so down to earth. Especially under the circumstances."

Kaplan relied on his own vast reading as well as conversations with his wife to increase the number of women in the book.

"For instance, Joyce Carol Oates will be quoted for the first time. The mystery is that she hasn't been quoted previously. She's one of those writers who are always being talked about for the Nobel, and so she's included, at least in part, as insurance in case that happens. Alice Walker appears in the new edition several times, including, 'I think it pisses God off if you walk by the color purple in a field somewhere and don't notice it.'

"I've quoted Kate Chopin, a turn-of-the-century writer who went out of favor partly because of what was considered the daring nature of her subject matter, but who was rediscovered in the past twenty years or so by the feminists. Here are the quotes: 'Mrs. Pontellier was beginning to realize her position in the universe as a human being, and to recognize her relations as an individual within and about her.' That's from *The Awakening*. So is, 'For the first time in her life she stood naked in the open air, at the mercy of the sun, the breeze that beat upon her, and the waves that invited her.' I have tried to include quite a few writers who have been discovered by feminists in recent years. I have added Zora Neale Hurston, who wrote *Their Eyes Were Watching God:* 'Women forget all those things they don't want to remember and remember everything they don't want to forget. The dream is the truth. Then they act and do things accordingly.' "

The Nigerian writer Chinua Achebe will be quoted, as will the Czech writer Milan Kundera. To make room for them, there will be somewhat less Henry James, less Emerson, less Oliver Wendell Holmes. Certainly not all of the quotes in "Bartlett's" are literary, and some of the new literary quotes are plain entertainment as well, such as the light verse of Richard Armour:

Shake and shake the ketchup bottle
None will come out and then a lottle.

"I've chosen a lot of slogans that are part of the popular landscape, like 'A woman without a man is like a fish without a bicycle.' I wrote to three prominent feminists, Barbara Ehrenreich, Gloria Steinem, and Betty Friedan, asking for their suggestions. Implicit in the letter was the invitation to submit their own work and not one of them responded. Annie said her theory is, 'We're so used to being left out we can't handle being included.' Quotes from leading feminists were taken from their written works. Besides writing to the feminists, Kaplan also wrote numerous others in his search for quotations. He also spread the word by sundry means that he was looking for quotes. And many came flowing to his desk, en route to publication.

"Lenny Bruce is quoted, about how humor has to be dark and destructive," Kaplan says. "Degas is quoted about how painting requires as much calculation as crime. Abbie Hoffman is in there for what he said about how sacred cows make the best hamburger. I've quoted from the movie *Star Wars,* 'May the force be with you,' and the witch's words in the *Wizard of Oz,* 'I'll get you, my pretty, and your little dog too,' as well as what the wizard says: 'I'm not a bad man, just a very bad wizard.'

"The Beatles are quoted, not just their lyrics, but also that comment about being more popular than Jesus."

Some of the quotes, Kaplan says, are almost historic in that they recall an event or controversy that should be included at least partly as a matter of record. "Along those lines, I included Janet Malcolm's quote about how all journalists are con men," he says. "As another example, I quoted Ayatolla Ruholla Khomeini's death sentence against Salman Rushdie: 'The author of *The Satanic Verses* book, which is against Islam, the Prophet, and the Koran, and all those involved in its publication who were aware of its content, are sentenced to death. I ask all Moslems to execute them wherever they find them.' "

Kaplan says he also has a quote from Rushdie, but not from *The Satanic Verses.* There is no point in stirring up trouble, he says. "I have him saying, 'Literature is the one place in any society where, within the secrecy of our own heads, we can hear voices talking about everything in every possible way.' I wanted something to commemorate the thaw in U.S. and eastern European relations, which is why I included Alexander Dubcek's socialism with a human face, the slogan of the Prague Spring in 1968."

Margaret Thatcher is quoted: "If you want something said, ask a man; if you want something done, ask a woman."

There are several new entries about civil rights. "I quoted Rosa Parks recalling her refusal to give up her seat on a Montgomery, Alabama bus in 1955: 'I had felt for a long time that if I was ever told to get up so a white person could sit, that I would refuse to do so.' The quote from George Wallace makes him sound pitiful; it is from his inaugural address as governor of Alabama in 1963: 'I draw the line in the dust and toss the gauntlet before the feet of tyranny. And I say, Segregation now! Segregation tomorrow! Segregation forever!' "

Nelson Mandela is quoted twice, once for something he said while he was in prison: "Only free men can negotiate; prisoners cannot enter into contracts." He is also quoted for the words he spoke when he was sent to prison and spoke again on his release: "I have fought against white domination, and I have fought against black domination. I have cherished the ideal of a democratic and free society in which all persons will live together in harmony and with equal opportunities. It is an ideal which I hope to live for and achieve. But, if need be, it is an ideal for which I am prepared to die."

Kaplan regarded it as mandatory, in documenting recent scientific history, to include what James Watson and Francis Crick said upon discovering DNA: "This [double helix] structure has novel features which are of considerable biological interest. . . . It has not escaped our notice that the specific pairing we have postulated immediately suggests a possible copying mechanism for the genetic material." Watson's remark to the typist of his and Crick's original article is included as a footnote: "We told her that she was participating in perhaps the most famous event in biology since Darwin's book."

Footnotes, Kaplan notes, are a useful way of getting extra material into "Bartlett's." Dan Quayle is a footnote for the slogan of the United Negro College Fund, "A mind is a terrible thing to waste." Quayle got it wrong in a speech and said, "What a waste it is to lose one's mind."

As for Ronald Reagan, Kaplan says: "I didn't think it would be historically accurate to make him look too good. Some quotes which are widely attributed to him I trace back to the original source such as 'Go ahead, make my day,' which was spoken by Clint Eastwood in a movie called *Sudden Impact,* which was written by Joseph Stinson. The new edition has a trademark quip he made all the time while campaigning for governor of California in 1965, 'Government is like a big baby—an alimentary canal with a big appetite at one end and no responsibility at the other.' I'm also including his definition of Republicanism as the party that wants to see an America in which people can still get rich. And then in 1986, at the height of homelessness in this country, he said at a press conference, 'It's difficult to believe that people are starving in this country because food isn't available.' "

Recently, when Kaplan mentioned during a luncheon speech how he planned to quote Reagan, somebody asked why he was picking on Republicans. "I answered, well I'm picking on Democrats, too. Kennedy, for example, is quoted in the last edition of 'Bartlett's' saying all these saintly things that were for the most part hot air, and the product of his speech writers in the first place. A tricky point there; with a politician I use the reverse of my actor/screenwriter rule. You quote them, not the speech writer, because the convention is that the speech writer is hired to help them say what they want to be saying in the first place. I tried to find quotes from Kennedy that made him more earthbound as when he said, 'My father always told me that businessmen were sons of bitches.' I liked that. I also wrote a gloss about the famous 'Ich Bin Ein Berliner' quote, which is actually unidiomatic. In German, I am told, when the word Berliner is preceded by the article 'ein,' it connotes a form of pastry, so what Kennedy really said was, 'I am a jelly doughnut.' "

Under his screenwriter rule—which represents a change from previous editions of "Bartlett's"—Kaplan quotes Orson Welles for the famous line of dialogue from *The Third Man:* "In Italy for thirty years under the Borgias they had warfare, terror, murder, bloodshed, but they produced Michelangelo, Leonardo da Vinci, and the Renaissance. In Switzerland they had brotherly love, they had five hundred years of democracy and peace. And what did that produce? The cuckoo clock."

Film critic Pauline Kael is quoted: "The words 'Kiss Kiss Bang Bang,' which I saw on an Italian movie poster, are perhaps the briefest statement imaginable of the basic appeal of movies."

Woody Allen had been in "Bartlett's" previously, but Kaplan—mainly because Allen is "so good and so funny"—decided to beef up his section. Among the Allen quotes:

"Not only is there no God, but try getting a plumber on weekends."

"How wrong Emily Dickinson was! Hope is not 'the thing with feathers.' The thing with feathers has turned out to be my nephew. I must take him to a specialist in Zurich."

"It's not that I'm afraid to die. I just don't want to be there when it happens."

"On the plus side, death is one of the few things that can be done as easily lying down."

"Eighty percent of success is showing up."

From another screenwriter, Francis Ford Coppola, Kaplan quotes the lines from *Apocalypse Now:* "I love the smell of napalm in the morning. It smells like victory." A second Vietnam quote comes from Philip Caputo's *A Rumor of War:* "You're going to learn that one of the most brutal things in the world is your average nineteen-year-old boy."

Several Vietnam veterans told Kaplan that in a way, the quintessential quote from that war was "Sorry about that," as in, "We burned down your village, sorry about that." But Kaplan says: "The problem with that expression as a quote for 'Bartlett's' is that out of context it is so generic it has little meaning. Just because an expression is common doesn't mean it's worthy of 'Bartlett's.' For instance, I would be reluctant to include the expression you see on car mirrors all the time, 'Objects in the mirror are closer than they appear.' "

Kaplan has added a good deal of music to the new edition. "It seems to me that in some ways musical lyrics are our street poetry," he says. "Michael Jackson's in 'Bartlett's' for 'We Are the World.' I've added a lot more rock and roll. I had as my technical advisers for this category two friends who are in their late thirties, early forties. One of them, Joe Kahn, submitted two tapes of what he considered the correct choices, as well as four single-spaced pages of commentary and characterization. There are six new entries for Dylan. Grace Slick is quoted, so is Bruce Springsteen, Arlo Guthrie, 'You can get anything you want at Alice's Restaurant,' and Chuck Berry.

"Anonymous remains a big category. Sometimes you know when something was first said but you don't know the actual writer, as in "We are the people of this generation, bred in at least modest comfort, housed now in universities, looking uncomfortably to the world we inherit.' Do you recognize that as the Port Huron Statement [the founding manifesto of Students for a Democratic Society] made in 1962?"

Another anonymous quote came from the September 24, 1982, Morbidity and Mortality Weekly report published by the government: "A disease, at least moderately predictive of a defect in cell-mediated immunity, occurring in a person with no known cause for diminished resistance to that disease." That, Kaplan notes, was the first formal definition in print of AIDS. He also quotes Surgeon General Otis Bowen on AIDS: "When you sleep with someone, you sleep with everyone that person has ever slept with."

Among the authors quoted for the first time are Jerry Siegel and Joe Shuster. "You've probably never heard of them, but you have heard their words." They are the creators of the character Kaplan calls the best known in American fiction: "Faster than a speeding bullet, more powerful than a locomotive, able to leap tall buildings in a single bound—look, up in the sky, it's a bird, it's a plane, it's Superman!"

Ann Landers is also included. To wit: "Women complain about sex more often than men. Their gripes fall into two major categories: (1) Not enough (2) Too much."

"For a while I was telling interviewers that for the first time 'Bartlett's' will have four-letter words," Kaplan says. "But actually there have been four-letter words in the past. I personally don't see how we can talk without them, but whenever I get into a discussion of this there is always someone who is offended and it causes a terrible ruckus without any positive gain. Suffice it to say I will be quoting language which is closer to our daily usage. To this end, Erica Jong is one of my new authors, as in her famous zipless such and such. If that bothers old loyal readers on puritanical grounds, well, such and such them.

"I'm planning to quote 'The opera ain't over until the fat lady sings.' It took forever to find out who said that first, but I'm fairly well satisfied it came from Daniel Cook, a columnist for a newspaper in San Antonio. It was very hot in the eighties, like Andy Warhol's remark about how in the future we'll all be famous for fifteen minutes was popular in the seventies. Warhol, by the way, is also the author of the observation, 'Sex is the biggest nothing of all time.' I won't be quoting that. I mean, that's his problem."

The first "Bartlett's," which appeared in 1855, was the work of John Bartlett who, like Kaplan, lived in Cambridge, Massachusetts. Bartlett owned the University Bookstore, which still exists on Massachusetts Avenue. It was Bartlett's breathtaking ability to recall passages at an instant's notice from the many books he had read that prompted the first edition as a kind of public service to other readers.

In terms of the breadth of reading and scholarly interests, Kaplan is a worthy successor to the original editor. "I used to feel guilty about how I spent all my time screwing around with words," he says. "In fact, once when I was in my twenties and I felt that I should be a social worker and work with poor people, I spent a day in Hoboken, New Jersey, taking vocational tests. Anyway, when the final evaluation came in, it said my verbal interests ran off the scale, but helping other people didn't even register."

Born in Manhattan, Kaplan was the son of a Russian immigrant father. His American-born mother died when he was "seven or eight" and his father, who owned a small shirt-manufacturing company, died when he was "eleven or twelve." Young Kaplan found himself in the "absolutely fantastic position of being an orphan with an absolutely fantastic guardian, a brother who was nine years older." Kaplan offers two quotes about his early years that seem in their pith and poignancy worthy of "Bartlett's": "You can always tell an orphan" and "The difference between no money and a small amount is much greater than a small amount and a vast amount."

The money bequeathed by his father was enough to finance his years at Harvard, which he entered at age sixteen, and to free him during the first years out to pick and choose the kinds of editing projects that piqued his interests. Twice while he was at Harvard, Kaplan took leaves of absence and both times he headed west. While out West, he bummed around, pumping gas, growing chili peppers, trout fishing for the first time.

"It meant much more to me than going to Europe. It was a much more eye-opening experience. One of the questions in any culture is: Who owns it? Who has the right to work within it? If you are the child, as I was, of an immigrant father, you might feel that perhaps you don't have the same rights as people who were born here. But spending time in the West demonstrated to me just how big America is and how it is open to interpretation by more than just Anglos, but also Indians and Chicanos and so on. No one has a right to be proprietary.

"The experience taught me to follow my own impulses. Or I could quote Joseph Campbell, who is in the new 'Bartlett's,' by the way, with that revolting expression, 'Follow your bliss,' which keeps turning up everywhere."

Over the years, Kaplan has engaged in an impressive array of editing jobs. At the age of twenty-two he prepared a collection of the dialogues of Plato, about which he knew nothing at first.

"One thing that ignorance does is make you work harder," Kaplan says. He edited a book called *The Pocket Aristotle* and, in his oddest work, he compiled an anthology of misogynist statements entitled *With Malice Toward Women*. The year was 1949, when the social climate was much more tolerant of such an enterprise. Kaplan does not disown the work: "I was eager to work. I probably would have done Satan's biography if that was the only opportunity I had."

Biography still ranks as his great passion as a writer and, although he won't be quoting himself in the new "Bartlett's," he has quoted Julian Barnes from *Flaubert's Parrot,* who wrote: "Biography is like a net, a series of holes tied together with a string."

His wife calls him the Pope of Quotations. "I think he's a great intellectual, but he claims not to be one at all. When I first met him, Joe was pathologically shy. And then because he claims to have been smitten by me, his tongue was tied doubly: he was shy and he was shy of me. Finally, after he had asked me out and we had had trouble talking on several occasions, I suggested we go to the Metropolitan Museum of Art. He was editing a book about art and I thought maybe he'd start talking if we got into a place where there are pictures. He didn't, and finally out of exasperation I turned to him and asked, 'What are your enthusiasms?' And that has always been a private quote in our relationship. It sounds so clunky: 'What are your enthusiasms?' At the time I had no idea that his mind spread all over the place. He cares about so many things, from books to reading magazines to watching television to talking to people.

"He also has what I call a trick memory. He can remember everything he's ever read, I mean everything. Just the other day he brought up some dinner party we were at thirty-five years ago, and he could remember the entry number above the doorway at Adams House where he lived fifty years ago as a sophomore. But, if you listen to him, he's not an intellectual and he doesn't have a trick memory."

As for whatever burden Kaplan might feel about being true to the culture and historically accurate and fair, he says he has done his best to include quotes that are generally familiar, to be as representative of the broadest numbers of concerns as possible, and to include quotes that aren't familiar but should be. Part of the joy of the task has been the chance to reflect his own vast learning as well as eccentricities; as Henry Miller once put it, "If you can't be fair, be arbitrary."

One of the burdens of the job is that it has a built-in endless-ness; like the urge to eat peanuts or to watch the ocean, the research could go on forever. What about that Jack Nicholson quote about how a movie is PG-13 if you cut off a breast but R if you kiss it? People keep suggesting advertising slogans, such as "Where's the beef?" and "I can't believe I ate the whole thing," but Kaplan doesn't want to include just one or two without taking inventory of the entire advertising culture. And so it goes, on and on and on. The only reason it doesn't go on forever is because the final manuscript is scheduled by Little, Brown for publication and, to quote not "Bartlett's" but the nature of life itself:

Deadlines are deadlines.

❧ ❧ ❧

Justin Kaplan says he no longer dreams in quotes and that he is hoping to settle on a major writing project that compels him. He would like to launch a new biography, but he is waiting to find "the real right electrifying idea." There have been numerous false starts which entailed extensive preliminary work on Ulysses S. Grant, Charlie Chaplin, Willa Cather, Irving Berlin, and now Stephen Crane. He says that the biggest problems with biography often come from dealing with the subject's living relatives who want to place unacceptable caveats on the writer. "Either you trust me or you don't," he tells them. "The first rule of biography," he says, in yet another quote worthy of "Bartlett's," is "Shoot the widow."

THE OTHER SIDE
OF MARY GORDON

t the age of thirty-nine, after five books and two babies, Mary Gordon says she is ready to forsake her self-
imposed exile in the country and reenter the world. So
once a week she leaves her family in New Paltz, New York,
and takes the bus into the city, where she spends all day
Monday and most of Tuesday. Late in the afternoon on Monday she teaches a seminar in fiction writing to twelve young
women at Barnard College, the same seminar she attended in
the late sixties, when she was at Barnard.

To these students she is the older woman, the one with
experience, the famous writer, and they are soft-spoken in her
presence, studying her movements in the classroom as if they
were studying the migration of a fascinating new planet. She
is barely over five feet tall, yet she is imposing, mainly due to
her bearing and the confident set of the shoulders, but there is
something about the face as well, with its classical balance, the
large eyes, strong nose, and full lips.

"This is a community," she tells her class. "My teaching
style is not based on the male model. I am not a priest, and you
are not acolytes." They will be called upon to evaluate one
another's work, not attack it: charity must reign. Finally, she
wants no excuses. They are to do the work and get it in on

time. "If you think you don't have time to write now," she says, "just wait."

When she was her students' age, Mary Gordon used to think of herself as a monster writer. But now, she says, her ruling passion is motherhood: Her daughter is nine, and her son turns six in December.

Yet, despite the distraction and the tumble of domestic life, she remains in many ways intensely literary. The bookshelf in her kitchen is stacked with novels.

When her son was born, she wanted him to have a godmother to reckon with, someone both fierce and wonderful, on the theory that it is harder to be a boy, harder to be a good man in the world, and that a powerful outside female influence would not hurt. She picked her old friend Toni Morrison.

She is clearly thrilled that her daughter is already showing interest in becoming a writer. For a while the child was working on her own book about five girls who go away to school and are each given the exact same room, but the differences in how they decorate the rooms and keep them up reveal the complex differences in their characters. "That's very good," says the mother, "don't you think?"

When the baby sitter starts looking up "lumbago" in the dictionary to tell the children its meaning, Mary Gordon can't help but interject herself: "What's that? Lumbago? Now why would you be teaching that to my daughter?" Her voice rings with delight, the surprised delight of someone who has caught an exceptionally flattering glimpse of herself in the mirror. She says that the most gratifying moment of motherhood so far came when she and her daughter, reading *Little Women* together, sobbed in tandem over Beth's death.

Mary Gordon lives in a world of many self-appointed literary mothers. Her studio has three photos of her favorites lined up in succession: George Eliot, Virginia Woolf, and Jane Austen. She refers to Virginia Woolf as her "impossible, unearthly literary mother." It was Woolf, of course, who wrote, "A

© Joyce Ravid

woman must have money and room of her own if she is to write fiction."

She took the words to heart, and when her first novel, *Final Payments,* was published in 1978 and proved to be an unexpected financial success, providing her with a kind of writer's dowry, she took the proceeds and literally spent them on a room of her own, a small cabin in the woods about fifteen minutes by car from her house in downtown New Paltz. On good days it is even a room with a view of the Hudson River.

Every summer, she and her husband, Arthur Cash, a professor at the State University of New York at New Paltz known in academic circles for his biography of British novelist Laurence Sterne, rent a house in Wellfleet for the month of August. It is big and old with slanty, settled floors and a ramp in back for the writer's mother, who is eighty-one and uses a wheelchair most of the time because of the progressive crippling that comes from the polio she contracted as a child. In the mornings the children attend day camp, which ends at 1

P.M. Their mother awakens early, runs, and then works until they come home.

Even on the Cape she tries to work every day. She says she feels itchy and crabby if she can't, "extremely displaced. Renoir said it was important to draw every day, even if the only thing you draw is an apple in the margin of your notebook. I don't care if it's only two sentences in my journal. As long as it's something," she says.

In terms of her lineage, Mary Gordon is a perfect flowering of an immigrant culture: she is half-Jewish, one-quarter Italian, and one-quarter Irish, a mix that is not as much a clash as a unique new thing. Her Jewish father converted to Catholicism. He met and married her mother, late in life for both of them, after being introduced by a priest who ran retreats.

As for personal identification with one group more than another, the Irish won out, and it is curious to Gordon how dominating the Irish sensibility can be, especially since she finds so much of it to be, if not negative, then troubling. "To be Irish," she says, "it to be mired in inaction. If you don't believe me, read Joyce's *The Dubliners*. Those stories are filled with people who just let life surround them.

"There is nothing intrinsically thin-blooded about the Irish," she says. "They have a love of liquor and the horses and love of talk, as long as the purpose of the talk is to amuse rather than reveal. The Irish seem to believe totally in the sacredness of the secret. To keep a secret is more sacred than to tell a story.

"At its worst, the Irish culture is a narrow-minded, death-dealing, body-hiding culture. All the Catholic countries propagandized against sex, but Ireland is the only country that produced men who actually believed the church. Yet the Irish are always interesting, partly because of their very hiddenness. One has a sense of breaking into a buried treasure: of discovering news."

But the place where she identifies the greatest vacuum in Irish contributions to the American culture is in literature.

She seems to view Irish-American writing as the literary equivalent of penny candy, a root-beer barrel of words. She says Eugene O'Neill and F. Scott Fitzgerald have the right-sounding last names, but for the most part their work was not concerned with exposing their culture. "You could go then to James T. Farrell, whose *Studs Lonigan* recorded—with vigor but, to my mind, with sloppiness that borders on the dime novel—the experience of the Chicago Irish in the 1920s and 1930s. You have to jump, then, to J. F. Power's brilliant tales of fifties priests. Then you could go on to William Alfred's *Hogan's Goat,* to Elizabeth Cullinan, to Maureen Howard, and William Kennedy. After Howard and Kennedy," she says, "there is no place else to go."

Until, of course, *The Other Side,* Mary Gordon's latest novel, in which she tries to take on the Irish and their fate here, to capture, in essence, the tension that occurs when a bright, tragic, gifted people who feel a blood call to doom graft themselves onto a culture that believes in bootstrap optimism, in the inevitability of advancement due to bustle and enterprise. The Protestant notion that day-by-day things improve in every way is the exact opposite of the Irish belief in the downward, mournful pull of Providence, of earthly tribulation.

"For the Irish," Gordon writes in her new novel, "unhappiness was bred into the bone, a code of weakness. The sickle-cell anemia of the Irish: they had to thwart joy in their lives. . . . You see it everywhere in Irish history; they wouldn't allow themselves to prosper."

The idea for *The Other Side* began years ago, when she was an only child on Long Island and would sometimes visit her friend Kathy and observe Kathy's grandparents. They had immigrated here and had a great story to tell, but little of it was ever shared. Like the Vincent he became in *The Other Side,* her friend's grandfather was a machinist, an engineer, and the most courtly man Mary Gordon can ever remember meeting. The grandmother had come here and worked as a maid and then as a "needlewoman," and she was peppery and feisty, railing against big business and for Roosevelt and unions.

The author knew that much and one other thing: when the grandmother had a terrible, disabling stroke, she also became deranged and started ranting, spouting venom and filth. "It was one of the most frightening things I ever witnessed," Gordon recalls. In real life, as in the novel, the husband remained caretaking at the side of this woman who had become a libel of her former self. If in the Irish character there is any undisputed universal, it is loyalty.

The original Ellen and Vincent were not articulate old people. "They were typical of their kind: They didn't use a language to communicate so much as to entertain," Gordon says. "Language is a carapace that hides the true pain, not that they were silent—they weren't—but you didn't get a lot of emotional information from them. They would find that unseemly." To flesh out the bones of the story, Gordon relied on her travels to Ireland. She has been there five times, once right after college, later with her mother, and then three times by herself for stretches of about ten days each to research *The Other Side*. The book follows Ellen and Vincent on their separate journeys from Ireland to this country, documents their meeting, their marriage, the three children, their grandchildren, and their great-grandchildren. The central action of the novel occurs on a single, heightened emotionally topheavy day. The family has assembled for a homecoming: Vincent, now in his late eighties, has been in a Catholic home for many months, recovering from a fall that occurred when his frail wife flailed at him after mistaking his grasp at her lap as sexual overture; in truth he was trying to pry pills from her grip so he could crush them and give them to her in her ice cream.

Ellen is bedridden, sometimes senile, sometimes aphasic; withered, too long in this life, reduced from her early pro-

Roosevelt days when she was a vibrant fighter. Then she was filled with the juice of conviction, her face was radiant, she had flames for eyes. But now she is stooped and nearly incontinent, not quite human.

The MacNamara family is not some rollicking, idealized clan. The hate in this family, Gordon writes, "unfolds, like a paper flower in water. It exfoliates, intricately, as if touched by some seasonal impulse. It unrolls and throws itself out like a bolt of cloth." How all these lives are shaped by shame, by that deadening brew of embarrassment and guilt and the need to keep things hidden, is an overriding theme of the book and, according to its author, an essentially Irish view of life.

When asked to identify the hallmark of her own Irishness, Gordon is a bit more on the positive side. She says she is a little suspicious of pleasure. But only a little. She likes to laugh a lot. And she has this tic, which she considers Irish, of a heightened moral consciousness.

At many provocations, both big and slight, she is capable of a fine sermonizing fury. At those times her voice is likely to tremble, not from a lack of conviction but from the opposite, the pure passion.

Mary Gordon has a serious face. The dignity and proportions of the features, the solemn evenness, function like a tattoo: Born to crusade. In old book jackets from her early work, with her bangs and dark pageboy and oddly elderly knowing eyes, she calls to mind St. Joan.

When Salman Rushdie's life was threatened last spring because his novel, *The Satanic Verses*, offended Muslims, Gordon was one of the leading New York authors who took to the streets to protest. She is extremely active in Catholics for Choice. "An eleven-week-old fetus is not a baby," she says. "It's tremendously important to choose to be a mother. For a child, any child, to be a curse instead of a blessing is a terrible thing." When she gives her Barnard students her address and phone number, she implores them to keep them absolutely private because her outspoken views have made her the target of death threats from the Catholic right.

Her fervor extends to ideas about writing. In class her advice on writing bristles with the righteous voice of well-deserved authority. This semester she has assigned the short stories of Kafka and Katherine Mansfield. "Kafka's not exactly on the vaudeville circuit," she says by way of half an apology. "But you will find that all the writers I like to read are extremely sad."

As for Mansfield, "Her stories don't get read much lately because she's not desperately chic. I am interested in Katherine Mansfield because I feel she's very female, in a way I don't feel Emily Dickinson, Jane Austen, and Virginia Woolf are particularly female. With writers like Mansfield and Colette, I am always aware of the female body in the middle of the prose. As women, we are often asked to read male writers and say how much we like what they choose to write about—rape, war, disembowelment—to show how cool we are. But when women write about motherhood and children and sexual love and the female body, it embarrasses people, and therefore a whole lot of writers get cut out of the respectable pie."

Gordon does not shy away from the female body. Her students would be well advised to read, for example, this passage from "Safe," a Gordon story in a collection entitled *Temporary Shelter:*

"I step out of the shower and begin to dry myself. I see the two of them looking at me: man and child, she in his arms. She stretches out her arms at me in that exaggerated pose of desperation that can make the most well-fed child suggest that she belongs on a poster, calculated to rend the heart, urging donations for the children of a war zone or a famine-stricken country. I take her in my arms. She nose-dives for my breast. My husband holds my face in both his hands. 'Don't take your diaphragm out,' he says. Just ten minutes ago I fed my child; just last night I made love to my husband. Yet they want me again and again. My blood is warmed, then fired with well-being. Proudly I run my hands over my own flesh, as if I had invented it."

In the classroom, Gordon is brimming with tips:

"If you want to create a character who is not psychologically astute, but you want to make the reader see the side of that character, one way to do it would be to make her a good observer."

"Be careful when you write about light and shadows and reflections. It is hard for most readers to get what you mean when you try to show how light strikes things. The danger is it makes them feel like they are back in fourth-grade science, and failing."

"Don't take one part of speech and force it to become another. If you do you'll be guilty of all kinds of tonal mistakes: He 'stilled into sleep,' he 'pleasured' her, they 'partied.' I don't like the amphibious use of language. A verb is a verb."

Afterward, when she is complimented on the high-Fahrenheit quality of her advice, she demurs. "If you think I force my views on students now, you should have seen me the year I taught at Amherst College in 1979. I remember telling one class that if anyone in it did not like *Persuasion,* by Jane Austen, not to tell me because if I knew that, I could no longer like or respect them as a person." She still has pockets of such ardor even today. She won't read anything by Hemingway anymore because "he's a sexist, and therefore he's a liar, and I don't read liars."

The Irish tic of always seeing everything in the starkest of terms, in black and white with no shadings, can precipitate attacks of conscience at the oddest times. Last year, during what was conceived as an innocent trip to Sturbridge Village with her children, she noticed as they moved from one perfectly replicated building to another her growing discomfort with the way nineteenth-century village life was being presented. She went on to one exhibit where a woman in an apron and a bonnet talked about all the uses of products that come from sheep. At another exhibit yet another equally mild woman in an apron and a bonnet talked about cooking corn-bread in a skillet on an open hearth. Yet again a woman in an apron and a bonnet extolled the joys of making candles from scratch.

Gordon found herself feeling overwhelmed by what she felt was an essential falseness of a place that would turn history into such a seamless idyll. Before she could stop herself, she turned to one of these women, wed to what she saw as a basically harmless Sturbridge Village script, and demanded: "Isn't the vision here pretty corrupt? Isn't it wrong to present an entire town and play only one note?"

With her children virtually dragging their mother from the exhibit, she continued: "Where's the hardship? Where's the poverty?"

Hardship and working-class poverty are not unfamiliar to the novelist. Her father died when she was eight, and although he doted on her, he was not the most provident of fathers.

While he pursued doomed businesses (one was a series of religious cards with great works of art rather than the cornier icons that Mary Gordon says most Catholics prefer), her mother was forced to find work as a legal secretary at a not particularly thriving firm, where she stayed for forty-one years.

After her father died, her mother, her aunt, and her grand-mother all moved into the same house and pooled resources. Practically the first thing Gordon tells an interviewer is, "Let me disabuse you of the notion of an extended family as a vast nurturing network. My family was not into play. The mes-sage always was: life is tough, and you can't fool around."

Her first marriage, to a professor, came when she was very young. She says she married out of insecurity. It was so long ago that her mother pretends it never happened.

Gordon says that shortly after she married Arthur Cash

someone in her family died, and she asked her husband to accompany her to the funeral as moral support. "I remember on the plane down to Florida I told him that the people in my family are the meanest people in the world. Well, of course, he is used to how I exaggerate, and when we got to the funeral, I remember I was there with my new baby, and instead of congratulating me, people kept coming up and saying things like, 'Well, it's about time' and 'At least you can finally afford to have children.' On the plane on the way back, Arthur leaned over and said to me, 'You were right. Those are the meanest people in the world.'"

"The most important event of my early life was my father's departure from it," Gordon has written in an essay entitled "David." He died after suffering a heart attack in the New York Public Library. He did not hold a traditional job but wrote odd, even vicious, diatribes. He adored Franco and was drawn to Catholicism because of its right wing. He believed in a conspiracy of international bankers. One of his articles was entitled "Roosevelt: The Antichrist."

Yet he was also the one who told her stories at bedtime, and they often palled around together. She remembers going into the city with him and visiting a bar in the theater district, where a very drunk woman put a hand on her hair and said, "Remember, always brush your hair a hundred strokes a day," and then passed out. Gordon remembers that her father "took the occasion to tell me that God loved drunks and thieves sometimes more than respectable people. I could not have been more than five."

Her first novel, *Final Payments* (with its wonderful first line: "My father's funeral was full of priests"), is about the insane grief that overtakes a woman who for years has taken care of an ailing father who then dies.

In her own life, Gordon recalls spending the first four or five years after her father's death in exile with books. It was only when she turned twelve or thirteen that she began to experience happiness again. At school she became a cutup, a sort of clown, and she remembers thinking that to make others laugh was to know joy.

She tells a story of being about four years old and in a dance recital. Her father was so excited that he got diarrhea and stationed himself in the back of the auditorium to be near a bathroom. But when his daughter came on stage, he could not help shouting, "There she is! That's my little girl!"

"He had a tremendous gift for children," Gordon says. "He was the only person who ever made me feel that special, and all my life I have known I would never be made to feel that special again. Despite his death, I was tremendously beloved by a parent gifted at love for seven years, and that's so much better than what most people get." Her father remains "the first object of romance," she says. "In the end, I named my son for him."

She named her daughter, Anna, for her mother.

Her mother lives three blocks from her house in New Palz. Gordon sees her mother several times a week, the most important being on Sundays and Holy Days of Obligation.

This summer, at the noon Mass on the Feast of the Assumption at St. Peter's Church in Provincetown, the most touching sight is that of Mary Gordon, with a characteristic look of determination on her face, wheeling her mother up a ramp into church: filial devotion personified. The mother has on a new blue blouse purchased by her daughter; she is fair, with a fine, pure-boned Irish face, with a wonderful soft puff of white Irish hair.

This is the modern church. Gone are the mantillas and the white gloves and the old, high ways of Latin, that sense of garbled secrets being sent to the sky. It is not total ruination, a great beauty gone haggish, but for anyone familiar with the Roman Catholic church before 1963, there is now always a small sigh for bygone standards. The current casualness

can be shocking, as if the Ritz allowed patrons to take afternoon tea in cut-off jeans and curlers, chewing gum all the
while.

"Don't present a falsely pious picture of me," Gordon says.
"I don't want to seem like one of the characters in my books."
The author has had a complicated relationship with the church.
She went to Catholic grammar school and high school. She
was taught by Josephite nuns, who she recalls as being "very
strict but also very dumb. They managed to combine being
very ill educated with being very strict about all the wrong
things. Everything seemed to center on neatness and appearance, and content was really pretty irrelevant." By the
time she was ten, she says, she was smarter than all her
teachers.

The second time she was married, it was by a priest, and she
has chosen to raise her children in the church, though they
also celebrate Jewish holidays (in honor of her father). And
because her husband is an Episcopalian, they sometimes attend those services as well.

Just before Mass begins on that gray summer day, she slips
out to the parking lot to get a Diet Coke from the vending
machine. When the vending machine balks at accepting her
coins, she pounds it slightly. "Oh, now look how God is
punishing me," she says. Then a whir and a clank. Pardon,
reprieve, forgiveness: the Coke. "Church means everything
to my mother. It is her whole life. It means everything to her
that I go to Mass," she says. "Everything."

She says she takes Communion. Yet isn't that the ultimate
signal that she agrees with everything the church stands for
when she more than admits she doesn't? Is not the act of
accepting the Eucharist into her body a way of saying "I agree
to your rules"?

She takes a swig of her soda. There is bravura in the gesture,
a faint air of felony, or at least hooky: the longer it takes to
drink her soda, the closer she comes to missing the Introit. "I

guess we should go in," she says. And then, confidentially, "Wait until you see who goes to this church. The median age of the parishioners is"—and this is said like the kid who is the cutup, with swagger and the wish to shock—"dead."

On the way back to the cottage, the elderly Mrs. Gordon says that she has tried to read her daughter's latest book, and she liked it very much, although there certainly were a lot of characters. Gordon says her mother reads books by only two authors: herself and Erle Stanely Gardner.

Erle Stanely Gardner?

"The man who wrote the Perry Mason series."

No matter where the elderly Mrs. Gordon's remarks begin, they seem to have a way of propelling themselves toward some religious point. A typical progression:

"Mary is a good daughter.

"Her husband, Arthur, is as good as any son could be.

"Every morning I say a Rosary for Mary and her family.

"I have, you know, a great devotion to Our Mother."

"Can Mommy ever get enough kisses?" It is late September, and the writer has just arrived home after her weekly overnight trip to the city. Lately she has been dreaming about moving the whole family to Manhattan, making that hard trade of serenity for stimulation. At a glance, New Paltz appears to be a worn-out kind of town, with lots of doughnut shops and three inexpensive motels, one of which is conveniently located next to a new business, a bar with exotic dancers. Her children are in public school, and although Gordon likes the democratizing nature of public education ("My children go to school with children who have cars rusting in their back yards, and I like that"), she also thinks that they need greater challenges than they are getting. Her son, David, is a slight, handsome, nimble child, sweet, an entertainer. "He's the person who is always doing funny things with hats: For his birthday he wants a tuxedo. He's Cary Grant."

She worries that Anna, now in fourth grade, is lacking

in compassion and sometimes calls her daughter Margaret Thatcher. But she was recently thrilled to discover that her daughter, who is pretty and exceptionally articulate (she uses words like "exceptionally"), has been choosing to sit next to a kindergarten child who sometimes cries on the school bus and has actually been offering comfort. Her mother beholds a trend worth embracing: "When I was Anna's age, I used to tell people my favorite color was orange because everyone else always chose blue, and I felt so sorry for orange."

The minute she arrives home, which happens to be at the dinner hour, there is a subtle surrender of the kitchen to her deft short-order skills (fresh fish, grilled; broccoli done so it's crisp and then lightly seasoned with sesame oil; a salad with apples and tomatoes).

The house is not excessively tidy, and the kitchen floor is an instant repository for the flow of books and boots and brief-cases. She prides herself on being able to put up with messiness. "Eighty percent of the yelling that goes on between parents and children is because parents are trying to get their children to be less messy," she says. "I have a great tolerance for certain kinds of chaos."

Her husband looks professorial, with his glasses, his fringe of gray hair, and his always thoughtful face, made strong by a square jaw. He is quick to give her those spousal updates that always greet a returning parent, coded bulletins about the children: "David is upset because he wants to watch 'He-Man' cartoons, something I told him neither you nor I particularly approve of."

Anna does her homework, some kind of genealogical study that requires her to list every known person in the family tree, living and dead. This includes Arthur's children from his first marriage, one of whom Anna happily notes was born in the same year as Mary Gordon: 1949. Mary Gordon does not discuss Arthur's family except to say the children are all grown and "in Hawaii."

At home, after being away for several days, there is the

usual onslaught of messages, only some of which seem to be conveyed properly. They range from the mundane—the times of Anna's soccer practices and David's painting lessons—to the solemn: Mary McCarthy, author of *Memories of a Catholic Girlhood* and a professor at Bard, is ill (she would die a few weeks later, of cancer) and has asked Gordon to take over a class in the Hardy part of Thomas Hardy and D. H. Lawrence. "God, I always thought she didn't approve of me, I didn't quite measure up," Gordon says. "Back when I was in high school I used to dream that maybe she would someday be my mother-in-law. Somehow I had learned that she had a son who was close to my age." And then, "I can think of worse things to do than spending the weekend rereading Hardy."

A couple of messages are garbled. She gives her husband a look that is both tolerant and upbraiding. Then, as she removes the dishes, she mutters under her breath, addressing the tablecloth, "God, if men would just stop pouring all their brains into their sperm they use to overpopulate the world, maybe then there would be something left over, so they could be . . . sensible."

She hugs and kisses her son and answers her own question: "No, Mommy can never get enough kisses."

Every weekday that she can, from 10:30 in the morning until about 5:30 in the afternoon, Mary Gordon goes to her studio in the woods. It cost her fourteen thousand dollars in 1979. Over the years she has done nothing to improve it: There's electricity but no running water. "I chose not to put in water," she says. "I wanted to be in a place where domesticity was impossible. You'll see: It has a screened-in porch that I've been meaning to sweep for months."

Gordon's cabin is so remote that she usually takes her dog with her, as company and as protection. On good days the river is in full view, but on this soggy fall day it is just a promise in the distance covered with mist.

To get to the cabin, Gordon must walk down a twisting

trail, a cordlike path through the woods. This walk is her transition time, from the world of soccer practices to the world of mind and memory.

Inside, the cabin is moist and dark and shadowed. It is as close to being outdoors as a house can be, a breathing feral place. There is a phone, if she really feels a need for other voices, and a sagging old sofa on which she sometimes cat-naps. This used to make her feel guilty until Toni Morrison told her, "It's all work, even the dream time."

On warm days she often takes a book and sits in a cushiony chair on the porch. "Really," she says, gesturing toward a thick bank of clouds, "there is a river out there someplace."

"You know," she says, "my family would be happy if I never wrote another word again. My children would love to have me at home at their beck and call twenty-four hours a day. If you were to ask my husband if he supports me in my work, he would answer, yes, absolutely, of course he does. And in his mind he is satisfied that he does. But what I notice is that he intrudes on my solitude by making mistakes. It bothers me profoundly that there's a mommy track but there is not a daddy track. It's not even factored into the equation, not a feather on the scale."

In her studio, beside the framed photos of Eliot and Austen and Woolf, there is a picture of Pope John XXIII, a photo of Gordon's father (when she was a child, she says, she resem-bled him to a degree that was comical), and a photo of the original Ellen and the original Vincent, in which the old woman is looking straight ahead, as if about to make some wry, wise remark, and her husband is looking protectively toward her. She kept the photo on her mantel during the composition of *The Other Side*.

Her hands graze against her desk. Here, on good days, peace comes dropping slow. Here, on good days, she writes and writes, always in longhand.

She loves it, her odd calling, that hard, sweet labor of summoning the entire universe by fixing herself in silence at one small part of it, at a desk, with a pencil, hour upon hour, lifting mist, finding rivers.

❦   ❦   ❦

The Other Side was considered by most critics to be the author's most shapely fiction to date, unified not by the mechanics of plot so much as place: the single setting of the MacNamara's family house. Judith Thurman, in a review published in the *New Yorker* on March 12, 1990, praised Gordon's sentences as matter-of-fact. "Poetic lushness has been suppressed," the critic wrote, saying the rich, thick sentences of the author's earlier work were "like the kind of lavish hair that outrivals a woman's face."

The reviewer compared Gordon's narrative style in this work to series of portraits with "classical composure, even a grandeur. A perfectly rendered solitary sitter dominates the foreground of each picture, and in the background an open window reveals a landscape, or a vignette from the past, or a room where someone is being married, flagellated, or born."

A collection of the author's nonfiction prose entitled *Good Boys and Dead Girls* was published in the spring of 1991. It received an excellent review in the *New York Times:* "Through these essays the reader understands, like the work of the writers and painters she most admires, Mary Gordon's work is buttressed by a powerful moral vision."

AT NOBODY'S
MERCY

There is something contradictory about Liberty City, with the sad irony of its name. The sun here is just as fierce and cleansing as it is in Kendall. The streets are wide. The cars are big. Two and two make four, but sunlight and palm trees should not add up to deprivation, should not equal a ghetto.

Liberty City is "that place," a vast area that begins just west of Biscayne Boulevard and stretches toward Hialeah. Filled with "those people." If a white man in a suit is seen near the projects here, he is generally taken for a bill collector.

The most obvious sign of despair is the grown men, in clusters, hanging around storefronts, hanging around bars and lounges like Old Hickory, the Palace, or Tiny's where there is a sign outside the men's room spelled this way: "No Drug's."

Even the men sometimes talk about how bad it is, how the teenagers are crazy, out of control, on every corner selling something they shouldn't be selling. The vogue among them is to sell drugs under the name of astrological signs: Want some Pisces? Some Capricorn? The men talk about how in the old days everybody on the block would whip your butt if you did something wrong; the whole neighborhood raised the

Miami Herald photo by Brian Smith

children. Today the kids don't even speak right; they don't as the saying goes, "know their Webster's." And after saying all this, the men take another sip of whatever it is they are sipping. The day has just begun.

If there is any sign of hope on the streets, it is the spectacle of the children dashing off to school. At seven in the morning, Seventeenth Avenue is alive, and it is alive in a way that is different from the partying on Friday evenings after the working men have been paid. The children arrive, holding the arms of parents or grandparents, aunties or cousins, older brothers or sisters. "Git," says a boy to his baby brother, as the child runs toward school. "And wave at me when they open the door and let you in."

Every day is typical. Every day is unique. But they always begin the same. The Star-Spangled Banner. The Pledge of Allegiance. Sometimes there is a crackle over the intercom, a message from the principal's office.

"Boysangirls . . ." he begins. One of a principal's unsung talents is pronouncing this as one word and Mr. Morley is a master. "For the first time in the history of Drew we have new furniture in the cafeteria. I'm asking you: You *must* take care of the furniture. We're going to paddle you if you stand on the chairs. If I find out that anybody is destroying the furniture, they're going to be paddled right here, in my office, today. One other thing. There was too much playing in the halls during the National Anthem. Boysangirls, we want you to work hard and have a pleasant day."

To the children in Mrs. Clapp's fourth-grade classroom at Charles R. Drew Elementary School, these messages are like a plane passing overhead. Sometimes the children pay attention, sometimes they don't.

Fourth grade is a special time. In some way it is the last year of innocence, before breasts, before braces. The boys don't like the girls because "they don't know how to play anything." The girls don't like the boys because "they feel on people in the wrong spots." On the field trips, boys hold hands with boys, girls with girls, and they readily kiss the teacher but not each other.

Jolonda Rudolph, a willowy girl with braided hair and wonderful big eyes, defined nine years in its essence: "When you are nine you don't believe in Santa Claus, but your mother and father still think you do."

Although they are young, there are things in life that have already made them sad. They have been sad when: my watch broke, I got a whipping, I was stung by a bee, when my brother swallowed a marble, when I didn't get what I wanted for Christmas. Also, stitches. Stitches have made them sad. These are the normal catastrophes of childhood. Artlyn Johnson, who is "Shortcake," for obvious reason, was saddest of all when her sister left for college. Other sources of sadness were more touching: "When my uncle died on Tuesday at 7:30." One girl wrote: "When they throwed us out of the house, when I dropped my mother's plant the one she loved, and when they stoled my mothers car."

If they could have one thing they don't already have, Andy said he would have the "three kinds of telekinesis," though he didn't say why. Brenda would like to go to Puerto Rico. One boy wanted a "big house with six stories, 30 bedrooms, 15 bathrooms, and a pool inside and out." One girl wanted "a $100,000 'lamazine' and a 'manchan.'" Corey McKnight would like "clothing with a matching bike to each pattern." Jolanda said she wanted to be "a grown-up and drive a Monte Carlo. That's my car."

At nine, the boys think they can be anything. So do the girls. Their aspirations are typical, but to them they are unique. When they grow up, they would like to be: a principal, band director, movie star, football player, teacher, secretary, psychiatrist, doctor, cashier, lawyer, truck driver, Army man, scientist, famous trumpet player, mailman lady.

Room 32. The trenches. Sandra, Deidra, Natasha, Tanzana, Kevin, Gregory, Paula, Letitia, Andy, Rodney, Artlyn, Javon, Mark, Patrick, Sylvia, Corey, Treska, Dylan, Angela, Melinda, Charleston, Edwin, Elissa, Kala, Karen, Wandra, Jolonda, Brenda, Myron, Clarice, Warner, Nicole, Michelle, Naidra, Vanessa.

What are their chances?

"Warning: Hubcaps and car accessories in this lot are protected with permanent code markings." This is the sign that greets visitors when they pull into the parking lot at Drew Elementary.

In the playground, bits of shattered glass accumulate overnight as mysteriously as grass grows. By morning the sandbox has syringes and empty wine bottles. There is an armed camp atmosphere. The windows have been boarded up. The classroom doors lock automatically. Mrs. Clapp never allows a child to leave her classroom alone.

Often on Monday mornings one teacher's door, which is in a separate wing of the school, is marked with the word "Pussy." She takes a pen and writes "cat" after each pussy. At least the door has a peephole; Mrs. Clapp has been requisitioning one for years.

It is rare when the school has not been victimized by vandals over the weekend. On a recent Monday, the sturdy glass outside the principal's office was pockmarked by blasts from a pellet gun.

This is not considered remarkable. It is a fact of life.

There is nothing remarkable about Mrs. Clapp's classroom either. There is little to distinguish it from a classroom at a white school. The books are the same, fractions are fractions, and 9 times 6 equals 54 anywhere. Like all classrooms this is where something will happen during the very early years to determine whether a child will succeed or fail. Every child is a story. Every classroom and every teacher. There is no way to tell them all.

There is little to distinguish it except maybe this: the pressures are more subtle. And the stakes are higher.

Mrs. Clapp: "If there is one thing that burns me, it's people coming into a school like this and saying that all these black children need is love, love, love. Of course they need love. But they also need to know how to organize. They have to be able to read. . . ."

Whenever there is a flower anywhere on the grounds, the response is: "Oh that's Mrs. Clapp's touch. You can tell." Because she works late, Mrs. Clapp has been accidently locked in the building more than any other teacher. She plans Saturday trips for the children. She brings in material for costumes for an upcoming class play.

Children almost always adore their teacher. These children adore Mrs. Clapp, a bosomy woman with large, bright eyes that she uses as a weapon of discipline and an instrument of approval. They like: the dresses she wears; the way she does her hair, her beautiful face. She lets us have parties. She spends money on us. See all that material—it's hers. She doesn't spank a lot. She doesn't embarrass nobody. She doesn't smoke. She doesn't drink.

"She doesn't sit. She is on her feet all day long, wearing her Mushrooms," said Kala Rolle, who every day shows up at school dressed identically to her twin sister, down to the last ribbon, bow or bead in their hair. The first reaction to Kala and Karen is to wonder how long it takes their mother to get them ready for school each morning. Kala says there is one absolutely amazing thing about Mrs. Clapp. "She never leaves the room. She never goes to the bathroom." Her eyes become wider and she shook her head at the incredibleness of it all. "Never."

Colleagues also salute her dedication. One day Mrs. Grace, who teaches remedial reading, tried to convince Mrs. Clapp to leave a few minutes early to visit a former colleague in the hospital. Mrs. Clapp said she would stay the full time.

Mrs. Grace stood in a windswept corridor, empty but for

the Cheetos bags and other debris. To herself she said: "No, Mrs. Clapp would never leave early. She would never bend the rules a little bit, even though the rest of us. . . ." The sentence trailed, and she made a gesture like a twig snapping. "She has that kind of morality about her. I used to be like that, in the old days."

Mrs. Clapp's classroom is on the second floor. That is fortunate, because at Drew the upstairs classrooms get one unboarded window. Hers is used for a display marked "photosynthesis." Little signs on manila paper say: Plants need air. Plants need water. Plants need sunlight. Beneath the window are ivy and roses. The window itself is streaked and blurred with dirt.

But the plants do grow.

Very similar scenes can be found in all schools, but classrooms are like snowflakes: no two are exactly alike. It is a world largely ignored except by the participants: the world of cursive handwriting, plurals and capital letters, pronouns and fractions, the patient repetitive world of training young minds, day in, day out, year in, year out, generation in, generation out.

The product is an abstraction; it is knowledge itself, something that cannot be measured. It is process, change, mutation slow and subtle.

8:10. Class begins. Mrs. Clapp has already written the dictionary study words on the blackboard: criticism, hostility, condemn, ridicule, shame. She has also written a thought for the day, the wisdom of Samuel Johnson: "Language is the dress of thought."

The letters of the alphabet line the top of the blackboard like a necklace. A typical lesson: penmanship. The secret of teaching seems to be to generate enthusiasm for tasks that require patience. How many times, since her career began at Douglass Elementary in 1958, has Mrs. Clapp instructed her class to take out a piece of paper and copy a passage? How many times has she taught the children the four key points for self-evaluation of one's handwriting?

"Did I form my letters properly and accurately as I should have? Form. Did I observe proper spacing? Space. Slant." Here she pauses and on the blackboard she writes a fat, mis-shapen cursive "A," leaning to the left, a silly "A." This causes laughter almost as unrestrained as the response to one of Artlyn's jokes. (Why did the teacher wear sunglasses? Because her students were so bright.) "And last, alignment. How many margins do we have?" The children answer: One. She shakes her head. Two? No. Three? No. Four? Correct. "We have four margins. Now what are the key elements of hand-writing?"

The children recite them from the blackboard:

"Form. Space. Slant. Alignment."

They are asked to grade themselves. The children are easy markers. They give themselves B, B+, or A−, all nicely formed.

It is the accumulation of such small moments that results in an education. There is nothing sudden about the ability to read and write on one's grade level. There are no bolts of lightning. It is as invisible and complex as photosynthesis.

Children can be cruel. They have not developed the subtle ways of displaying prejudice that adults have learned.

The children in Mrs. Clapp's class have nicknames for each other that make them sound like a platoon: Big-time, Lover-boy, Shortcake, Curly, Cheeks, Grenade Head, God Our Father, La Machine, Godawful, Skinhead.

Many of the nicknames are affectionate; some are not. Mrs. Clapp monitors these names, to make sure there is nothing "degrading" about them. On a recent day, a child in Mrs. Clapp's class was called "Old Black Sambo" by another child. She took the insulted child aside: "Look in the mirror. What do you see? That fine nose. Those high cheekbones. You are a very handsome boy." The other child was reprimanded.

On the playground at Drew, it is fighting words to call somebody's mamma anything, but the worst insult of all is: "Your mamma's a Haitian."

There is one Puerto Rican child in the class, Brenda Serrano, who speaks English with a black inflection. There is one white child, Andy Jackson, whose mother is a psychologist on the school staff. The children like Andy and would not mind if there were a few more whites. "It's hard on Andy," said Dylan Mobley, who is called "Curly" for obvious reasons, "because in the skits we do, he has to play all the whites."

No attempt has been made to integrate Charles Drew, except in the exceptional arts program, attended by junior high children from more than seventy schools. The faculty at Drew is integrated: in 1970 many black teachers were transferred to other schools and whites were brought in. In education circles, this is still referred to as the Big Switch, and it has created as many problems as it has redressed. There are cliques now, and resentments among the new blacks and old, new whites and old.

Mrs. Clapp knows there is jealousy among the staff. There is grumbling about how it's easy to be the best teacher if you have the best students. The funny thing is that she has always taught the best students.

"She was a brilliant girl," says Mrs. Charlotte Ford Clark, the dean of students at Bethune Cookman when Mrs. Clapp was a student there. Throughout her career, Mrs. Clapp has been one of "Clark's girls." Clark had been principal at Douglass and brought Mrs. Clapp with her when she became the first principal at Drew.

"When she showed up at Douglass, she worked with the gifted children," said Mrs. Clark. "People forget that gifted children need gifted teachers too. In some ways it's more of a challenge, because they get bored and turned off more easily."

Mrs. Clapp made enemies this spring when she lobbied for Lilia Garcia, the white art teacher, as Drew's candidate for teacher of the year. There were some factions who wanted to support a black teacher on principle. Mrs. Clapp has another principle, one she stresses to the students: color doesn't matter; be who and what you are.

Only a few of the children know what prejudice means. Some of them call it "prejudism." Artlyn thinks it means "a different race, like Jewish."

"When my mamma was little," says Artlyn, who just got glasses a month ago, "they had fountains that said 'for colored only.' "

Paula Gaymon, the winner of the fourth-grade spelling bee, defines it this way: "A bigot. If you're one color you want other people to be your color." She is one of the few who can define integration: "Black and white together."

Integration. Prejudice. The children do know about both even if they don't realize it. There is not a child in the class who doesn't know the story of Charles Drew, and this is how they tell it:

"He was a scientist who discovered plasma and that's why we have blood banks. He died in North Carolina in 1950 when he was driving a car and he fell asleep. They took him to a white hospital that wouldn't let him in. He died on the way to the black hospital."

"That happened," says Paula Gaymon, "in the days of . . . oh what do you call it?" She thought for a minute, eyes looking up, a characteristically shy smile on her face. "Oh, yes, in the days of Jim Crow."

Mrs. Clapp is very lucky. All her children read on at least their grade level, if not above. When she first started teaching at Douglass, there were books in the classrooms that had never been cracked. Every now and then she propagandizes on behalf of reading. A typical speech on this subject is like a sermon. It is delivered in an extremely pleasant voice, warm, full of authority.

"Children, I want your full attention." There is some whispering going on, and a few conversations. "We can sing at the same time, but we cannot all talk at the same time." Silence. "I am not accustomed to addressing the backs of heads. Turn and face me when I speak." All eyes on the teacher. "As you know, I am a tiger about reading. As far as I am concerned, no one, *no one* reads as well as he possibly could." She seems to veer from the topic: "Let me tell you about something that happened the other day. I was with my son Edwin in the car. I started to get out of the car and I rushed back in because I saw a pit bull." She leaves the anecdote hanging.

"I want you children to show how eager you are. Reading is the key to living. If there is a big old sign on an elevator that says 'Out of Order,' what happens if you can't read it?" You die, the children answer, in singsong. "If a bench has a sign that says 'Wet Paint' and you are wearing a beautiful new dress, what happens?" It's ruined, the children answer in their exaggerated chorus.

"I will never forget a woman in my neighborhood when I was growing up in Jacksonville. She couldn't read, and she was dependent on my mother and grandmother to read important documents for her. Tax notices. This lady was at the mercy of my grandmother and mother, and they could have taken her. If you can't read you will be at the mercy of just anyone. And I don't want you children at anyone's mercy."

And then, back to the beginning, the tie-in. "Act like a pit bull. Be as tenacious as a pit bull. Grab onto those skills and don't let go."

Mrs. Clapp's class is the good news. All is not sweetness and light at Charles Drew. Mrs. Clapp teaches a resource class. Resources: assets, things that lie ready for use. There is a tracking system at Drew and for each grade, there is a teacher with a resource class. Some children in Mrs. Clapp's class are driven long distances to attend her class. Their parents know the education their children can receive here. Patrick Knight is the son of Dewey Knight, a Metro commissioner. Artlyn's father and mother are teachers. So is the mother of Karen and Kala. Jolonda's father is the minister at Mt. Zion Baptist Church.

The other classes at Drew are truly unhailed worlds. One teacher has a student who attends only cafeteria—free breakfast, free lunch. He is on the playground the rest of the time. There are children at Drew who wear the same outfit every day, all year long. There are children who undergo traumas beyond comprehension and beyond the healing powers of the school system. The personality of one sixth-grade boy was altered radically after he witnessed one parent slowly knife the other to death. He attends the principal's office; he is always there.

Mrs. Grace, the remedial reading teacher, sat one day in the library, teaching a twelve-year-old boy. All of a sudden she said, "Steve, I am really proud of you." She called to Miss Holland, the librarian. "This is the first page he's ever read, truly."

Haltingly, with extensive coaching, this is what Steve read:

> A fat cat sat on a mat.
> The fat cat is Nat.
> Pat Nat, the fat cat.

"What the public does not understand," said Mrs. Grace, "is that it is in their own best interest to care about these children. You will deal with these children. Now or later."

In a classroom, under the guidance of a skilled teacher, anything is a tool of learning. Of all the activities that teach children, perhaps none is more formative than the class play, and Mrs. Clapp's children have been asked to present one, about the contributions by blacks to art and literature. The avowed purpose is to honor culture, to teach children to recite great words. But more than anything, such a program serves the socialization process. It teaches poise.

Normally Mrs. Clapp is an even-tempered sort, chronically jolly if anything. She says she prefers not to paddle the children, and most of her reprimands are verbal. Sometimes she will hold a group of children after school for a few minutes. The offenses: pinching people, showing off, wasting time. A typical lecture: "Why was it that when I left the room for one minute today, I came back to find you chasing someone? You want responsibilities. You want to pass out things. But with every little responsibility you have a duty."

A sense of responsibility is the chief lesson of the class play, one the children have not yet learned. One day, after rehearsal, the class received a vintage tongue-lashing.

"Freeze," Mrs. Clapp said, pacing the room. The children were as still as snowmen under a cold sun.

"I have been noticing attitudes," she said. "I have not been pleased with our rehearsals. You children know that I compliment you when you deserve it and I reprimand you when you deserve it." Mrs. Clapp likes to discipline with her eyes. On this day she stared with anger at one child who was reading, and finally exploded: "Put your eyes out of that book, little girl, and put your eyes on me."

Mrs. Clapp directed her first comments to the girl who will recite a Langston Hughes poem, "I Am a Black Child," in the play.

"You are projecting well, Elissa. I wish the others would project as well as you do. But cut out that kneeling gesture. It doesn't work. Don't kneel all the way to the floor; we like your voice at the mike. Kneel just a little and keep your face next to the microphone when you say: 'Give me, I beg you, a world.' Kneel deep enough so you can grow proud and tall.

"Some of you are speaking too slow; others, too fast. And some don't even know their parts. Some of you sound like you have a mouthful of grits, there's no other term to describe it. Some of you have an attitude that you are special and you don't have to work."

She paused. Drew a deep breath. "When I cast this play, I tried to include every soul so no one could go home and say, 'Mamma, I don't have a part.' It's a joy, it is a privilege, to be on stage. To me that is what school is all about: it gives you the feeling you're important.

"I am kind of burned up. You will be representing yourself, your family, your class, your fourth-grade group, Drew. You are relating a story. You are relating a story of a people who were plucked up. They didn't come here because they wanted to. They were plucked up. They were brought here. They didn't come as the Cubans or the Haitians. In spite of all those things they have maintained themselves and contributed to the culture.

"Get home in front of that mirror tonight, and practice. Get mamma, get daddy, get your grandmothers to listen to you. If you don't want to be in the play, I can assure you there are many many seats in the audience. If you don't improve, I am not going to threaten you. I promise you—I promise, not threaten—that you will not be part of our next program. Teachers are human, too. I am not my usual cheery self. I am not pleased."

The bell for dismissal had rung midway though her speech. Now that she seemed finished, the students stirred. Through clenched teeth came an odd incantatory sound. The sound grew and became decipherable. "Unmelt. Unmelt. Unmelt."

"Oh yes, all right, children," said Mrs. Clapp, still not smiling, "unfreeze."

Education is a difficult subject to write about. When it is covered, it is usually on the upper echelon: Supt. Johnny Jones Indicted. Phyllis Miller Decides Not To Run. Ben Sheppard Dies. Unless there is violence, nobody pays much attention to what happens in the classroom. Schools are small worlds operating in a vacuum of public attention, unhailed, for better or for worse.

Charles Drew Elementary is located at 1775 N.W. Sixtieth Street. The northern borders of the campus are at Sixty-second Street. This is where the first fire was lighted after the murder of Martin Luther King in 1968. The biggest change since then is that the street has been renamed Martin Luther King Boulevard.

Next door is Drew Middle School. Twice there has been big news out of Drew Middle. In 1968 a student shot and killed another student and wounded a teacher. In 1977, the U.S. Supreme Court ruled that teachers may physically punish students. The decision was passed on a paddling at Drew in 1970. Drew Middle School is also where Johnny Jones served as principal before being named superintendent in 1977. Solomon Barnes, indicted with Jones, was an assistant principal there at one time.

The children in Room 32 pay as little attention to the larger world as the larger world pays to them. To them, the larger world in which "Dr. Ben Dies" might as well be a thousand miles away. It is another voice over the intercom. One day in March a small portion of the school board meeting was broadcast, and Chairman Miller offered a eulogy for Dr. Sheppard. No mention was made of Johnny Jones, suspended after being indicted for grand theft in connection with the "gold plumbing incident." The eulogy was followed by a hymn. The refrain, "Gloria in Excelsis Deo," filled the classroom, and the children laughed, not out of disrespect, but at the funny, unfamiliar sound. Jolonda Rudolph understood that somebody, she had no idea who, had died, and had covered her ears. "Oh," she said, "I don't want to hear this. This is going to give me bad dreams."

For twenty-two years, Mrs. Clapp has been part of the Dade County school system. She started her work at a salary of about four thousand dollars a year and these days she is earning about twenty thousand dollars. In all the time that she was being interviewed, Alyce Clapp avoided only one topic: Johnny Jones. At the end, she did, however, have some words on that subject too.

"There is something you have to understand about blacks. We will often talk about something among ourselves, but not in front of others. That does not mean there is a lack of concern. On the very first day that the news broke about Johnny Jones, I arrived in school shaking, really shaking. I have known Johnny Jones over the years—not socially, but we have been at many meetings together. I have heard him speak. At one time I taught his daughter. In his career he has had to handle millions of dollars. I don't believe he would do something like that. My husband says I'm being naive, but before I believe it, he would have to go on television and admit it. I remember him at Bethune Cookman, pledging Kappa. He was always something, always on the way up. That man could move mountains. It gets me right here." She grasped an imaginary knife with her right hand and plunged it in her heart. "Right here." And then her large bright eyes turned shiny, and she started to cry.

The class play went very well. No one forgot lines, squirming was at a minimum and everybody projected.

The finest moment in the presentation came at the end. It was a summing up. Elissa Reynolds recited the poem by Langston Hughes. Elissa is a tall girl with a mature face. She would like to be a teacher when she grows up. She is one of those children who radiates dignity. For the program, she wore a colorful turban and dress. In reciting the poem, she never took a bad pause, never broke rhythm, never once faltered. There was in her voice a rich and unwavering resonance, a grace beyond anybody's ninth year.

This is what Elissa said:

I Am The Black Child
I am the black child
All the world awaits my coming.
All the world watches with interest
To see what I shall become.
Civilization hangs in the balance.
For what I am
The world of tomorrow will be.
I am the black child.

You have brought me into a world
About which I know nothing.
You hold in your hands my destiny.
You determine whether I shall succeed or fall.
Give me, I beg you,
A world where I can grow proud and tall.
I am the black child.

❧ ❧ ❧

Mrs. Clapp is still teaching the fourth grade at Charles R. Drew Elementary. Times have changed in Miami since that initial portrait in 1980 when the entire city of Miami waited, tense, coiled, fisted, for the verdict in the trial of a gang of white policemen accused of beating a black man to death with their heavy police-issued flashlights after he failed to stop for a red light and then beating his motorcycle to make it appear as if he had been in an accident. The riots that followed caused eighteen deaths. When the schools reopened, Mrs. Clapp knew that she would have to draw a lesson about what had happened. She looked out at row after row of expectant faces and clouded expressions: young minds housed in the hard bones of reality. She took a piece of chalk and in clear looping cursive, sick at heart, she instructed them in the proper spelling of riot, coma, victim.

The school, both inside and out, appears to have prospered. It was recently repainted and landscaped, in part because it was chosen as the site of a visit from the vice president of the United States in February 1989.

"It was," says Mrs. Clapp, "Dan Quayle's finest moment." In the school office is a report card of Quayle's visit signed by George Bush, in which Quayle received A's in everything but geography. For choosing to visit a school in a place many travelers might ignore, he was given "A+."

On the first day of school in the fall of 1990, a heightened day for students, when they have to put the brakes on summer fun and settle down to the business of learning, and a heightened day for teachers as well, filled with melancholy because last year's class is now truly gone, vanished like a wave, a fifth-grade girl poked her head inside Alyce Clapp's Room 32 at Charles R. Drew Elementary. She told her former fourth-grade teacher, "Hey, it looks like you have the same ones this year as you had last year."

"Not exactly the same ones," said Mrs. Clapp, shaking her head sadly, extending her arms for a quick hug. "I don't have you."

There is something ageless and unaging about a classroom, a quality that often extends to the teachers, who also seem somehow spared the usual inroads of time. Alyce Clapp looks now as old, and also as young, as she did in 1980, a handsome woman with flashing eyes and a mobile face surrounded by a dark springy corona of curly hair.

The biggest change in her appearance is that now she, like her students and like most of the other teachers, has elected to wear the same colors of blue and white to school every day. Charles R. Drew was the first public school in Dade County to adopt a uniform for its students. The decision was based on the wish to create one less distraction for students and to avoid the envy that arises when some students arrive decked out and others wear the same outfit every day, uniform or not. It is a voluntary system, and the school receives one free uniform for every ten purchased for distribution to children who cannot afford to buy a uniform. Out of 850 students at Charles R. Drew, about 150 are on uniform "scholarships."

If the first day of school is melancholy for teachers, it is also filled with hope because, of course, new waters are rising. In the fall of 1990 Mrs. Clapp's class had seventeen boys and twelve girls. There are two sets of identical twins, male and female, and several second-generation children—those whose parents or older siblings or cousins or aunts and uncles had Mrs. Clapp in the past.

She is famous for several specialties. One is eyes everywhere. The other is a way of overwhelming the class with words, an oratorical style that echoes old-fashioned preaching, in which seemingly unconnected remarks build to an overall point. But rather than rely on the gospel as a source of inspiration, she uses the news and everyday life. This year's students got their first pep talk on the first day. There is something artful in her lectures; the presentation is itself a performance, the way she moves, now quick and darting, then, slow and majestic, and the way she speaks, at first soft and distant, building to a sonorous peak.

She begins by standing in the front in silence, waiting for the menace of her silence to grow. Behind her are the sayings she has posted in the waning days of summer, short one-sentence homilies like "Learning is a journey that never ends." When, finally, all the chatter has died and each child's gaze is solemnly trained on the teacher, she says, softly:

"You are gifted. I expect even more from you because you are gifted."

A slight stirring in some corners; a whispered exchange or two.

"I will not talk to people who are talking." More silence. "I believe in paying attention to your teacher. I'll tell you something else I believe. I do believe in calling your mothers.

Maybe you people think you're so brilliant you can act anyway you want in class. This is the first day of school. How
you act today will color the entire year. Research has shown
that the first impression is the lasting impression." Now she is
roaming the room, an impressive figure in her white dress and
blue vest with those piercing eyes. She turns on her heels and
bends a bit, putting her face near that of a small boy. "I taught
your daddy," she says. The cadence is stern, filled with quiet
power. "You go home and you ask him if Mrs. Clapp puts up
with talking all day long." Then, tall again, louder: "You are
GIFTED. What does this label mean to you? This assessment,
this evaluation? You have been given a gift from some Supreme Being. You owe it to yourselves and your families to
cultivate this gift. And then, after you pack in all the knowledge you can, the most important thing is how you use it.
That person killing people in Gainesville? I would guess he is a
very smart person. But he is using his smartness the wrong
way. Tonight for your homework I want you to write a paper
with four or five sentences about what it means to be gifted.
That's your first assignment. For your second, please take
home your math books, and I want you to do pages two,
three, four, and five. . . ."

Every year Mrs. Clapp's former student Elissa Reynolds
drops by Room 32 and recites "I Am the Black Child" for the
new fourth-grade class. Mrs. Clapp keeps in loose touch with
the other children in that class now lost to time, and she
knows where many of them are in college, but of them all, the
student whose fate she most admires is Paula Gaymon. Paula
was famous in that class for knowing the answer to everything, yet she never bragged or acted big and important.
Name a subject, Paula had an answer.

Today Paula is at Spelman College in Atlanta. "I guess,"
says her old friend Elissa, "you might say the black child has
grown up." Paula says, "Every time I go home I drop by and
see Mrs. Clapp. The most vivid thing I recall from fourth
grade was her taking the children and putting them in front of

the mirror we had in class and she would tell them they were beautiful and important. Mrs. Clapp always seemed to have extra time and Friday afternoons she gave us watermelon or some other treat. She writes to me at college and she often encloses money, ten or twenty dollars."

Most of the decorations in Mrs. Clapp's room change from year to year, but for a long time now the display about oasis has remained. She used tempera on plain brown paper with glaze to create a colorful mural, and each new class of students is allowed to make the hues a little deeper, to refurbish and renew. But it remains permanent, a symbol of the class and the school.

THE POET
AND THE
BIRTHDAY GIRL

Victoria Hospital, private room: That's where Vivian Kahn was born on April 16, 1943. She does not hesitate to remind people of this fine beginning, especially when her birthday is approaching. Every year there is a big celebration. One time Vivian Kahn went to a Tony Orlando concert: "He kissed me once. He kissed me twice. And he called me one of God's special children. Which I am."

Her mother, Hannah:

"When you learn your child has Down syndrome, one of the first thoughts is: How will I get through the first Christmas? The first major holiday. And then you think, how will I get through the first Mother's Day? The first day of first grade, when all the other children are enrolling in regular classes. And then you think, how will you tell her about the womanly processes?

"But you can. And you do."

"How was work today, Viv?"

"Fine."

"What did you do?"

"Well, we said our address and when our birthday is and our social security number."

Vivian's speech is exceptionally clear for a person with her impairment, and her vocabulary reflects her mother's love of language. "Marty said that on my birthday he's going to play music. He said he had something cooking up his sleeve and we're really going to town. Ronni said she's going to give me a present." It is dinnertime and Vivian looks up quickly from her plate, anticipating her mother's disapproval. "I told Ronni a card would be plenty." Vivian swallows hard and repeats herself, "Plenty, Hannah, plenty."

Hannah: "One thing with retarded kids. They're not jealous. They are noncompetitive, nonmanipulative. One gets something, they're all happy. Call it pure soul or pure light or whatever you want to call it."

Vivian Kahn goes to "work" every day at the Association for the Development of the Exceptional, on North Miami Avenue. She is small, four feet seven inches tall, and dresses young for her age: Hannah says that size 14 Polly Flinders fit the best. She joins fifty other retarded adults who are taught how to count, how to take a bus, how to answer the phone. Her mother drives Vivian in the morning, and she is given a ride home to their apartment in the afternoon. Her mother, who has had a job selling furniture at Whitecraft Industries' showroom for forty-one years, arrives home a couple of hours after Vivian, at 5:30. A few minutes before her mother's blue car pulls into the parking lot, Vivian goes to the window and looks for her, so she can wave a greeting at the woman with silver hair. Hannah has a remarkably energetic stride for a woman of seventy-two; it is the always-hurried movement common in mothers of young children. When she is alone, Vivian can take care of herself. She can watch television or type a letter or answer the phone as long as "I don't give no information to wrong numbers. Frank taught me that. He taught me not to climb and not to touch the stove too."

Frank Kahn was Vivian's father and the stepfather, though he disliked the term, of Hannah's two sons from a previous marriage. Hannah Kahn was nineteen when Melvin was

Photo by Keith Graham

born, twenty-one when Danny came. "No one could have been more scared with a baby than I was. I remember the doctor told me, as long as you've got a healthy baby, they'll probably turn out all right no matter what you do." Hannah Kahn's first marriage is a phase of her life about which she is uncommunicative, yet it has figured in some of her writing. For in addition to the steady prosaic life amid the rattan,

selling the étagères and convertible couches, Hannah Kahn is a
poet of some note, once considered a leading candidate for the
title of poet laureate for the state of Florida. "Ex-Wife" is an
early poem about which she says today: Too obvious, everything about it. The sentiments, the rhymes:

> Wonder if my shadow
> ever interferes,
> do they know their laughter
> as an echo of my tears?
>
> Wonder if her love
> is stronger than was mine?
> I who only asked for bread—
> She whose bread was wine.
>
> Sometimes when the shadow
> is intensified,
> I can hear him breathing
> softly at my side,
>
> I can feel his fingers
> reach across the night
> and rest upon my eyelids
> shutting out the light—
>
> I have heard him tapping
> on my window pane
> and when I rose to answer
> found out that it was rain.
>
> Wonder when their beings
> merge within a flame
> does he ever call her
> by my name?

Dinner over, Vivian helps clear the dishes. She inquires after
dessert. "When God gave you to my house, Vivian, there

must have been a contract requiring dessert with every dinner." Dessert is an apple. After dinner, Vivian says, "I'm cold, I'm chilled."

"What should you do when you're chilled?"

"Put something on."

Vivian was Frank's first child. Hannah had wanted a girl, and when Vivian was born Frank told Hannah, "It's a girl. You got what you wanted." Hannah recently came across the hospital bill: ten days, one hundred dollars.

Vivian has fetched her sweater. "Hannah," she says, very businesslike, "Take your pills."

"See," says Hannah, reaching for her pills. "She watches over me."

She touches her daughter's soft pretty hair. "I was born with nervous hands," she once wrote. "What they loved they had to touch."

Hannah Kahn found out that Vivian had Down syndrome when she was eight months old, just after Christmas: "We went to the doctor for a routine checkup. She was dressed in white shoes, a blue organdy dress. For the first time her hair was long enough for a narrow ribbon bow."

Frank and Hannah Khan were left alone with Vivian in the examining room. The child's chart was on a table, open. The doctor had written, "Did you tell her that Vivian is a Mongoloid child?"

Hannah:

"In those days nothing was known about retardation. No one knew anything about an extra chromosome. Lightning strikes. I felt that I was the only person in Miami who had given birth to such a person. I can still remember the words of the doctor: They Are Unfinished Children. During Pregnancy Because Of Some Endocrine Or Other Deficiency In The Mother That We Do Not Know, The Unborn Child Is Not Completed. She Can Never Go Beyond The Mental Age of Five Or Six And It's Best For You And Your Other Children That She Be Placed In An Institution When She's Thirteen Months Old. There Is No Doubt About Our Diagnosis. See This, These Special Epicanthal Folds In The Eyes. (But her eyes are impish. . . .) Their Little Fingers, Short Curved Like A Fish. Their Hands Are Short And Stubby. (Her fingers which we had counted and recounted. She's double-jointed. . . .) These Children Usually Are."

At home that night Hannah performed the usual tasks in a trance. She prepared the dinner, talked to the boys, cleared the table. Frank took Vivian into her room, changed her, gave her a bottle, and put her to sleep. Hannah thought: I should have known. Should I have known? The pregnancy was so easy, too easy. I told the doctor the baby wasn't kicking as much as the others had. He said, "We'll take care of everything, Mrs. Kahn." At the hospital the nurses remarked on what a good baby Vivian was, how well she slept.

Frank came into the living room, dressed for the card party they had planned on going to. Hannah Kahn was incredulous. "Get dressed," Frank said softly. "Everything goes on." Hannah remembers only one detail from the evening. "I drank cup after cup of coffee. It tasted like blood."

"Frank established the rhythm. Frank set the pace. Without him I don't know how I would have survived. . . ."

"We never actually sat down and told the boys something was wrong with Vivian. We said she was slow in some ways but advanced in others, like her dancing. Both boys were always good with Vivian. I remember Melvin used to go to the beach with the debating team, and every now and then he'd ask me if Vivian could come along. I told him, Melvin, the other boys aren't going to want Vivian to come along and he said oh, they do. Vivian walks around and she attracts the girls and helps us make friends. Danny told me that whenever he took Viv to the playground, he never thought she was slow. He simply assumed all the other children were very advanced.

"In whatever way Danny and Melvin might have been hurt by it, they certainly got to be more considerate people through their association with Vivian. By far she has enriched me. Without Vivian I would've had such an ordinary, take-for-granted life."

"Child," the mother once wrote, "give me your hand that I may walk in the light of your faith in me."

From a letter Hannah Kahn wrote to a friend shortly after her husband's death in 1975:

"Vivian's relationship with her father was unique; everyone who knew them grieved doubly when he died, wondering how Vivian would adjust. She's been wonderful. He taught her well.

"I don't have to tell you how grief comes in waves. Vivian sometimes sets the table for three instead of two.

"About six months ago he re-wallpapered our kitchen. The icebox goes in a niche. . . . He already wasn't feeling well—moving the ice box was difficult. I told him no one would know if he didn't paper behind the icebox. He looked at me, smiled and said 'I would know.'

"Tomorrow I have to go to the lawyer's office and sign a new will. . . . Vivian's future is my greatest concern."

From "Betrayal":
I walk among the headstones in my sleep—
I read the names, the dates. I place two stones
Upon your grave. I ask you to forgive
That in some strange, distorted way I live.

From "Metastasis":
The cells divide
and multiply
My body is their battleground
I am the field they occupy.

Hannah Kahn had a mastectomy seven years ago. During a recent visit to the doctor "something showed up on the scan." Hannah now rehearses the reality of the future: "Someday our life together, as it is now, will end. Vivian's not going to be by the window and I'm not going to get out of the car." She is looking into Haven School, the possibility of placing Vivian there five days a week to accustom her to separation. "It has always been my unspoken dream that something would happen to her before something happened to me so Vivian would be forever sheltered."

"Hannah," says her daughter, "now please don't forget your pills."

Vivian Kahn has never been to her father's grave. She thinks he is buried in the clouds. On his birthday she always waves to him in the sky ("That's where Frank is, he's in heaven") and sings "Happy Birthday," including the second verse, "We love you, we do." "Frank didn't want Vivian to see him sick in the hospital. Instead they spoke to each other over the phone. He never wanted Vivian to go to the cemetery. He didn't think she could handle the thought of the underground thing.

"At the time of Frank's death I was very worried about the effect it would have on Vivian. I didn't understand that for a child like Vivian who has two parents, when one dies, her life didn't change very much. She was in the same house, the same bed. There was no break," says Hannah, "in the rhythm."

When it came time to tell Vivian about the womanly processes, this is what Hannah Kahn did:

"Frank would die if he knew this. He was a very modest man. I never sat down and told her. I took her in the bathroom with me and showed her and tried to behave as naturally as possible because I have discovered with Vivian if you're casual, she's casual. With Vivian, I don't know how much she needs to know. At Vivian's job, at A.D.E., they keep stressing Who-man Growth and Development, as Vivian pronounces it. I don't know what they're telling her. I don't know what she understands. I'll never forget the day Vivian was watching 'All in the Family,' and Vivian is yelling 'push, push' and I ran into the living room to see what was happening and Gloria was having a baby and my daughter's coaching her."

"At A.D.E. they say, this is reality. This is actuality. The children should know about these things. I look at Viv, and I see a child, in many ways, a child of eight or nine, and I keep thinking: Who would want their eight- or nine-year-old child thinking about getting married?"

Only once did Vivian ever cross Hannah. That was when Richard gave Vivian an engagement ring, a diamond. Hannah told Vivian to return it. Vivian put it in her pocketbook.

Vivian often chooses to wear the clothing that Richard has told her turns him on. "What does that mean, Viv? Turning someone on?" "Actshully, Hannah, it means I light up his life."

Vivian has a notion her mother would like her to cool it with Richard: "I think she wants me to be just friends."

Would she like to be more than friends?

"Be honest now. I would love to, but I don't know if my mother's going to let me."

Why Richard?

"Because he thinks I'm beautiful and so on and so on."

What's sex?

"I would suggest sex is good, you know why? I'm not embarrassed in saying it. Now making love is when you're kissing on the lips. My mother won't let me kiss on the lips. Sex means when you get VD."

Babies?

"I do have my dolls, Princess from Hungary and Granny from Russia. They are not real babies, they're dolls. But the only thing is how is my mother going to put up with it, it's a big job, supposing he starts doing something in his diapers."

Where do babies come from?

"Babies," she says, "can come from anywhere. The mother's stomach, a hospital, could come from God."

Vivian Kahn begins the celebration of her birthday on January 1st, with references to surprises and cake. On the first day of April she announces, "It's my month." This year was the first year in a long time that Hannah Kahn allowed Vivian to be her true age: forty. For years Vivian's age was frozen at sixteen. Hannah: "It was easier that way."

The public festivities lasted two days. On Friday April 15 Vivian received flowers at A.D.E. and everybody gave Vivian a kiss. There was a wondrous cake from a Cuban bakery. Vivian got to sit in the middle of the cafeteria next to a person of her choosing. She chose Richard. As the birthday girl, she was given the first piece of cake, but she made certain that Richard received the next piece. "Here Richard, this is the second piece." Marty, a man in his fifties who has spent his life in institutions and who has a gift for playing the piano without being able to read music, told Vivian "You ain't seen nothing yet." Then he sat down at the piano and played Vivian's favorite song, "You Light Up My Life." She got up and sang, "So many nights I sit by the window waiting for someone to sing me a song." Vivian has told her counselor at A.D.E. she would like to be Debby Boone, or a secretary. Ronni gave Vivian more than a card, she gave her a bracelet and kept saying, "Happy Birthday. Many more 'til next year." Vivian clapped her hands and touched her bracelet: "I've never had it so good. The cake and this and the flowers." Marty was asked by popular acclaim to play "those Marine songs" which he did, and at the end of the hour, he got up, received a smattering of applause, and looking at his scruffy shoes when he spoke, which is his custom, he said, "I told you, you ain't seen nothing yet." On the next day Hannah and Vivian attended the annual luncheon of Women in Communication at the Omni, and Vivian stood before the hundreds of women in attendance to receive some birthday applause. A private party followed, at the Kahns' residence.

Hannah Kahn's *Eve's Daughter* was published in 1962. Her latest collection, *Time, Wait,* will be published soon by the University Presses of Florida. By far "Ride a Wild Horse" is her most successful poem. Published first under the title "Into the Sun" in *The Saturday Review,* it has been in more than twenty textbooks and anthologies:

Ride a wild horse
with purple wings
striped yellow and black
except his head
Which must be red.

Ride a wild horse
against the sky—
hold tight to his wings

Before you die
whatever else you leave undone—
once ride a wild horse
into the sun.

Vivian has written two poems:

The Pink Carnation
The Pink Carnation is wearing a white sports coat
all dressed up for a date.

The Ocean View
I look across the Atlantic ocean
I see Europe
the ocean waves are dancing just like diamonds.

When Hannah Kahn is asked the difference between prose
and poetry, she answers with a quote from one of her poems:

I wanted to write about the old men
Who looked at the dinner menu for a long time,
And then ordered doughnuts and coffee.

"I wanted to say, as quickly as I could, these men were poor
and could not afford to order what they wanted. A prose
writer might have said the same thing, but in a more complete
way. A poem is as much what you don't say and what you

imply as what you do say. A poem gives the reader the chance
to add to or complete the thought.

"A poem can be about anything. It contains a certain moment you can almost take a picture of. It should capture a
feeling or an essence or a scene. Something that stands out,
that is not blurred into the momentum."

A certain moment:

After the guests had departed, Hannah and Vivian Kahn sat
down to a light supper of gefilte fish and a salad and chocolate
mousse cake. ("I like my life," says Hannah, "but sometimes I
don't like the facts of my life.") After dinner Vivian sat by the
phone to collect more calls. More than once, she admired the
flowers from her nieces and nephew. Vivian examined her
gifts: the doll from Mexico, the Lollipop bloomers from Aunt
Sylvia, the handkerchiefs. She wanted to play her new record,
"Elvira," sung by the Oak Ridge Boys, but she decided she
better wait by the phone. Whenever it rang, and it rang a lot,
it was for her: Danny and Phyllis in Spokane, Leslie in Washington, D.C., Estelle's son in California. Vivian decided that
on the next day she would like to wear one of her new dresses.
She thought it would be nice if her mother took her for ride
past Victoria Hospital.

At eight o'clock Hannah said, "Viv, I think it's time. I think
this is the time you were born."

"Oh, you think so Hannah."

"Think so? I know it. It's 8:20, Viv."

Vivian rocked back and forth on the sofa. Her chin was
buried in her neck, concealing the wide happy smile. The
short stubby fingers clapped in delight. "Victoria Hospital.
Private room."

"That's right. Nothing but the best for my daughter."

"Hannah, do you think we could go out on the terrace and
say hello to Frank?"

The older woman stood, and crossed the room, her stride

erect and swift, as usual. She opened the sliding glass door and made a sweeping motion with her hand, ushering her daughter onto the balcony. "That's because I am the birthday girl, right," said Vivian. The two women stood side by side. They held each other's hands. They looked up. The night was cloudy and still. Vivian took her free hand and raised high the short bent fingers. She waved at the sky. In a soft shy voice she said, "Frank, it's my birthday today. Right now I will be born, be born, sure, Frank. Thank you for carrying me home from the hospital." Then her hand still raised, her face uplifted, Vivian stood utterly still and listened as only she can listen. "He says he remembers me," she said, her head beginning to rock. "He's singing 'Happy Birthday.'"

🐦 🐦 🐦

Hannah Kahn always said she hoped her daughter would die first, the daughter, Vivian, about whom she wrote poems, the daughter fixed in a perpetual youth because of Down syndrome, the havoc of that extra chromosome, the clunkiness in the very number of the genes.

> They always have such lovely names;
> Melissa, Isla, Valerie, Dale:
> As though in naming them there was
> A premonition of their bleak
> Commitment and the barren days.
>
> The world in which they live is small;
> Controlled, constricted, limited,
> With fences they may never climb,
> Doors that are too often locked,
> Language they may never learn,
> And yet their names reflect the sun.

After her cancer had begun, Hannah began looking around for institutions where Vivian could move after her death. But she could not envision a facility that would be remotely adequate.

Hannah was certain that the reason Vivian had survived the death of her father was because both women kept him alive in their conversation. When Hannah died, who would keep her alive for Vivian?

Where was the group home that believed in magic?

Like most writers, she lived partly in the past, mining childhood memories for some of her best work. It had been a hardscrabble early existence, a typical immigrant story. Her father was a scholar, a dreamer, a ladies' man, and an orator. Her mother was forced to support Hannah and her younger sisters, Estelle and Sylvia, as a "turner" on an assembly line in a pocketbook factory, checking the seams of the lining and then tucking it back into a purse as it moved on a conveyor belt. Whenever possible, the mother would lease a railroad flat, a long hall with rooms coming off it, and using one room for herself and her daughters, she would rent out the other rooms to make a little extra money. Hannah's first poem was written when she was fifteen; it was playful, mock tragic in tone. She wrote it in an effort to win the heart of an older man. She felt she needed to win his favor with her wit; her appearance would never be adequate: "I was so homely, no girl was ever as homely as I was," she used to say, but the pictures she would then produce to prove her point conveyed an opposite impression of someone with fine strong bones and big eyes whose main flaw was the shyness that kept her from advertising them.

> I wish I were to go crazy
> Because then I would not have to wait
> For death, the glory.
> People would look at me and say
> She was a brilliant woman.

In the end, her output was slim, two small volumes, *Time, Wait* and *Eve's Daughter*. But what there is has been praised by the best, including Maxine Kumin and Gwendolyn Brooks. The high point for Hannah was an invitation from Gwendolyn Brooks to give a reading at the Library of Congress during the year she was poet in residence.

In Hannah's hands, words had shape and color, they were like glass, they caught the light. "The sun is older than I," she once wrote, "But I will be the first to die."

In the final two months of Hannah Kahn's life, time changed character. It moved mockingly, too slowly and then with agonizing swiftness in no set pattern, a mitosis of the minutes themselves. She would not let her grandchildren come and visit. Even her daughter, Vivian, was sent away. But Vivian knew what was happening. "She knew," says Hannah's sister Estelle, "in her own little way. Sometimes she would ask me, 'Is Hannah going to get better?' And I would answer 'She's trying.' And that would satisfy her at the time."

"I became very close to her in the end," says her sister Estelle, the middle one. Sylvia had always been close to Hannah. She often took care of Vivian, and Hannah used to say that without Sylvia she would not have had a social life. But Sylvia was far more than just a babysitter; she was Hannah's dearest friend, her nurturing soulmate.

"Closer," Estelle says now, "during that last year than we'd ever been before. Sylvia and I took turns staying with Hannah. I made her walk the hall outside her apartment as many as seven trips in one day. She would lean against me as she walked. She did not want two people helping her because she thought it would embarrass the neighbors to see her so weak. She liked to walk to a window overlooking the pool, and she enjoyed how nice it was to get a different aspect every time you looked through it, sunset, sunrise, some sense of the world outside.

"I never lied to her. I never said anything's going to be fine.

What I said was, 'Hannah, you must walk so that you'll have strength to bear the chemo.' Hannah, the born hostess, famous for her carrot cake and mandelbrot, those hard flat almond cookies, could not eat. But she would eat for me. I would try to make something, and sometimes Hannah would say, 'That smells good, maybe I'll try a bite.' And I would say very reluctantly: You want to taste some? I didn't want her to think I was forcing her. But naturally I had a big plate waiting in the kitchen, hoping she would try to eat something. And whenever she did, I would tell her, 'Gee, Hannah, I don't know what we're going to do. You're eating us out of house and home.'

"She discouraged company, but when someone from outside the family persevered in the wish to stop by, Hannah insisted on putting on a colorful muu muu, lipstick, earrings, a bracelet: the works. She was putting on the mask. After the visitor left, then came the pain, the fragmentation."

"For some reason her legs always felt leaden to her, so I would rub them, massage the skin with lotion. Sometimes we'd be up almost all night, and we would talk of our childhood, reminisce, and it seems to me that it soothed her, all the talk."

It appeared to Estelle that during those moments Hannah would lighten, would seem to forget about her silver hair and the dry aching skin and the pain everywhere (by then the cancer had moved into the bones). She would banish that dying fake and become young again, a gawky girl who read incessantly, sometimes stirring to help her sisters set the table for their simple dinner of canned sardines and Marshall's tomato herring, fresh rolls, and hot cocoa in a glass they kept covered with a plate to keep it warm. Oh how Hannah listened to Estelle, wrapping herself up in all the old stories, pulling them close to her like a pleasing old shawl: shared experiences are as thick as blood and they had both. Together, they could almost smell the salt air outside their childhood apartment on Coney Island. Together, they could summon the day their mother lost her job and how she came home with a box that night containing a wonderful indulgent dessert: cake with whipped cream and fresh strawberries and only after they have finished did she say she had lost her job, "I brought the cake to sweeten the news."

We didn't, the two elderly women would agree, know how poor we were.

We weren't, they would further agree, really poor:

We had, they would then say, all that love.

Remember the play *Liliom*, they would ask each other and their faces would beam at the thought of that swank afternoon long ago when they went into city and sat in the balcony of the Eva Le Gallienne theater and thrilled to the passions on stage. You know how Mama got the money for the tickets? one would say. And the other would answer, of course I know: she walked to work for months so she could have the nickels carfare cost.

And then the talk would turn to further examples of her thrift. They would remember the meals she sometimes prepared for the people who rented the rooms in their apartments, how smart she was to serve the potatoes first and after the edge of hunger was gone, to bring out the chicken. She worked hard, at home and at the factory. Sometimes it shamed her to leave her girls to go to that place where they made the pocketbooks: she wore a big hat to hide her face. . . .

The two sisters knew each other so well that as the night wore on and their energy waned they did not even have to talk in complete sentences; just a word, like *Liliom*, or strawberry, and they were borne backward, giddy and girlish, to a continent that no longer exists. Sometimes words were not even needed: a look, or a raised eyebrow, and they entered another dimension. The further Hannah burrowed back inside time, the closer she moved to being beyond it.

It was exhausting, a heavy labor of remembering, and afterward the sleep that followed was deep and still, a child's sleep, filled with dreams of cake and fruit and visions of three small girls following their mother as they walked on the beach by the water, embraced by the warmth from the sand.

But of course sleep like that could not last. There was always something to disturb it, something shrill, sharp, intruding. The phone would ring, a blinding shaft of daylight would invade the room, a sudden burst of pain would jab at Hannah, and she would return to her elderly dying self. But at least she did not worry about Vivian. Hannah's son Danny and his wife, Phyllis, told Hannah they would take care of Vivian, that she would move in with them. Phyllis promised Hannah that Vivian's room would be as pretty as the rooms of her two grown daughters had been.

She did not die alone. When the final hour came on January 13, 1987, she was at home in her apartment in the company of her sister Estelle, her housekeeper, and her older son, Danny, and his wife, Phyllis. "I've told Danny this over and over," says Estelle. "By his promise, Hannah could die in peace."

Not long afterward a group of friends gathered and started the Hannah Kahn Poetry Foundation. In a sense her work predicted this. She once wrote a poem in which she imagined that after her death someone will catalog her work, gather "scattered bits that were her life, her moods, her subtle mind, the scraps of paper shaped like little kites that will not fly again in any wind."

> The poet dies . . . the poem then becomes
> the living word

The foundation identifies poets of great merit and brings them to town for a public reading. A year ago, Gwendolyn Brooks came to Miami and gave a reading paid for by the group and next year the Israeli poet Yehuda Amichai has been invited. The group thinks Amichai is worthy of the invitation because like Hannah's work his work is all muscle and no fat. During a recent meeting a member read aloud a snippet from his work:

> I think of forgetting as a slowly ripening fruit, which
> once ripe will never be eaten. . . .

And someone added softly, that the purpose of the group is to keep the world from forgetting about Hannah.

The members are the lawyers, housewives, professors, people of business, all of whom were somehow touched by Hannah during her lifetime. Many studied writing with her. Fred Witkoff, a dentist and the group's president, told Hannah's son Melvin in no uncertain terms that time will show that Hannah was a great poet, among the best. "He told me," said Melvin, "that she was even better than, say, James Dickey."

Billie Witcoff, Fred's wife, tries to offer Hannah Kahn's carrot cake at all the gatherings of the foundation in which dinner is served. "The recipe Hannah used is very easy. It comes from the label for Hollywood carrot juice. Hannah, being the creative spirit that she was, changed it a little. She split the 1 and 3/4 cup white sugar into 1 cup white sugar and 3/4 cup brown. You'll see that in Hannah's recipe you don't have to grate anything. That was her way: to take what for most people is complicated and to find a way to make it simple."

Hannah once wrote, "I will make a poem out of plain words that a child could know."

She also made a poem out of her child, turned someone plain and simple into a pure moment of glad grace.

Vivian lives in Seattle now.

She is no longer the little girl.

"Hannah had a great fear of Vivian presenting herself as a young lady, but Phyllis feels differently," says Estelle. "She no longer wears her frilly clothes; she wears suits, heels. She's forty-eight now and she looks it. She's starting to show wrinkles. She has a job, doing piece work for electronics and computer companies from eight in the morning until quarter of three five days a week. She takes the bus, she transfers, she crosses the street. She has her own savings account, her own checking account, she even has a VISA. Once in a while, on Hannah's birthday and on Frank's, she treats Danny and Phyllis to dinner at a nice restaurant. Sometimes Viv even palms the manager of the restaurant, gives her five dollars to play her favorite songs, like "You Light Up My Life."

"Hannah left Vivian financially secure. I used to wonder sometimes if Hannah wasn't trying to save all her extra money for Vivian after she was gone. She lived so modestly. But now we know the reason. Hannah wanted to make sure Vivian had enough money to survive."

Phyllis says Vivian leads a quiet life. After work, she listens to music and does puzzles and word games. Her favorite TV show is Lawrence Welk, which comes on the cable. She goes to bed early.

She had a picture of Hannah on her bureau and she asked Phyllis for permission to put it in a drawer: "Do I have to have this picture up? It makes me sad."

Phyllis says, "Vivian lives in the now; she lives in the moment. She calls January 13th the day that Hannah left me."

Sylvia's daughter Leslie says that when she used to visit Hannah and Vivian she was always a little put off by the unreality of their life together: "They lived inside a veil. It was very sweet, and very delicate, but it had its own restrictions. Phyllis has given Vivian more responsibility. She irons her own clothes. She gets herself up early for work. She's a woman. She's lost twenty pounds. She's been told: your body matters.

Because Hannah gave Vivian such a great foundation, she now has a new beginning."

MONICA'S
BARREL

First you have to pack the heavy things, the cans of tuna
fish and fruit cocktail so that you don't crush anything
treasured and fragile, like the box of corn flakes clearly
labeled Leonard. Long ago Monica learned to assign by name
all the major items in her barrels because that keeps people
from fighting about who gets what.

Monica tries to send four barrels a year to Jamaica, sturdy
cardboard cylinders filled to the brim. She has been here four
years, but she has not forgotten the poverty there, what her
life would be like if she'd stayed. The brightest prospect
would be a job at the bra and underwear factory, making fifty
dollars a week in an economy where five dollars buys a pound
of rice. In the United States, Monica earns about two hundred
dollars a week, living-in Monday through Friday as a housekeeper for a family with three children. She says that she has a
perfect boss who even lets her keep her baby, Ivor, with her
and who pays for his Pampers, too. On weekends, she moves
out to her own two-bedroom apartment in Little Haiti with a
sofa set she bought on time (eighty dollars a month) at the
furniture place up the street and protects with plastic and a
color television and a shelf full of carefully arranged ceramic
statuettes.

Monica is always radiant. She is trim, with an easy smile and obedient hair that responds favorably to the chemicals in a curly perm. Her face is a sculpture, all planes and angles.

She likes her work as a housekeeper and calls herself a

professional, pronouncing professional in that Jamaican way that combines a native lilt with hints of a British education, combines song and royalty. She prides herself on how well she takes care of her employer's possessions, the children and the crockery, shining both. There is only one thing she hates doing and that is getting on a ladder and dusting the paddle fans.

Monica's apartment costs four hundred dollars a month. The extra bedroom is generally occupied by friends who want temporary shelter before finding places of their own. Right now Abner and Velma live there and pay half the rent. Once in a while, on Sundays, everyone who has the day off gets into Abner's blue and white truck and goes to the beach to barbecue, and, if the beach goers are lucky, Monica has made meat patties or, even luckier, her famous curried goat. Monica can make anything, including wedding cake, the kind that takes weeks because of having to soak the raisins and the nuts in rum.

On Saturday nights the house comes alive. Monica and her music: how she loves her tapes. But by day she is often out, on her mission, harvesting the flea markets and tag sales and discount stores for bargains and bibelots, setting them aside in a corner of her bedroom waiting for the pile to grow until it swells finally and magnificently into a bundle big enough to warrant the purchase of a barrel for ten dollars at the Jamaican Grocery on seventy-ninth Street. The man who sells her the barrel is friendly, but she always inspects the barrel anyway to make sure it's not warped and tests the lid with a knowing tap before handing over the money.

Here is what is in Monica's most recent barrel:

Sunsuits and dresses from K mart, bags of clothes her boss gave her filled with things the children have outgrown: Oshkosh overalls and Lacoste shirts, some slightly stained but all usable, marked for Kerry, Andrew and Stacy. There are five brightly colored size 10 dresses for girls that cost $9.99 each. These are brand new, and whenever something is brand new, tags and hangers are pointedly included. For this barrel she was lucky enough to find for seven dollars a pair, four pairs of high heels, all different sizes, in pretty party colors: white and yellow, pink and peach. She packs shampoo and lotion and toothpaste and toothbrushes. She includes a few of those little soaps from hotels that she gets from her boss's husband's business trips. There is no such thing as a barrel without a twenty-pound bag of rice. And you have to have red beans: those people waiting in Jamaica, you don't want to disappoint them.

This barrel has a box of grits, some canned corn and canned peas and two boxes of macaroni and cheese. Monica always likes to include the centerpiece of the food items, a big ham in a tin. Processed food from America is considered something of a delicacy. The only dependably plentiful food in Jamaica is fruit—wonderful fruit with sap, with bolts of moist heavenly flavor, fruits like mangos and sapodillas and naseberry—even so, the children especially prefer the foreign and renegade taste of Del Monte canned fruit with its thick sweet sauce. It is easy for Monica to picture them, their young eager faces, as they witness the ceremonial opening of the barrel and to hear that gasp of breath, that rushing sound that signals their joy. Usually everything in a barrel is laid out, as if in state, for everyone to look at, to circle and admire. Only after the full munificence of the bounty has registered is the can of fruit from America opened. Monica imagines them eating it the way children who grow up in a culture in which food is not taken for granted tend to eat, not in greedy gobbles but slowly, silently, with respect.

For the children, there are also toys and trinkets, balls and pencils and hair clips and barrettes and ponytail holders and chocolate eggs (bought at half-price after Easter). There are many, many candles, and Monica laughs her quick laugh at the notion that this is because Jamaicans are romantic. Oh, they like romance but they also live in a country in which the electricity is forever going out.

As one of the final acts before sending the barrel out, she goes through her closet for any clothes she doesn't want and asks her friends to do the same. Toward the top of the barrel Leonard, the recipient of the corn flakes, once again scores a luxury item: this time a stack of Lipton tea bags bears his name. (Who is this Leonard? What kind of king?) Clearly, it would be better to be him than to be Sonya, who upon the opening of the barrel, will surely curse her reputation for practicality, decry her drab fate. In her name, labeled for all to see, comes a huge bag of detergent plus about twenty Brillo pads.

"Leonard?" says Monica. "Oh he's just a cousin," and she laughs, but this time there is a touch of the islander in the sound. It still has heart, but it is protected too, surrounded by private waters, not quite scrutable.

Last packed are the perishables, the codfish, the garlic, and the onion. It is important to keep these items as far from the clothing as possible. The codfish is meant to be combined with a vegetable called ackee to create the Jamaican national dish, and so its presence is akin to a patriotic salute.

The barrel is an abundance from an abundant land. Only milk and honey are missing.

The best barrel is the heaviest, taking at least two men to lift, sometimes three. And then off it goes, to cargo at Jamaican Air, which charges forty-four dollars for the first one hundred pounds. Forty-four cents a pound for every one after that, and five dollars for paper work. The airline tries to guarantee that within three days the barrel will have arrived in the place Monica and her friends love in a homesick travelogue way that often overcomes exiles. Oh how they miss the beaches, the view, the sun, the waterfall near Montego Bay. The excitement.

Yet she never forgets how lucky she is to be here, where she can fill barrels instead of waiting for them.

And so the gifts are also an offering in the religious sense, a way of thanking the gods and appeasing them. This task, like tides, like seasons, is agreeably haunted by the endlessness of its phases. The minute one barrel is gone, another is begun.

❦   ❦   ❦

Monica has changed jobs in recent times and she has managed in her typically thrifty way to save enough money to provide passage to this country and housing for her older children she had left behind. Her new job as a certified nursing assistant required three months of training at a special school where she was taught how to give medication, take blood pressure, make beds, and dress, feed, and bathe patients. Currently she earns ten dollars an hour, working six days a week from nine to six, caring for an eighty-six-year-old woman. She and her new husband live in a house with her children. In a corner of her bedroom, there is a pile of unopened goods, including a bedspread and sheet set for her mother. Still radiant, still trim, she is still sending barrels back to her extended family in Jamaica.

Epilogue:

TRISH, TAMARA, & TENNESSEE

Students often ask me how I got into journalism and how I go about my work. This essay is for them.

"Who reads the papers?" asked Mrs. McGrath, my third grade teacher.

Everyone's hand was raised.

"What do you read?"

"The comics."

"Anything else?"

"Sports," said the boys.

"Anything else?" My hand alone remained in the air. "The front page," I said. And then, as proof, I recited several recent headlines: "Six-year-old Peruvian girl has baby." (It turned out she was really twenty-four having been born on a leap year day.) "Estranged Wife Attacks Husband in Chicopee Melee." "Fair-goers felled by Tainted Tuna."

I grew up in a family of newspaper readers. They loved to recite headlines to each other. "Oh, listen to this," I remember hearing my uncle exclaim, "Canadian Jury Acquits Man in Death of Sleepwalking Wife." Or my mother, shouting with glee: "Here's a good one. This is clever, this is better than Haiku. Someone found a watch that had been lost for fifty years and the headline is: 'It's About Time!' " Just recently, my sister sent me a headline from the *New York Post* about a

Roman Catholic prelate's Father's Day blast at radical feminists. It was all done up in boldface capitals: "GOD IS A MAN."

My mother says she could gauge the transition in the lives of her six children from child to young adult by remarking the exact moment in which we gave up reading the paper by spreading it and ourselves out on the floor and instead sat in a chair properly, holding the pages at a suitable reading distance in our arms.

I was the kind of child who read insatiably: tickets, recipes, the back of cereal boxes, Nancy Drew, Trixie Belden, the Brownie Scout series, and the classics, particularly those involving orphaned, recalcitrant, or endangered children, which means almost all of them. I don't know why I liked newspapers so much unless all that tumult somehow seemed familiar, reflecting, I suppose, an inner landscape. I reveled in the particular vocabulary of newspapers, the clubbish appeal of all those special code words, all those "alleged" and "acquits." Husbands and wives who were having trouble were "estranged." You never got into a mere fight if you could have a "melee" instead. People didn't wear clothes, they were "clad" in them. Legislators—often called solons—did not think something over; they mulled, as in the common newspaper locution, "Solons Mull." People in newspapers frequently vow, probe, reiterate, claim, assent, quell, or become embroiled and they often pursue, especially doggedly. Whenever possible, they express "cautious optimism" and the measures they take are always either "strict" or "unorthodox." It was reassuring that in a world overwhelmed by change some things stayed the same. No matter what happened to popes and kings and presidents, the Springfield paper had a little front page box containing "Today's Chuckle." The Holyoke paper, published then in the afternoons, had a similar box indicating the precise time of sundown that day, urging drivers to illumine their "vehicular lamps" about thirty minutes beforehand. What a resonant old-fashioned phrase, even for the fifties: vehicular lamps.

I also liked what I now know is technically called the "weather ear," that part of the paper by the masthead that says: "Cloudy today, fair tomorrow." Once a year, it said "Big Fair tomorrow." Bad puns thrive at newspapers; "big fair tomorrow" referred to the Eastern States Exposition, a popular autumn event in our farming area where people could get their weight guessed and look at cows and sheep of exhibition caliber.

Best of all, in newspapers people behaved recklessly. They teemed with impulse, especially at taverns in Chicopee. They were the exact opposite of the surface quiescence and normalcy that characterized those father-knows-best Eisenhower days when all America seemed to be caught in the most mythical of myths, The Happy Family.

Still, it's a big leap from avidly reading newspapers to actually working for one, but it was the only career I considered other than becoming a poet, which did not work out because my output was sparse and my poems bad. Anytime I could, I used self-consciously evocative words such as bittersweet and honeysuckle, neither of which leant itself to ready rhymes, unless you count belt buckle.

In junior high I studied with Mr. Dudley, who taught us how to diagram sentences (which I enjoyed as a kind of chess) and gave us exercises in which we were supposed to write a serious expository theme with each sentence conforming to a prescribed formula: simple, simple compound, simple compound complex, interrogatory, exclamatory, hortatory, and so forth.

Here's an example from June 1961, entitled "Have We Learned?" which earned a grade of B +. The quest for perfection was stymied, according to the menacing red ink that has not yet faded, because of punctuation problems and even more insidious, in sentence three, an errant "noun clause—not asked for."

How Adolph Eichmann has been making news lately! Hardly a day goes by without a newspaper review, television account or magazine report covering the Eichmann trial, because the verdict of the trial will be of lasting importance for years to come. When the sentence has been revealed, many thoughtful people hope it will serve as a prevention of future oppression of any race. In some ways, though, it seems unfair to have Eichmann bear a punishment by himself for crimes committed by several hundred German officials. But the revelations at the trial and a possible death penalty for Eichmann may be the only way to reveal the horrors of crimes committed by the Nazis during World War II, and it may alert the young generation to the dangers of past horrors being repeated in the future which is a loathsome thought. Do we dare hope to learn a lesson from history? Facing reality in its grimmest phase is an extremely hard thing to do, and I only hope that the world can do it. Do not let Anne Frank's diary be in vain!

I can look back at these words with embarrassment at the strident generalizing voice. There's none of what newspapers call "sourcing" or attribution. I wonder, for instance, where I came up with "several hundred German officials" rather than some other number. I wince at the final line, filled as it is with teenaged myopia, but still I feel some fondness for this piece of writing, surely my first editorial, and I will always be grateful that I had a teacher who believed that language has shape. From Mr. Dudley, I learned to look upon sentences the way architects look upon houses, as if they are living, with bones.

I spent my high school years in uniform studying Latin with the Ursuline nuns, who billed themselves as a teaching order of the highest quality; they were known as female Jesuits.

It was a very Irish Catholic school. Every other girl was named Mary or Kathleen. The nuns practiced an odd patchiness in terms of what they stressed and what they didn't. The scholarly pursuit of science was considered not only unlady-like but potentially dangerous: all that bothersome business with Bunsen burners, with their distinctive sensuous shape and their suggestive trade in ignition and flame. Sports was taught only now and then and in such a way to make it clear that exercise was the handmaiden of chastity; once we lay on the floor on mats and spent an hour circling our ankles (that famous trouble spot).

Latin was *the* big subject. Our teacher, Mother Mary As-sumpta, used to brag about how Assumpta was the past per-fect participle in Latin for "having been assumed" as if all the world craved a name that proved a grammatical point. She taught Latin with such passion that to this day snippets of the *Aeneid* are lodged in my brain like something caught between the teeth. I'll be stranded at a traffic light or waiting for the new cashier at the supermarket to figure out the price of lemons, when all of a sudden, across the years, whipping through the wind tunnel of time, those words about how the ancient warrior was propelled by fate from Troy to the shores of Italy fill my mind with their old rhythms: *Arma virumque cano, Troiae qui primus ab oris Italiam fato profugus.*

At my Catholic college I dropped the uniform but con-tinued my struggle to master the accusative. I liked it. Al-though I possess a tin ear and have never been able to make myself understood in a foreign language of the live variety, I still hear the music in Latin cognates. When I learned, for example, that the word "gregarious" has its origins in the word "grex, gregis," meaning herd or tribe, I felt I had been let in on a family reunion attended by me and the alphabet. From Latin I learned that words are like people: they have ancestors.

In what was a doomed effort to sound sophisticated during those years, I occasionally remarked in the most bored, super-cilious, irritating tone, "College is what I do when it isn't summer." What saved me from a case of cosmic adolescent ennui was *Tatler,* the school paper. During my first week at the College of New Rochelle, I walked across campus and volunteered my services.

My first assignment was to write a poem to accompany a moody black-and-white photo of a tree with empty branches. I recall only a fragment, *limbs limning spaces.* I wrote movie reviews, covered appearances by guest lecturers such as Robert Penn Warren, and wrote editorials about the need for coed education, employing headlines of a frankly biased nature such as: "Are Female Ghettoes an Anachronism?"

The paper had as its professional adviser a retired editor from the *New York Sun,* a tall distinguished ancient man who taught us a great deal about technique, including how to do a headline count and the names for the different kinds of typeface, my all-time favorite being agate, the tiny five and a half point letters often used for scores and lists. To me agate equals obscurity, pure and simple.

Upon graduation, I went on to the Columbia Graduate School of Journalism. I am sure that the principal reason I was admitted was my work on that four-page weekly. Print is king, I tell my students. Clips are gold.

I attended Columbia during the height of the protests against the Vietnam war. Morningside Heights in the fall of 1969 was Mark Rudd territory. It was *the* place to be in school. We were dedicated to weathering our jeans and ending the war. We refused grades. One had merely to attend a few classes and not vandalize the equipment in the ersatz newsroom and one received a diploma.

We were arrogant and petulant and very young. Every now and then real journalists would come to the campus and one or another of us would be interviewed about student unrest. We thought of these interviews as a kind of job audition.

We all expected to graduate from Columbia and waltz into the city room of the *New York Times,* and I remember the shock I felt in June 1970 at the gap between what I saw as my potential and the world's utter ability to go on as if I'd never been born.

What followed was a series of apprenticeships: a summer at a small Connecticut daily, five weeks at an old-fashioned Boston tabloid, a year of tape recording actualities for radio stations, a year at the *Boston Globe,* another year at a fashion paper.

These first jobs occupied me in my early twenties and I learned something of value at each of them. At the small paper in Connecticut I learned that I didn't want to stay in a place where the biggest news was a Chamber of Commerce contest to guess the exact moment when a ton block of ice in the center of downtown would melt into nothingness on the hottest day of the year.

My five weeks at the *Boston Record American* in 1970 could have taken place fifty years earlier. The newsroom was on an upper floor. There were occasional fires in the pressroom below, but employees were ordered not to budge until the flames licked the windows. The air conditioning consisted of a water cooler and salt tablets. There was a single dust-covered dictionary in the room, its dust being a point of pride. If a word had to be looked up, it probably wasn't worth using. Once I wrote a story about a restaurant opening and showed off my college education by referring to cooking as "colloidal chemistry." "This expression," said my editor, underlining the offensive phrase, "is not even worthy of the S.S. Pierce Christmas catalogue." Language can sometimes be too simple, but rarely. The same editor used to say: "Short words in short sentences pack punch." The rigor it takes to stick to what's plain can be learned on a newspaper more quickly and lastingly than anywhere else. Hemingway's work is the most famous example.

My radio job involved going to press conferences and tape recording important personages. I would show up at public events, point the mike in the right direction, then click on the machine at the appropriate moment, and listen. This job showed me how little I wanted to make these star-dusted celebrity-soaked moments the routine of my work as a reporter. The enmities of the press corps, even its bonhomie, wore thin very quickly. I wanted to cover the singular story singly.

At the *Boston Globe* I covered the suburbs of Quincy, Braintree, Weymouth, and sometimes Milton. As a suburban reporter I found out just how deadly it can be to go to those nightly civic meetings and cover selectpeople as they considered—I mean mulled—bond issues for new school annexes. I can still recall the headlines from those days: "Drug Clinic Upsets Neighbors. Halfway House in Milton Protested. Town Wants Halfway House Elsewhere." And then, a few weeks later, "Town Still Wants Halfway House Elsewhere." Night after night of this kind of work made me despair of ever actually interviewing the kind of people who populated the newspaper headlines of my childhood, the kind who teem with impulse, whose words and actions are a true unburdening of the heart, in the way a vote for sewer pipes can never be.

Fortunately I was cut loose from my suburban beat for a week in order to write about hockey groupies at the Boston Garden. The Boston Garden was not then and is not now a place guilty of what might be called excessive charm. What attracted me to this story were the young girls themselves, the heartache of what it must have been to be these pale-skinned camp followers with bad teeth, daffy for a group of older men who couldn't have cared less that these children were skipping school and devoting their entire lives to a useless idolatry. They were twelve, thirteen, fourteen and compensated for the emptiness in their lives by filling themselves with lore about the athletes—their age, place of birth, height, weight, whether they shot left-handed or right-handed, their pluses and minuses. The girls headed local homemade fan clubs, which were different from finely tuned national organizations, and resembled, in the fierceness of the battles as to who got to head which club, the kind of turf wars one associates with gangs. I remember one of them telling me that she had tripped recently and received a scar on her forehead in the shape of a backward number 7 which in the mirror could be read correctly and in that way served as a tribute to Phil Esposito, the player whose number was 77. During games, they would run out to the parking lot and write their names in the dirt on players' cars.

But the comment that I found most haunting came in response to an ordinary question:

"Have you been able to use this pursuit in a positive way, for instance, in your schoolwork, when you do go to school?"

"Oh, yes," she answered eagerly. "Last year my teacher asked me to write a composition about what I would most like to be. So I wrote, 'Hockey ice.' "

"Why?"

"Because then the skaters would skate on top of me and they would think about me even when they weren't with me."

This remark struck me as wrenching and original. Suddenly the stakes were raised. This was not a trivial story about a dead-end hobby.

This was obsession.

The *Boston Globe* remains in my mind the model of a great newspaper for writers of feature stories. There is respect for prose, for the simplicity of language but also for its richness. Features are understood to be different from news accounts. A good one is like a good poem or a good short story. It is an exercise in economy, the art of the quick study (though not always so quick) and the art of the glimpse (though sometimes the glimpse turns into a panorama).

Why didn't I hitch my star to the *Globe* indefinitely? Like most young people starting out I had one major asset going for me, my impatience, and one going against me, my impatience. The fire in my belly threw out indiscriminate flames. I wanted to make the leap from correspondent to staffer more swiftly than the management there thought agreeable. I left for a much less interesting job at a fashion paper. Instead of covering selectpeople, I was now covering hemlines. I remember the kind of calls that came into that office, the desperate vanity in the voices:

"Quick, you must tell me the name of a good hairdresser in Cleveland."

"I have to know the top three colors for next fall and I must know now."

My favorite:

"Are you covering the charity ball on Friday?"

"I believe so."

"Will you be there with a photographer?"

"Probably."

"Well, be on the lookout for a woman in a one-armed caftan by Halston, forest green with silver sequins, and when you see her be sure you do one thing."

"What's that?"

"Take her picture."

Eventually I was fired, on the grounds that my pantyhose surveys were "not of sufficiently in-depth quality to warrant continued employment."

I think at one point I had applied at every major daily between Portland, Maine, and Miami, Florida. I once submitted what I considered to be a beautifully pasted scrapbook to a newspaper which not only declined to hire me but also failed to return my clips for over a year despite my weekly entreaties. I waited and waited. Finally, in a miracle of belated efficiency, there arrived in the mail the outdated collection of what I considered my finest flowers. I opened it up and settled down with a cup of coffee to look at myself in the mirror of my prose. A note from one editor to another fluttered forth.

It said:

"If this person possesses any talent, I fail to see it."

As discouraged as I sometimes became, I never tried to get a job as an editor. Reporters, especially young ones who don't see how mutually beneficial a positive relationship with editors can be, see them as power-mongering bonus-seeking sellouts, defrocked writers who have lost the steely fortitude to do what Jimmy Breslin once described as standing outside in the rain knocking on doors that rarely open. Before I wised up, I harbored the conviction that because editors are often writers who no longer write, their revenge is to ruin the work of those who do. I thought: editors don't edit, they ruin. They don't cut, they disembowel.

My favorite story about predatory editors comes from the old *Chicago American* many years ago. An old coot of a copy editor, famous for changing reporters' words willy-nilly, campaigned mightily for the opportunity to cover the Spanish-American war. He was finally sent to war as a kind of retirement present. His first dispatch tried to capture the devastation of a village. It began, "There's nothing left but a half a dozen adobe huts, and half a hundred hounds. . . ." It was changed to "six clay houses and fifty dogs."

One of the old saws of the newspaper profession is that it doesn't matter how often you switch jobs: you end up taking your contacts (and your ghosts, of course) with you. After my failed career as a fashion reporter, I craved a job at a more mainstream paper and by chance I heard that the *Trenton Times* had been bought by the *Washington Post* and was to be run by a greatly gifted editor and a former Marine named Richard Harwood, who was looking to hire a few good men, and women.

The *Post's* ownership of the *Times* was short-lived. As soon as the *Post* forked over sixteen million dollars to buy the paper, the old owner let it be known, "You could have got it for twelve million." Within a few years the *Post* abandoned its effort to bring big-city journalism to what may be the most small-town state capital in the country. But in the meantime about twenty or so young people were hired and told to be hard chargers. We were baby reporters. We tried anything. We worked incessantly, night and day, all weekend long, and from that experience I formulated the one piece of advice I give to all my students just starting out, "Work twice as hard as everyone twice your age." None of us earned much: reporting is not a get-rich-quick scheme. We longed for fifteen-dollar-a-week raises, our lifestyles improved considerably with ten-dollar raises, and we wondered if we had the moral fiber to refuse a five-dollar raise as insulting. With what little money we had, we threw impromptu dinner parties constantly. Recently when Ben Bradlee retired as executive editor of the *Post* he was quoted as saying his fondest memories of the business were the gatherings when he was a young reporter where someone made a pot of spaghetti and someone else brought along some wine and the night was squandered while everyone railed against politics and corruption, all the while toasting truth and each other.

I covered neither politics nor corruption, but I did try to pursue the quiet truth in the private lives of ordinary people. One of my first assignments in Trenton was to cover a Polish debutante ball. This was an important local event in a town filled with ethnic divisions and allegiances. As part of the research, I went to people's homes during the weeks beforehand and watched as they prepared centerpieces and decorations, cooked savory food, and caught up on the news. They discussed the retirements and graduations (with the deepest pride for those who had finished medical school), the marriages, and the deaths. The talk filled the room with an almost physical weight. It had the density of a real object, as real as the Kleenex corsages piling up on one work table or the odor of cabbage and sausage from the kitchen. I produced the usual dutiful report, concentrating on the facts of the event— how many girls were being presented, the name of the band that would be playing, the cost of the tickets, the ingredients of the presentee's punch (fruit juice and ginger-ale)—all the while ignoring the real news, which was the talk itself and how it bound the community like a tightly stitched seam, unnoticed, yet certain and strong.

Like most young journalists, my mind was coltish in nature, scampering from one subject to another. I went to science fairs and learned how to make grass grow on wet sponges. I got to meet, in person, the 1975 National Arc Welding Champion. I wrote about a teacher who was fired for not smiling. A twenty-six-year-old housewife, arrested for fortune telling, was proud that she never advertised: "In this business, if you're good you never have to wave a banner." A psychometrist (someone who tells people about themselves by communing with a certain object of their choosing) spoke of the importance of breathing certain colors: "Turquoise is great if you want to lose weight. . . ." A race track chaplain by the name of Homer Triculese told me he had learned two things on the job: "Horses bite and all jockeys have the same prayer."

At first I loved the idea of spending each day on something new, even an Easter egg hunt at the Trenton "Y" on an unseasonably hot April day: "The kids milled. The dust churned. The wind was hot. The sun was like the wind. It's 10:15, and the kids are antsy. Okay, start, said the organizer, and with that the children tumbled into the field with a chaotic inevitability, like groceries breaking out of an overloaded shopping bag."

One time in the space of a week, three major events occurred, a trinity of woes. A huge fire destroyed the civic center. Then day after day of nonstop rain soaked the town. Then pipes bringing water to the city broke, causing a serious shortage. Flame, flood, and drought. As a feature writer, I was sent to interview a high-ranking Jehovah's Witness. "Is it," I asked politely, "the end of the world?"

He had the look of someone lost in long thought. Finally, he hunched forward reassuringly.

"The Bible," he said, "doesn't even mention Trenton."

Eventually, in Trenton I began to feel my usual frustration, a certain restless wish to reinvent myself through my work.

Although there is a wonderful intrigue in not knowing what you're going to cover on a given day, it gets old after a while, the roulette. It starts to seem important to refine your vision of what you want to write about even at a paper. Like a novelist, good journalists have a theme. For instance, if Tracy Kidder worked for a newspaper, his colleagues would say his beat is genesis. He seems drawn inexorably to creation, whether it be the creation of computers, homes, or young minds. Richard Rhodes has written a book about the history of the atomic bomb. Subsequently, he wrote a memoir about his mother's suicide when he was fourteen months old. On the most fundamental level both these books cover the same territory: cataclysmic disruption. Norman Mailer loves an anti-hero. Joan Didion covers irony; in his last three books Joe McGinness has gravitated toward domestic tragedy; Phil Caputo says he can't write unless it's about war. In my pieces I think I am most often drawn to people walking the edge, curiously undefeated.

In my career I seem to act out the migratory habits of a bird, and after Boston and Trenton I stopped briefly in Washington where I free-lanced and decided it was not my city and proceeded south to Miami. By then I was thirty, it was the late seventies, and Miami was shedding its reputation as a sleepy backwater with a couple of glitzy winter months and was becoming the World Capital of Abundant and Unusual News. Story possibilities abounded. I was still free-lancing, and I was reading a lot. Having been drawn to newspapering, at least initially, by a love of literature, I found that in the crush of daily deadlines I had fallen away from that old passion. By renewing my relationship with words in books, I hoped the words I put on paper would experience their own renewal.

I had always wanted to work for a magazine and *Tropic* Magazine of the *Miami Herald* was (is) always looking for free lancers, especially of the rent-desperate variety. Over the years people working there have composed an unusual assembly of Thorny Personnel Problems and Unmanageable Free

Spirits, my kind of people. They have reveled in life in a city on the verge of discovering its own unsung rhythms, an incredible chorus of fleeting felons, drifters, lost souls, necessary wanderers, political exiles, cowboys, Southern belles, alligators, crusty pioneer settlers, ex-husbands, ex-wives, and ex-cops, survivors of various upheavals, including crazy childhoods, revolutions, imprisoning summer heat, hurricanes, tropical downpours, and roaches inside one's house as big as kangaroos, which we called kangaroaches.

Like the thick twisting branches of the mangrove trees rising out of the swampland, stories grew and flourished effortlessly.

It was not a matter of struggling to find topics I wanted to write about so much as choosing from among the possibilities. Choice was the important factor. Not one of the stories in this volume resulted from the traditional hierarchical arrangement in which an editor "assigns" a reporter to write about something. As the writer Mary Morris observes about herself, "Sending me on an assignment is like telling me to go to a party and fall in love."

Trish, Tamara, Tennessee. In time the people in these stories took on a first-name casualness. My choice to listen to these people reveals some kind of hidden kinship that says as much about me as it does about them.

Some of the stories grew out of the regular news pages: Kenny White, Christine Falling, and Wendy Blankenship had all been front-page news in Miami. Carol Fennelly made national news out of Washington, D.C. Tennessee Williams had also been reported on the front page, as beleaguered in Key West, his island retreat, harassed for his homosexuality and his prominence. I had always loved his work. I can't now recall how I got his phone number. It may have been listed under T. Williams on Key West. Or perhaps a bored literary agent dispensed it. I was plainly amazed when he took my call and agreed to fix a time for a meeting. I had never been to Key West, that wonderful honky-tonk town, but I had heard

Jimmy Buffet sing its praises and it was with an almost child-like eagerness that I boarded a bus and traveled the 150 miles for the six hours it takes to get by local to Key West, passing over numerous bridges that span a flat blue horizon of sky and water. I checked into an inexpensive room, at the Eden House, and then walked a dozen blocks or so to the writer's house. Small, white, unimposing, it had a friendliness that made my knocking at the door seem less intrusive than it might. The door was presently opened by a youngish man who informed me that the author was at lunch.

"But," I sputtered, "we had an appointment."

"Well," he shrugged.

"I'll come back later."

He shrugged again, and gave me a suit-yourself look.

Three hours later, I retraced my route from the Eden House to the author's front porch, only to be told that the eminent writer was in his room, sleeping off lunch.

This time I didn't say whether I would be back. I simply left, but three hours later, at six in the evening, I showed up again.

To my surprise, Williams himself answered the door and although he appeared somewhat groggy from the midday nap and other distractions, he not only posed but posed in style. For the remainder of that evening and all the next day and much of the following morning, photographer John Pineda and I quietly accompanied him at dinner, at a production of one of his plays, and at the Pier House for drinks on the verandah. When we thought we were finally finished, just as we were preparing to leave for the airport, and a taxi idled outside his house, he turned to us and asked in his unmistakable drawl, "Would you like to see my shrine?" Pineda, ten years my senior and a real pro, reached for his strobe and told me to cancel the taxi and reschedule our flights. In that way I learned a crucial truth in reporting, if not in life: When someone says, "Would you like to see my shrine?" ignore the pressure to be elsewhere and say yes.

On other occasions the subjects approached me about writing their story. Trish's sister Meg wrote to me at the *Herald;* David Montalvo's mother called. Mr. Zepp was a well-known fixture at newspapers in south Florida. He used to show up in all the newsrooms he could. Dressed formally, with a proud demeanor and a hat-tipping unctuous manner with security people and elevator operators, he insinuated himself so insistently that editors and reporters actually tried to avoid him. Usually, the most rookie reporter would be required to hear him out, again and again. At *Tropic* we decided to do the story in the hope that this would quiet him once and for all.

We found out about Tamara Jones when she visited the magazine as a child model in the company of her mother. The little girl caught everyone's attention, her precocity especially, the oddly adult way in which she behaved and spoke.

The woman in "The Time of Her Life" is a friend whose driven schedule has always amazed me.

I met Monica through Velma, who sometimes babysat for me. After my daughter celebrated her birthday, Velma took the discarded candles and rinsed them. When I asked why, she said they were for her friend Monica's barrels.

Hannah and Vivian Kahn were at a dinner with an editor, who then suggested I contact them. At first Hannah was reluctant to be interviewed. I didn't press the point, but made it clear that if she changed her mind I would be available. A month or two later when I called she said yes. I think she was acting out of some kind of fierce maternal logic—her hope was that the prominence her daughter might experience as a result of a piece in *Tropic* would be yet another protection for Vivian if Hannah died first.

Mary Gordon and Justin Kaplan are writers whose work I admire for different reasons, and in both cases the imminent publication of a major new book became a convenient excuse to suggest an interview. Gordon's novels and short stories and essays have always struck me as brave (in terms of the terrain she is willing to explore) and beautiful. Her narrative voice is indisputably her own: lush, quick-witted, powerful. Kaplan's exploration of the lives of Mark Twain and Whitman are wonderfully unencumbered pieces of prose held together by all the meticulous scholarly underpinnings one would wish for from a biographer. In dealing with editors, it is important to disclose anything that might be construed as a bias or vested interest, and when I explained that I knew Justin and his wife, Anne Bernays, socially, my editor said she foresaw no problems, given the nature of the story.

The profile of Mrs. Clapp is the only piece in this volume that grew out of a deliberate effort to find someone doing a particular kind of work. On "60 Minutes" I had seen a touching portrait of a brilliant teacher in Chicago teaching Shakespeare to grade school students in a poor neighborhood and I had the thought that there were probably equally fine teachers in Miami. Throughout my career as a journalist I have frequently found excuses to visit a classroom or a school where a good teacher is hard at work affecting, as Henry Adams put it, eternity. Reporters are like cops: on a daily basis they are often forced to confront the worst of what can happen to people. A visit to a classroom functions for me as an exercise in soul restoration. I found Mrs. Clapp by going to a public library in the Liberty City section of town where I was told about several dedicated teachers, one of whom was said to outshine all others. Mrs. Clapp is not an attention seeker. She has been in that same classroom in that same school for years and years. Her medals and her stars come from the successes of her students. She has a dignity and a sense of boundary that are profound. She resisted all my efforts to visit her at her house. It was her teaching self that was under scrutiny, not her home life. I stop by and visit her class every few years. We are friends but from a professional distance. I always address her as Mrs. Clapp.

The supreme pleasure of journalism is in telling the story well; that is its ultimate glamour. When I started out, I longed for the chance to travel out of town, to what I presumed would be fascinating cultural meccas. Most of my out-of-town work has taken me to backwaters, places like Jay, Florida, where in 1970 a lake of oil was discovered beneath its surface, turning people who owned the mineral rights to their property into overnight millionaires and the people who didn't own mineral rights or property into angry neighbors. In Jay all history is divided into two parts, "before oil" and "after oil." When I made my visit in 1980, the residents seemed to know almost everything about each other; they had a saying that as long as a person pays the electric and water bills, the neighbors will take care of the rest of the business. They knew about the woman who had the queer habit of keeping her first husband's ashes on the mantlepiece, and they all remembered him before he was ash. The town's only restaurants consisted of coffee shops, and my editor at the time, Lary Bloom, had explicitly encouraged the photographer and me to treat ourselves to dinner at a nice French restaurant. "Hey, it's okay. Spend as much as you want," he said, obviously aware that the toniest local establishment was Pizza Hut.

John Doman, the photographer who had been assigned to take Mr. Zepp's picture, expressed the essence of out-of-town assignments when we were sitting in the dining car of the Silver Meteor. The day had a dingy cast like the color of the alleged chicken on our plates. We were tired from the long ride and felt greased with dirt. We were hoping Mr. Zepp would retire early and we wondered about the journalistic ethics of bodily forcing him into his roomette. Doman was trying to raise his voice above the monotonous roaring clack. He started saying something about how when he left Ohio, he thought he was trading leaden skies for golden ones. He was hoping for jazzy assignments, French food, first-class accommodations, the works. He gave his plate a sad glance; clearly he was mistaken. He shook his head and sighed, "It's all Akron in the end."

Maybe so, but maybe that's not so bad. Perhaps it depends

on where you find your glamour. After all these years of reporting and never once finding myself on the Champs Élysée, I have learned to seek my glitter in unlikely places like the Boston Garden or the Dade County Women's Detention Center. I remember one lunchtime. Standing single-file, the women accepted the compartmentalized metal trays and a white plastic spoon, the only utensil permitted. The hands of some of the women trembled: prison palsy, withdrawal from drugs, from liquor, from the outside. Arms had scars. Burns, fights, needles. Jewelry was not allowed, but there was no way to remove the tattooed bracelets. Some, still young, had no teeth, or very few. I saw one empty mouth that was the handiwork of a motorcycle gang.

"They took pliers and pulled out two of my teeth."

"Why?"

"For entertainment."

"You let them?"

"You're the third person who's asked me that. Of course not. I didn't have a choice."

When the food was good (chicken, bologna) very few spoke. When it wasn't good (mystery meat, mystery soup, mystery starch) conversation richocheted throughout the room. I think of settings like that, or the parking lot at the 7-Eleven where I hung out with Trish as more, well, *fun,* than, say, attending some White House briefing. Oh, sure, I'd go to the White House once, but only in a spirit of exploration. Many journalists live by certain lofty precepts and mine is this: never interview a mayor. By mayors I mean the entire raft of humankind who occupy some high office somewhere and whose primary goal in communication is obfuscation. On a routine day-in, day-out basis, give me your basic alleyway and let me listen to the found poetry in the speech of Trish. I'd rather attend Vivian's presentation to a Medical School class in genetics than a formal lecture on DNA. Let me really hear Christine Falling and by documenting her "streak of mean" show as vividly as I can the effects of abuse and abandonment. Give me Kenny, the twelve-year-old killer, sad because the ice-cream man ran out of lollipops the day of the murders. The point is you don't have to travel far afield to find something worth writing about.

Journalism is not a popularity contest. I try not to expect the people I write about to like what I wrote even if I liked them and thought what I wrote was fair.

As for technique, the question I am asked most frequently is, "Do you use a tape recorder?" The answer is no. There are lots of reasons. One is a certain mechanical ineptitude which makes me so wary of all machinery that even in the presence of a tape recorder I am always obsessed about whether or not it is working and it gets in the way of my doing what I should be doing, which is a truly creative listening that takes years of practice. When I first started out, the people I interviewed had a disconcerting tendency to sound not only exactly alike, but also exactly like me, filled with cosmic, adolescent ennui.

Reporting requires deft social skills, an ability to get along with all sorts of people in a variety of awkward situations. A student once told me that the reason she couldn't write an article about the donation of canned goods to the local survival center was that she was terrified of talking on the phone with people who were older. A reporter must learn to be assertive, but it helps to remember that you are never as important as the person you are writing about. I always tell myself: cultivate a certain beigeness. Tracy Kidder was so adept at becoming inconspicuous doing the research for his book *House* that the carpenters wanted him to start wearing a cowbell around his neck. A writer is there to serve the subject, not the other way around. As Anna Quindlen of the *New York Times* says, "A reporter who thinks he's important is a deeply flawed, deluded individual."

Just how hard should you try to get a story? All reporters eventually formulate the standards of behavior they can live with. Badgering is never pleasant, and in feature writing it seems distinctly against one's self-interest. The key is access, to establish a spirit of cooperation between writer and subject. Edna Buchanan, Pulitzer-prize winning crime reporter and author of a journalistic memoir entitled *The Corpse has a Familiar Face,* used to say that she would always call people for an interview twice. If someone refused to speak to her on the first try, or had hung up in anger, she would wait sixty seconds and try again. By then some people had changed their minds. Would she call a third time? "Oh, no, that would be harassment."

I always try to do my homework so that I don't make people repeat information that is easily known with a minimum of research in advance. I always try to plan some questions ahead of time, but I try not to marry a sheet of preordained questions. What often works best is to go with the flow established by the subject. I remember a time when a young colleague and I interviewed a famous singer who had just undergone eye surgery at Massachusetts General Hospital. I was so in awe of the woman that I couldn't think of a thing to ask. The other reporter read from a list of questions in a voice devoid of the normal rhythms of speech:

"Are you afraid of going blind?"

"What a question," she responded.

It wasn't the question; it was the tone, the dissonance between what the subject was feeling and the perfunctory voice of the reporter that defeated the possibility of a conversation. No conversation: end of interview. It's a contradiction to say "make yourself relax," but you have to learn to make yourself relax.

I have never found the general question, the sweeping interrogatory, such as "are you happy?" to be as effective as more concrete ones. When I interviewed a couple on their seventy-fifth wedding anniversary, they had nothing in the way of an animated response to the question, "Well, what's it like to be married for seventy-five years?" I asked if they had any pictures from that day, and they didn't. Stumped, I turned to the woman and asked if she could remember what she wore.

Her answer was lively and detailed. It became the lede:

"Seventy five-years ago today, a slim and pretty girl got to act rigged up in a hand-made worsted skirt (ten cents a yard), a pale pink-and-white styled blouse (six cents a yard), a plain satin hat (one quarter), five-cent stockings and a dollar pair of shoes."

An interview is more than just a series of questions. It is a conversation. It is formal portraiture. It is a snapshot. It is a mutual collaboration. By requesting the interview, you have led the subject to believe you think what he or she has to say is important. Even if you and the subject don't like each other, you presumably like the larger story itself. It would be hard to demonstrate the ways in which Christine Falling could be called likeable, but her larger story—the tragedy of her early years—filled me with an indignation that became the passion fueling the story.

During an interview I try to use all my senses and to remind myself that what you see can be as important as what you hear. I remember once talking to a woman who had a problem she wished would disappear and with a vengeance she took a sponge to an already perfectly clean kitchen counter, wiping it over and over and over. Her words tried to make light of her distress; the gesture contradicted her words.

Sometimes I choose to capture people less by what they say than by describing the objects with which they surround themselves. People who are media-savvy, like Carol Fennelly, have an official agenda. What she said when she spoke to me was one thing: a brave sloganeering torrent about helping the homeless. What she expressed beyond words in her tiny room and the worldly goods gathered there seemed to be filled with far more insight. The way to really listen to Monica was to watch her pride as she laid out and examined all the goods and trinkets for her barrel and to observe the careful way she packed. Item joined item in a procession as cadenced as it was stately.

If someone doesn't want to answer a question, I might rephrase it, but if there is still no answer, I always back off, at least for the time being. A lot of reporters say they save their bombshells until some level of trust and intimacy has been established, but if there is trust and intimacy, there don't have to be bombshells, certainly not in the sense of some kind of entrapment for the purpose of a cruel or extreme unveiling.

Some interviews go nowhere. In a way the least propitious approach is to sit across from a stranger, firing questions. I like at the very least to mingle that sedentary style with a more active one, to capture people at their work or in the midst of an ordinary activity.

You don't have to include everything you are told and everything you witness in what you write. In Trenton a woman from an impoverished section of the city was interviewed on the day after her ten-year-old son was found murdered. He had disappeared several days earlier, on the way to a store for a loaf of bread. "He was a good boy," his mother said. "He loved animals and was always hugging and kissing on the dog in the backyard. He was devilish, like a mosquito on a horse's back, but he was sweet. One time he says to me, 'Mommy, who makes the most money?' and I told him doctors do. So he said he was going to be a doctor." Several reporters stopped by her house that day. Only one, a columnist from the *Trentonian,* mentioned the can of beer on the kitchen table in front of her, which no one saw her either touch or drink. Later, her grief at the loss of her son became mingled with her outrage at being linked in print with alcohol, which she not only avoided personally but also disapproved of. Just because you possess a so-called fact doesn't mean you can dispense it, scattershot, in a piece of writing. In any story, there is an ultimate truth you are seeking to convey, and this requires careful selection of details. The mention of the beer can was not only extraneous, but also misleading.

Sometimes I have a notion about a piece even before I start. Obviously, Kenny White's childhood would have enormous

rather predictable irregularities in it, despite the initial headlines calling him a model student and focusing on his family's
affluence. Mr. Zepp was a nettlesome sort in his old age; I
assumed some of that irritating behavior muddied the purity
of his crusade when he was young, though I hardly expected
him to behave so perfectly in character as he did when he
received the letter from the Pentagon and refused to accept the
very vindication he had fought for so hard. On the other
hand, I try to avoid too much preconception. Part of the great
"high" in reporting and writing is that sense of discovery.

As for drafts, I do as many as I have to in the time I have to
do them. As I often tell my students, despite their groans,
"Rewriting is a privilege."

The kind of journalism I do requires my physical presence.
Conducting interviews only by phone would be like seeing
the world in black and white or never tasting salt.

In the matter of how to quote someone, I will correct
grammatical slips if they are a mere distraction, but I am more
likely to preserve them for their symbolic character, for what
they reveal about a person's character, background, or prospects. The same holds true when someone says something
that reveals an ignorance about the world; Christine Falling's
strange and botched sense of history is in keeping with her
strange and botched present. In a similar vein, I remember an
interview with a survivor of Miami's race riots in 1980. Michael Kulp was a teenager in a car being driven by his older
brother Jeffrey. Passing through Liberty City on their way
home they encountered a crowd that had gathered to protest a
verdict vindicating a pack of white policemen in the beating
death of a black insurance agent who had run a red light. The
crowd stoned Michael's vehicle. A rock crashed through the
windshield, hitting his brother. The car stopped and both
young men were dragged out onto the streets and beaten.
Michael, brain damaged, survived: "I thought I knew about a
job that would pay me $5 an hour but I don't think that will
come through so I think now that I'm improving from my

recent operation I have to go back to my old job, driving a car between Norristown and New York, and that's only $4.50 an hour. Sometimes I had to make trips to Delaware too. Have you heard of Delaware?"

I would be loathe to show a subject a completed interview before publication. That is simply not done at newspapers or magazines. Books are different. J. Anthony Lukas, author of *Common Ground,* has said that he allowed each of the three key families in the book to review the portions of the manuscript about them, with the agreement that he would change any errors of fact that they could prove. As a courtesy, I often check quotes for accuracy. Basically I agree with what Justin Kaplan tells his subjects: Either you trust me or you don't.

There are times when I've been intimidated by the celebrity of my subjects, but a subject doesn't have to be famous to be intimidating. It's always hard, that initial phone call, and there have been plenty of times when I had to fight off demon misgivings about the initial meeting as well. I was afraid to meet David Montalvo at first, but of course David is used to reactions like mine. His first gesture upon introduction is to extend his hands, to touch. I am sometimes asked if I have any misgivings about interviewing some of my more disfranchised subjects. Is it in their interest to talk to me? Am I exploiting them?

I interview them not to exploit them but because what they have to say is so important. Most of them have told their story in their actions, but they are not journalists and cannot write what they have to say about the world in a way that would reach a large number of people, and it seems to me that one of the more crucial roles of the reporter is to give speech to the speechless.

Not only do I write as many drafts as I can, I also do as many interviews as my editors and my subjects will permit. Generally, not always, but generally, it's good to have time on your side. Editors always try to hurry you, and it is crucial to put them off as long as possible. It takes a certain amount of hanging out to be able to recognize the emblematic moment when it happens. Anyway, no one ever remembers how long it took you to write something, but if you're lucky someone may remember what you wrote.

Consider the work its own reward. You may have hopeful fantasies about some good ensuing from what you write, but as often as not, even when something good happens, the subject will be less than entirely appreciative, as when the truant officers from the Boston School system rounded up the children at the Garden and forced them back into class.

As for my audience, I tend not to think of a vast undifferentiated bloc of thousands upon thousands of newspaper subscribers but more specifically about individuals I would like to have read what I have written. I realized this when someone happened to ask me in passing whom I envisioned reading "Monica's Barrel." First of all, I imagined what Monica would think when she read the piece.

Before I used Monica's name, I made certain her immigration status was aboveboard. I could imagine the Immigration and Naturalization Service using my story to pick up Monica and force her to leave the country if she were an "illegal alien," a term with Martian overtones used by our government to keep us from acknowledging the humanity of some of the people who have fled to this country. I hoped that Monica's boss would read this, would see her generosity. I hoped a reader might recognize that Monica's diligence and goodness were worth a lot more than two hundred dollars a week and would contact her and offer her something better. I thought it would be fun to know what a psychoanalyst would think of Monica, of all her scurrying and squirreling. The barrel could also be seen as a bribe, something to keep away the evil eye of those who had stayed behind. Fear of the envy of others can be a powerful motive in many human transactions. Her generosity possessed a delicious doubleness; her kindness took the homely form of tuna and Brillo pads and codfish but it contained messages about larger subjects, such as racial inequities, envy, and religion.

I am always fascinated by the elements of fiction in journalism, the lifelike details in an account that are not (as in fiction) *like* life, but life itself. It is one of the most powerful forces in journalism, the power of what is real. Some people make what I consider a false distinction between journalism and fiction. It is often assumed that the principal job of nonfiction is to convey information and the principal job of fiction is to convey life. Novelist Pat Conroy once said that in our society, journalists are the "designated watchers" and novelists, the "designated feelers." My favorite journalism and fiction are in fact the kinds that do both.

When all the interviewing is over and it's time to write, I ask myself: What would I say about this story if I could tell people only one thing? Only five? If I have done my fieldwork properly, I am now an expert and must try to repossess the naivete and curiosity of the person who doesn't know anything about the subject. Many reporters I know describe the process of reporting as falling in love. The process of writing is falling out of love. It's similar to a plane's landing when the engines are thrown into reverse. Research is public, animated, like a party. Writing requires detachment, quiet, solitude, what Graham Greene called an icicle at the heart. An inner voice must always urge: "Cut to the energy, write to the best moments." After I have found what I think are a few good words, I review them, put them up for soldierly inspection. If they don't meet the measure, I try to follow George Orwell's advice: "Murder your darlings."

If I am having trouble knowing how to start, I try writing the story as a letter to a friend. If I am still having trouble, I write the ending. There is no one supreme approach to organizing one's material, but there are two usually weak approaches: telling the reader everything in the order in which you found it out, and telling the reader everything you found out. The tried and true chronological approach, "Once upon a time," is tried and true because it so often works so well.

The question I have the hardest time answering about my work as a reporter is "What is your favorite story?" In a way, being a veteran journalist is like being a parent with a huge brood; almost every story has been the noisy favorite at one time or another, including pieces that aren't in this volume for any number of reasons. Of the ones that are here, I can think of many ways in which each makes the greatest claim on my affection.

How do you choose?

My best answer is, I think, less a dodge than it is an attitude of optimism: My favorite story will always be the next one.

But even the breezy good will of that sentiment is tinged by the recognition of just how frightening and perilous and delicate the process of journalism can be and of the terrible trust it requires on both sides to go through someone else's truth to get to your own.

*The essays in this volume originally appeared
in the following publications:*

"The Disturbance," *Tropic Magazine, The Miami Herald,* May 24,
1987

"Mother Knows Best," *Tropic Magazine, The Miami Herald,*
September 21, 1980

"Sandy's Baby," *Tropic Magazine, The Miami Herald,* August 11,
1985

"The Time of Her Life, " *The Washington Post Magazine,*
August 26, 1990

"A Room of Her Own," *The Washington Post Magazine,*
January 27, 1991

"Zepp's Last Stand," *Tropic Magazine, The Miami Herald,*
November 11, 1979

"Lethal Weapon," *Tropic Magazine, The Miami Herald,*
August 16, 1987

"The Twisting of Kenny White," *Tropic Magazine, The Miami
Herald,* March 10, 1985

"The Babysitter," *Tropic Magazine, The Miami Herald,* June 5,
1983

"Three Scenes from the Life of a Tormented Playwright," *Tropic
Magazine, The Miami Herald,* April 1, 1979

"The Pope of Quotations," *Newsday Magazine,* March 10, 1991

"The Other Side of Mary Gordon," *The Boston Globe Sunday
Magazine,* November 12, 1989

"At Nobody's Mercy," *Tropic Magazine, The Miami Herald,*
April 13, 1980

"The Poet and the Birthday Girl," *Tropic Magazine, The Miami
Herald,* May 8, 1983

"Monica's Barrel," *Tropic Magazine, The Miami Herald,*
August 9, 1987